1

I Got Fired as a
COURT WIZARD
so Now I'm Moving to the Country to Become a
MAGIC TEACHER

Vol. 1

Story
Rui Sekai

Art
Kyou Kitazawa

Character Design
Daburyu

Adaptation
Kiyomi Tanabe

In cooperation with
Hifumi Shobo

CONTENTS

I Got Fired as a Court Wizard so
Now I'm Moving to the Country
to Become a Magic Teacher

1st Period

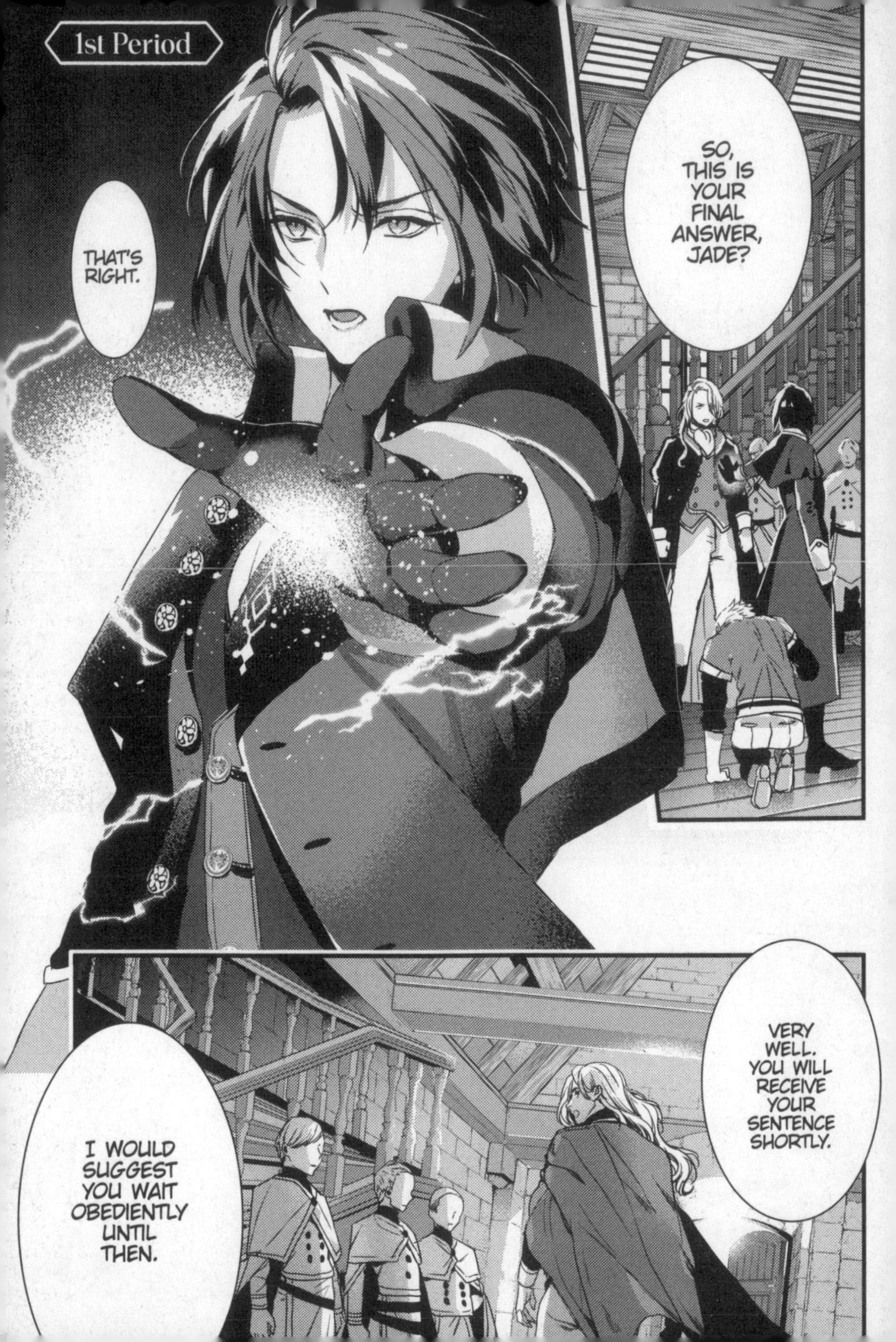
SO, THIS IS YOUR FINAL ANSWER, JADE?
THAT'S RIGHT.
VERY WELL. YOU WILL RECEIVE YOUR SENTENCE SHORTLY.
I WOULD SUGGEST YOU WAIT OBEDIENTLY UNTIL THEN.

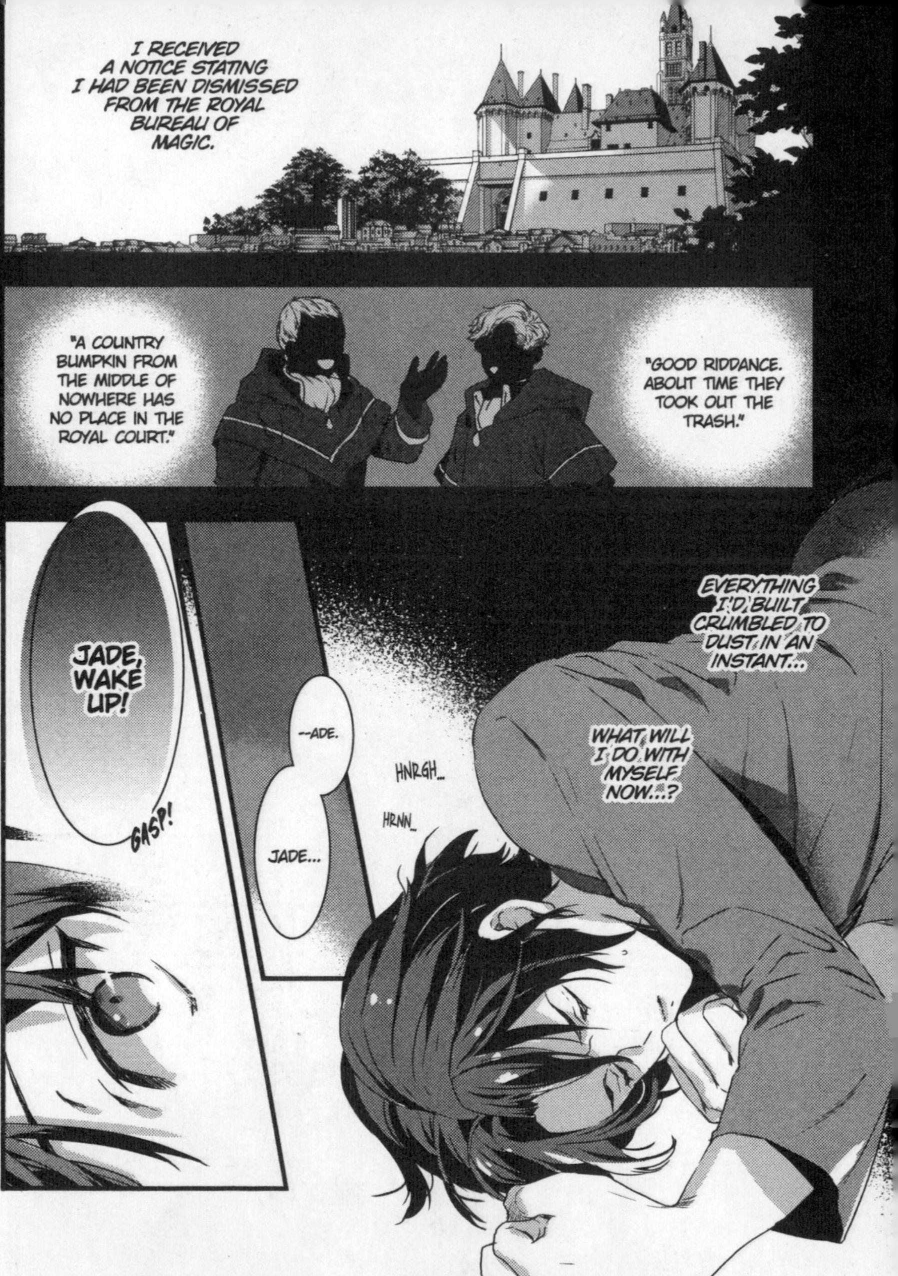
I RECEIVED A NOTICE STATING I HAD BEEN DISMISSED FROM THE ROYAL BUREAU OF MAGIC.
"GOOD RIDDANCE. ABOUT TIME THEY TOOK OUT THE TRASH."
"A COUNTRY BUMPKIN FROM THE MIDDLE OF NOWHERE HAS NO PLACE IN THE ROYAL COURT."
EVERYTHING I'D BUILT CRUMBLED TO DUST IN AN INSTANT...
WHAT WILL I DO WITH MYSELF NOW...?
HNRGH...
HRNN...
--ADE.
JADE...
JADE, WAKE UP!
GASP!

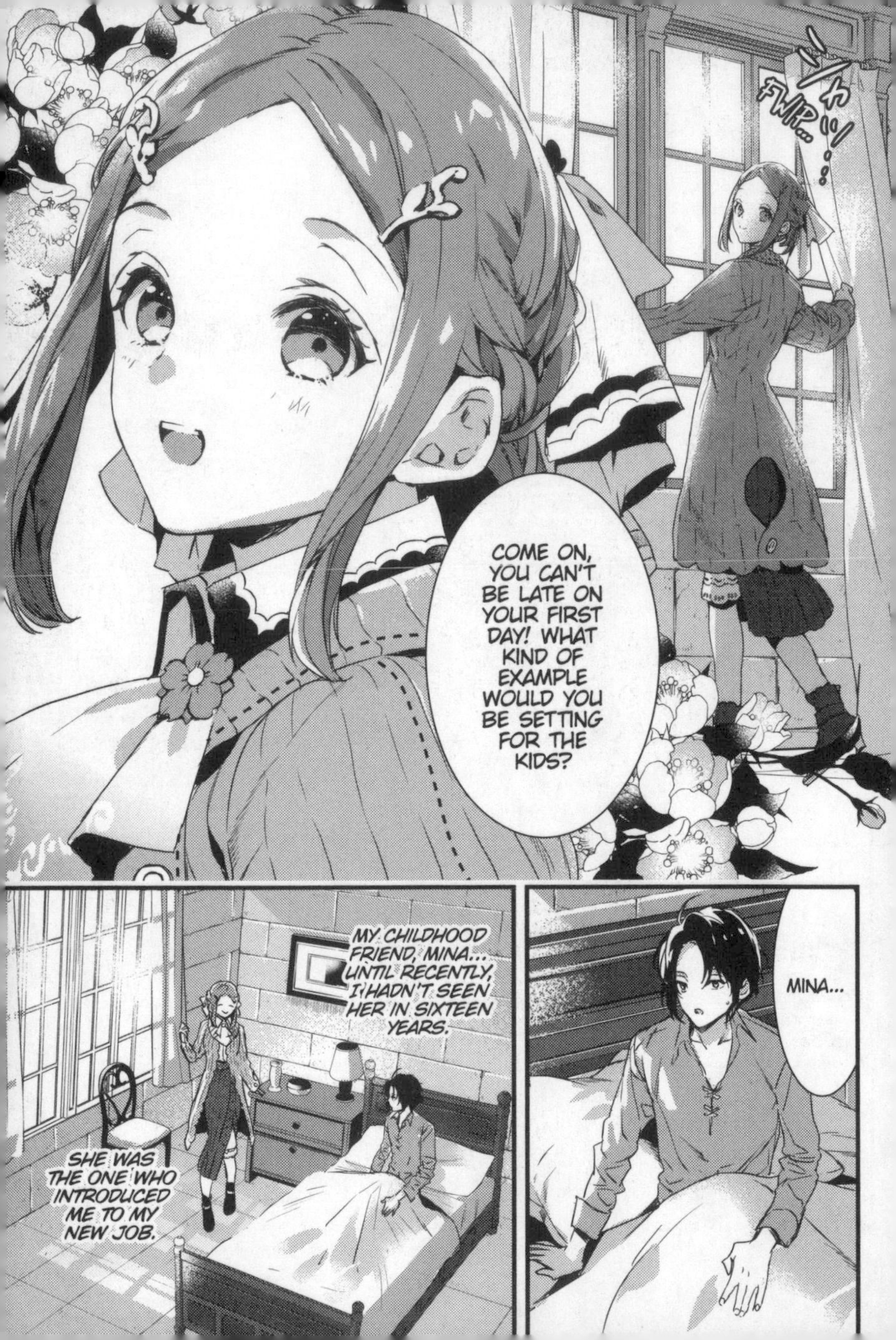
FWIP...
COME ON, YOU CAN'T BE LATE ON YOUR FIRST DAY! WHAT KIND OF EXAMPLE WOULD YOU BE SETTING FOR THE KIDS?
MINA...
MY CHILDHOOD FRIEND, MINA... UNTIL RECENTLY, I HADN'T SEEN HER IN SIXTEEN YEARS.
SHE WAS THE ONE WHO INTRODUCED ME TO MY NEW JOB.

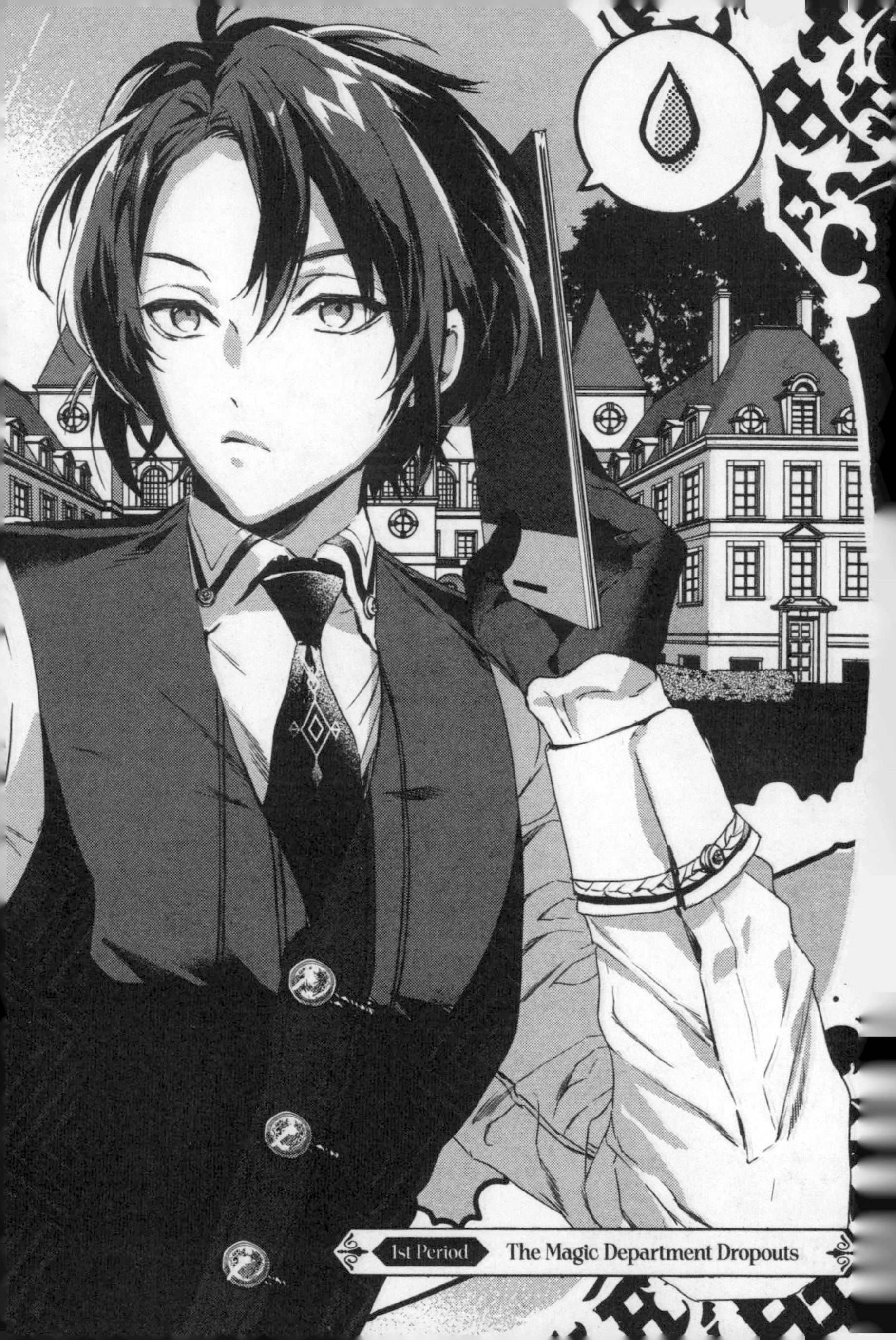
1st Period
The Magic Department Dropouts

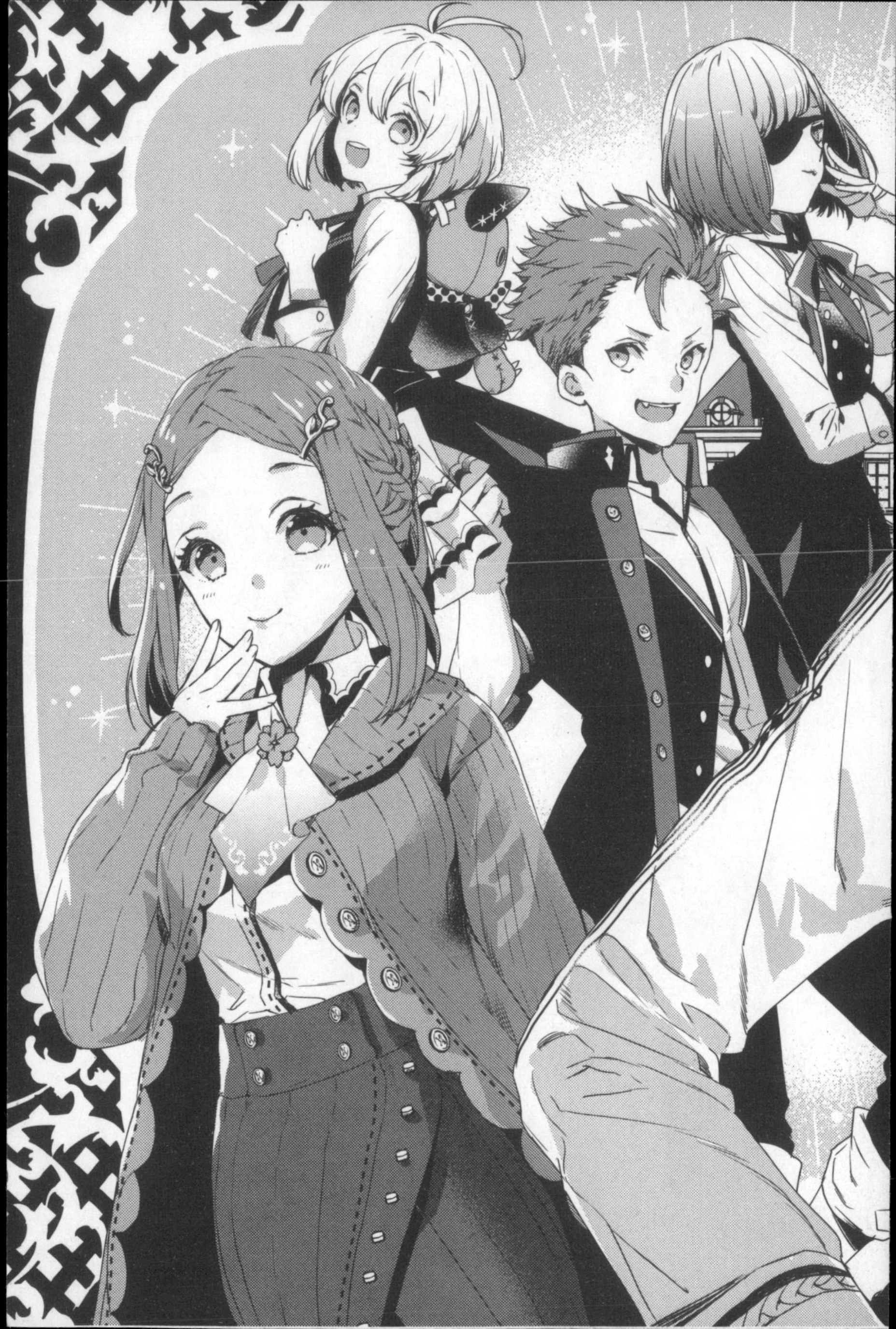

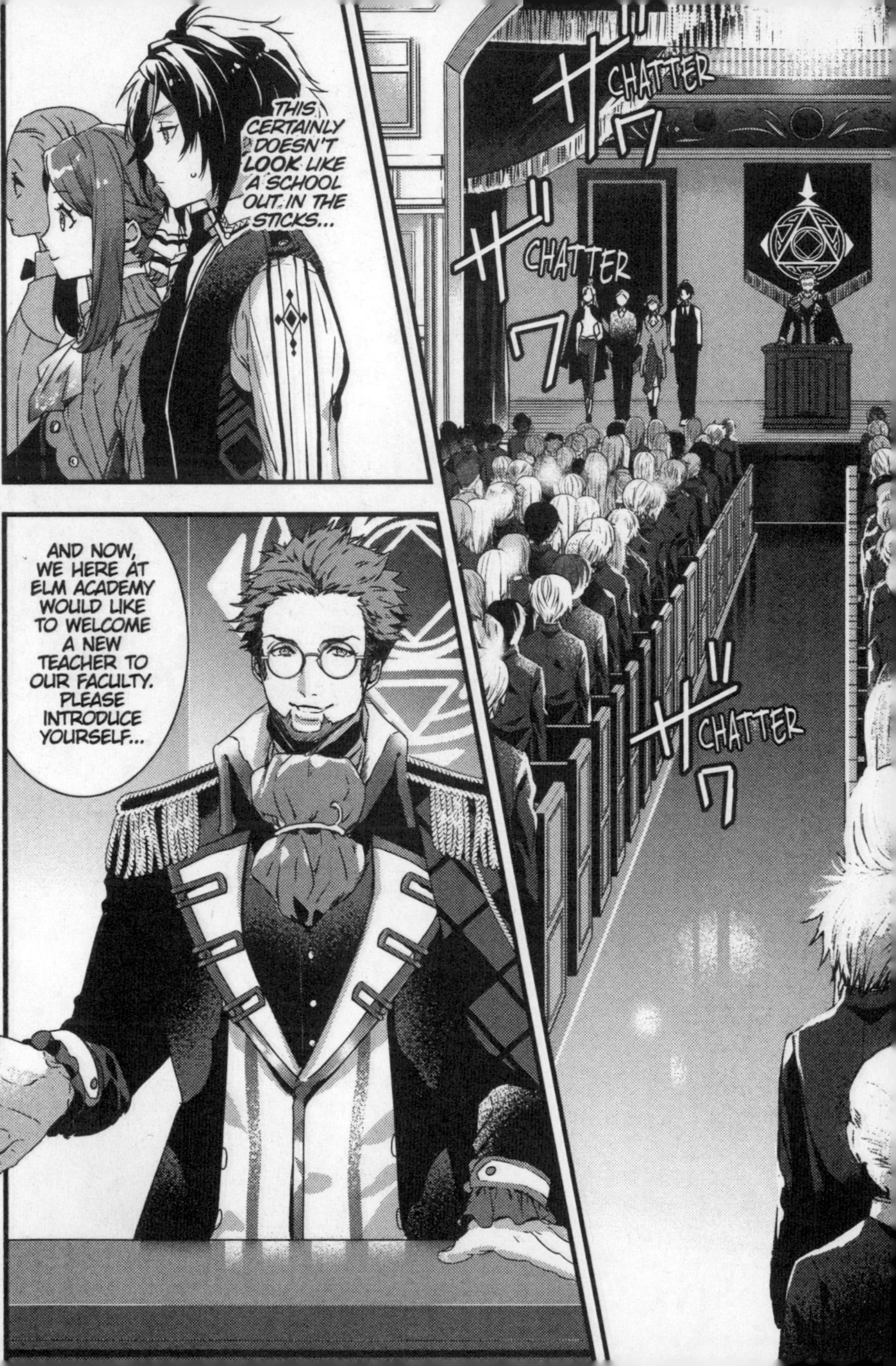
CHATTER
CHATTER
CHATTER
THIS CERTAINLY DOESN'T LOOK LIKE A SCHOOL OUT IN THE STICKS...
AND NOW, WE HERE AT ELM ACADEMY WOULD LIKE TO WELCOME A NEW TEACHER TO OUR FACULTY. PLEASE INTRODUCE YOURSELF...

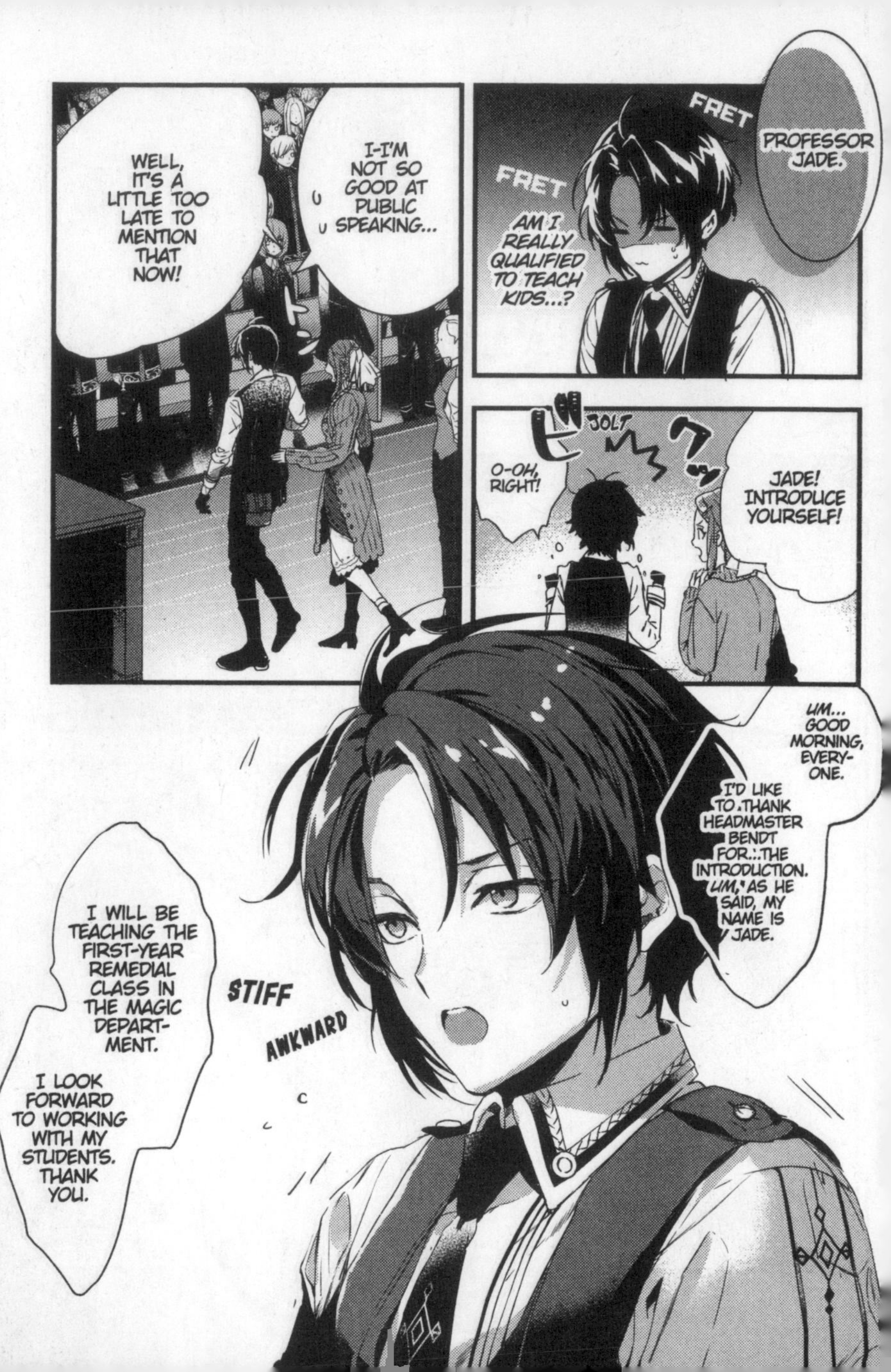
PROFESSOR JADE.
FRET
FRET
AM I REALLY QUALIFIED TO TEACH KIDS...?
I-I'M NOT SO GOOD AT PUBLIC SPEAKING...
WELL, IT'S A LITTLE TOO LATE TO MENTION THAT NOW!
JADE! INTRODUCE YOURSELF!
JOLT
O-OH, RIGHT!
UM... GOOD MORNING, EVERY-ONE.
I'D LIKE TO THANK HEADMASTER BENDT FOR... THE INTRODUCTION. UM, AS HE SAID, MY NAME IS JADE.
STIFF
AWKWARD
I WILL BE TEACHING THE FIRST-YEAR REMEDIAL CLASS IN THE MAGIC DEPART-MENT.
I LOOK FORWARD TO WORKING WITH MY STUDENTS. THANK YOU.

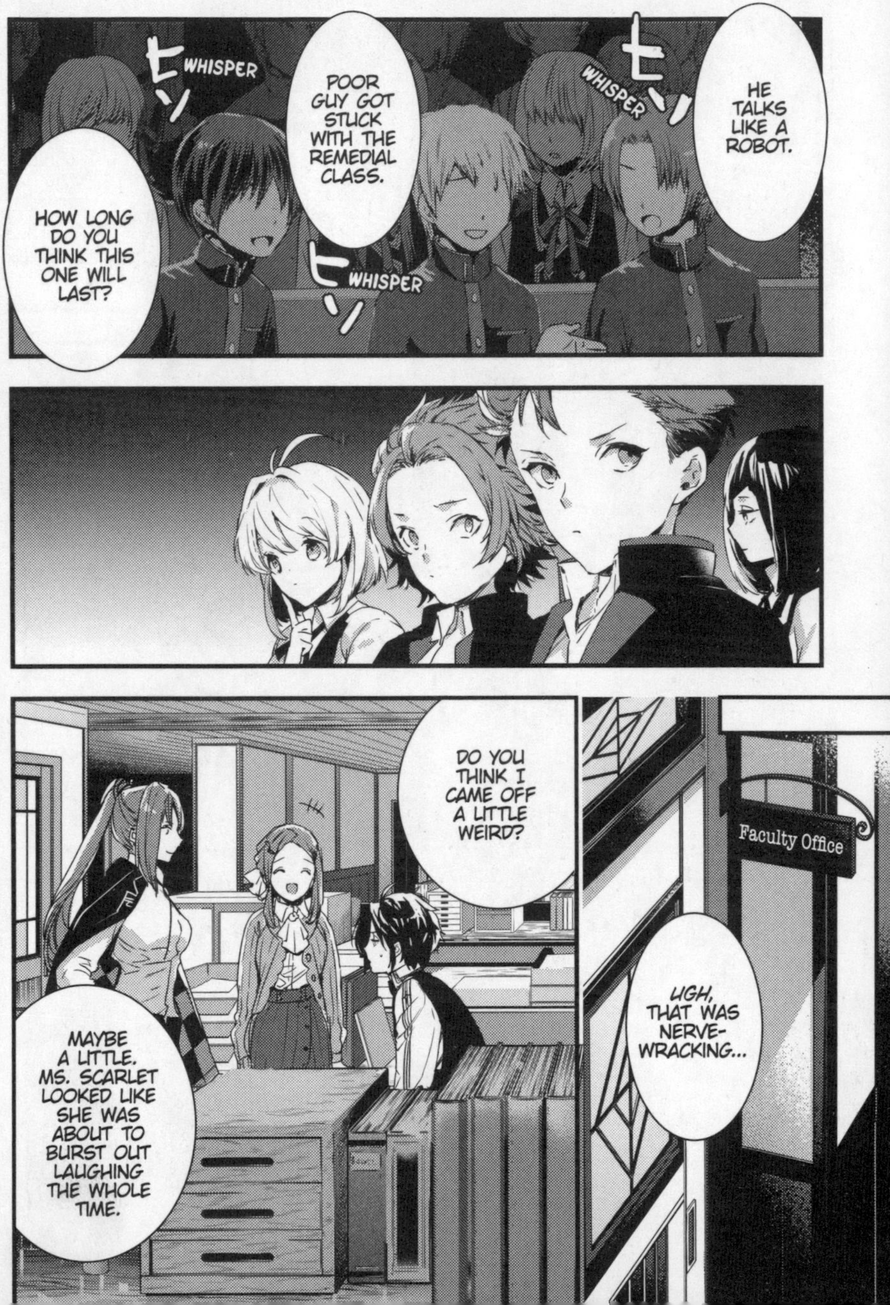
HE TALKS LIKE A ROBOT.
ヒソ WHISPER
POOR GUY GOT STUCK WITH THE REMEDIAL CLASS.
ヒソ WHISPER
HOW LONG DO YOU THINK THIS ONE WILL LAST?
ヒソ WHISPER
Faculty Office
UGH, THAT WAS NERVE-WRACKING...
DO YOU THINK I CAME OFF A LITTLE WEIRD?
MAYBE A LITTLE. MS. SCARLET LOOKED LIKE SHE WAS ABOUT TO BURST OUT LAUGHING THE WHOLE TIME.

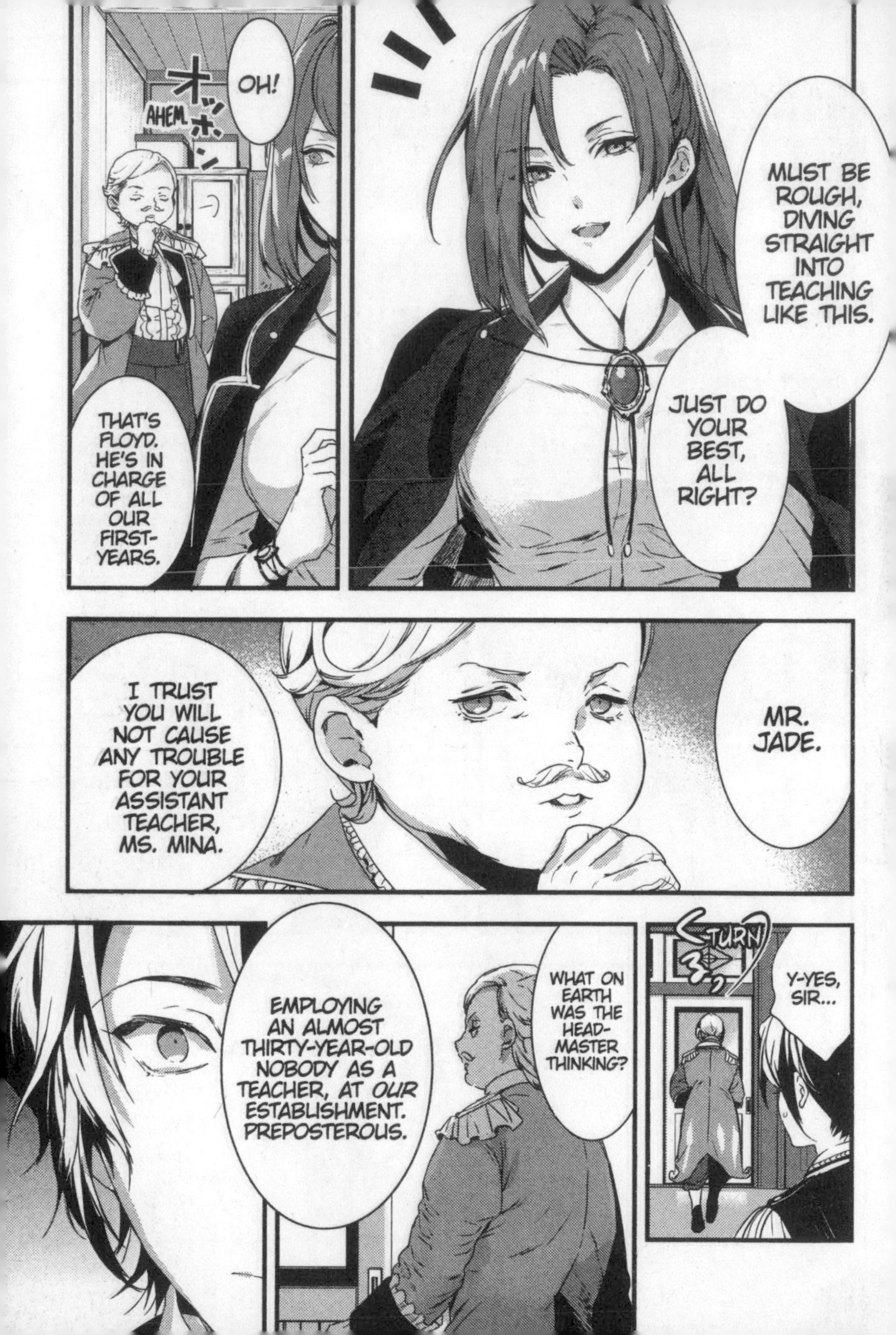
MUST BE ROUGH, DIVING STRAIGHT INTO TEACHING LIKE THIS.
JUST DO YOUR BEST, ALL RIGHT?
OH!
オッホン
AHEM.
THAT'S FLOYD. HE'S IN CHARGE OF ALL OUR FIRST-YEARS.
MR. JADE.
I TRUST YOU WILL NOT CAUSE ANY TROUBLE FOR YOUR ASSISTANT TEACHER, MS. MINA.
Y-YES, SIR...
TURN
WHAT ON EARTH WAS THE HEADMASTER THINKING?
EMPLOYING AN ALMOST THIRTY-YEAR-OLD NOBODY AS A TEACHER, AT OUR ESTABLISHMENT. PREPOSTEROUS.

CALL ME CRAZY, BUT I DON'T THINK MR. FLOYD LIKES ME VERY MUCH.

I PROBABLY DON'T LOOK TOO RELIABLE FROM WHERE HE SITS.

OH, DON'T WORRY ABOUT HIM. YOU NEED TO FOCUS! FIRST IMPRESSIONS ARE IMPORTANT!

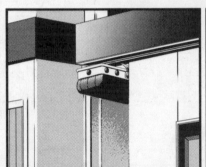

THIS IS OUR CLASSROOM.

HA HA... A CLASSIC STUDENT PRANK.

HOLD ON.

PAT

I SHOULD GO IN FIRST.

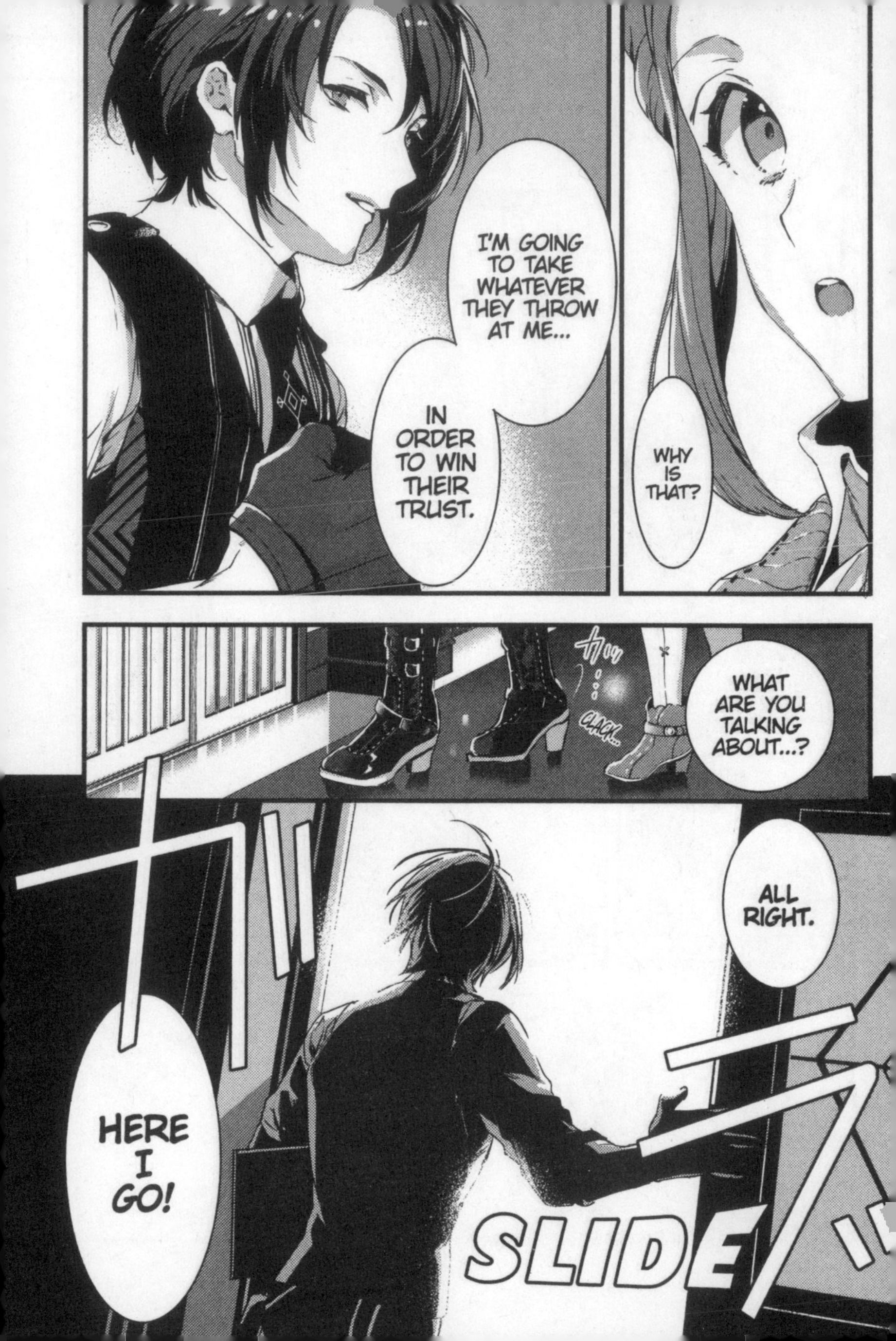
WHY IS THAT?
I'M GOING TO TAKE WHATEVER THEY THROW AT ME...
IN ORDER TO WIN THEIR TRUST.
WHAT ARE YOU TALKING ABOUT...?
CLACK...
ALL RIGHT.
HERE I GO!
SLIDE

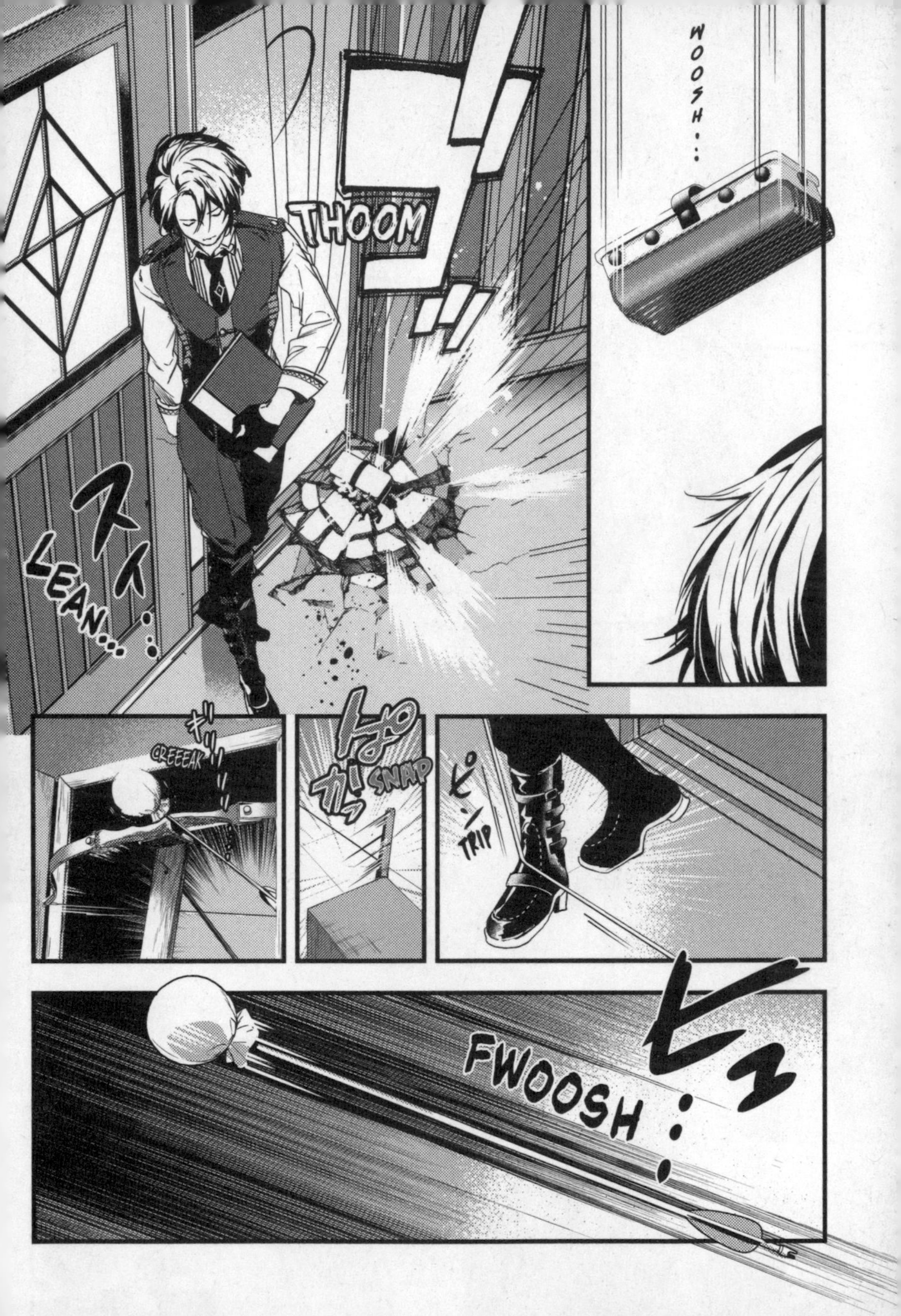
WOOSH...
THOOM
LEAN...
TRIP
SNAP
CREEEAK
FWOOSH

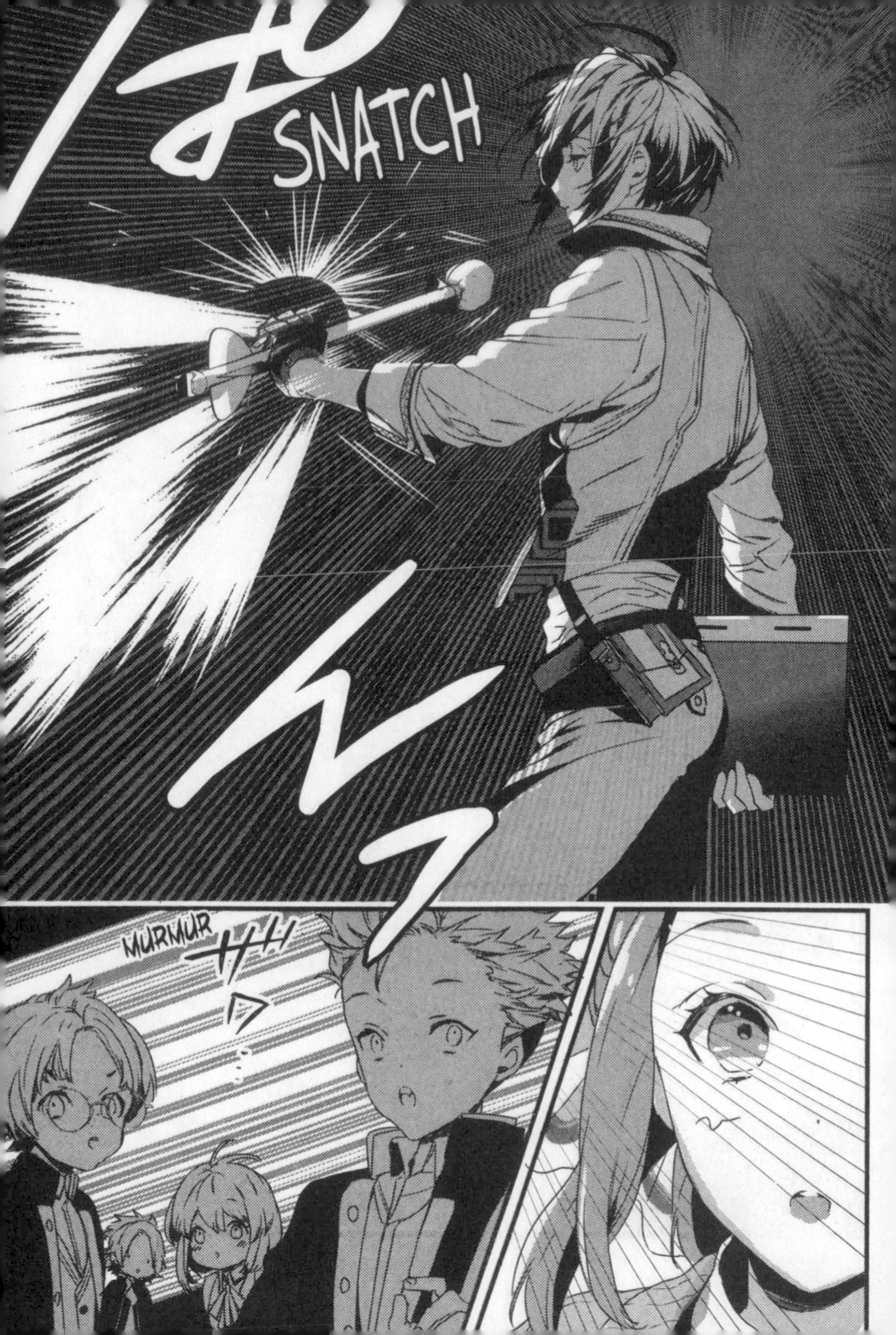
SNATCH
MURMUR

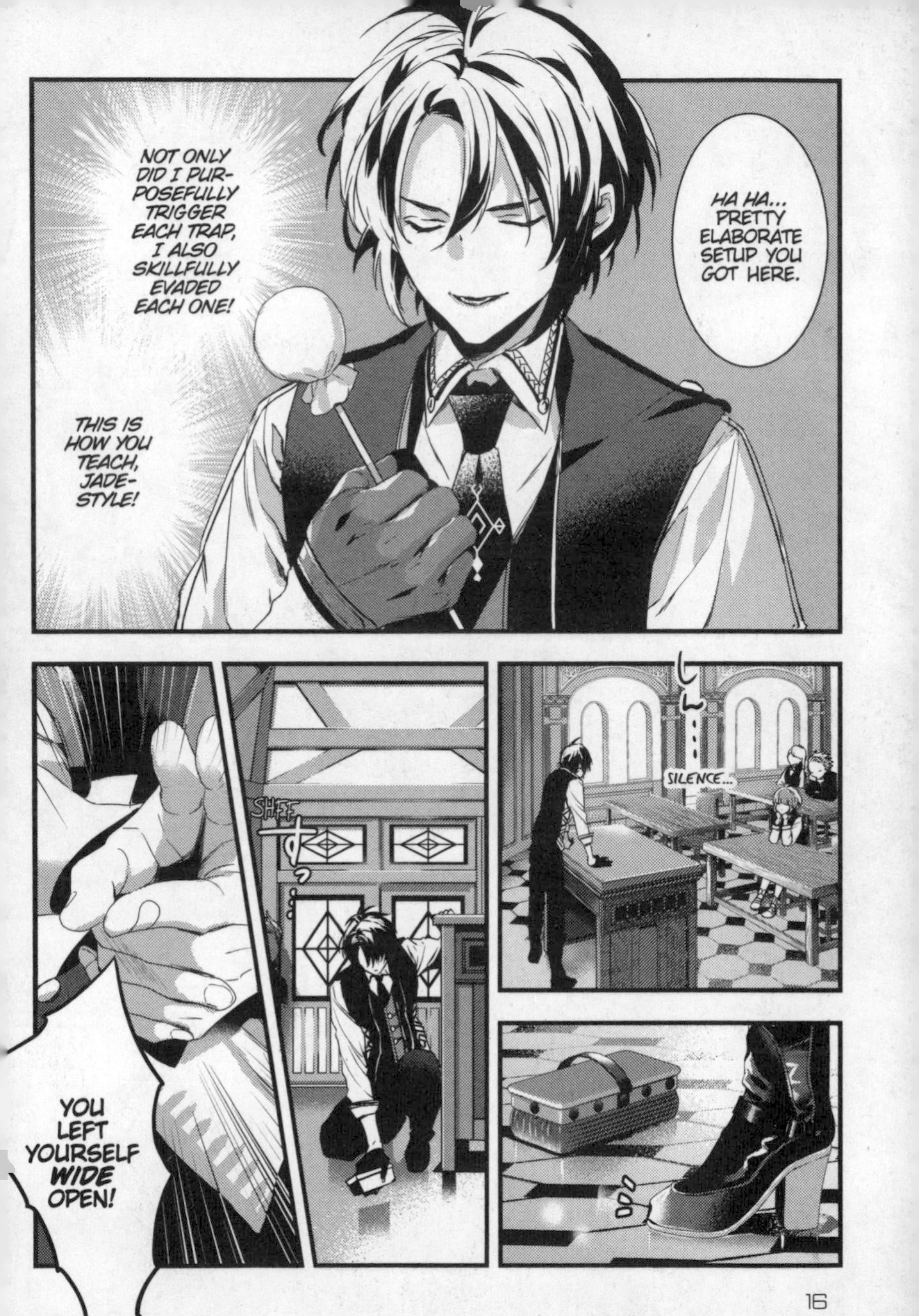
HA HA... PRETTY ELABORATE SETUP YOU GOT HERE.
NOT ONLY DID I PURPOSEFULLY TRIGGER EACH TRAP, I ALSO SKILLFULLY EVADED EACH ONE!
THIS IS HOW YOU TEACH, JADE-STYLE!
しん…
SILENCE...
SHFF
す…
YOU LEFT YOURSELF ***WIDE*** OPEN!

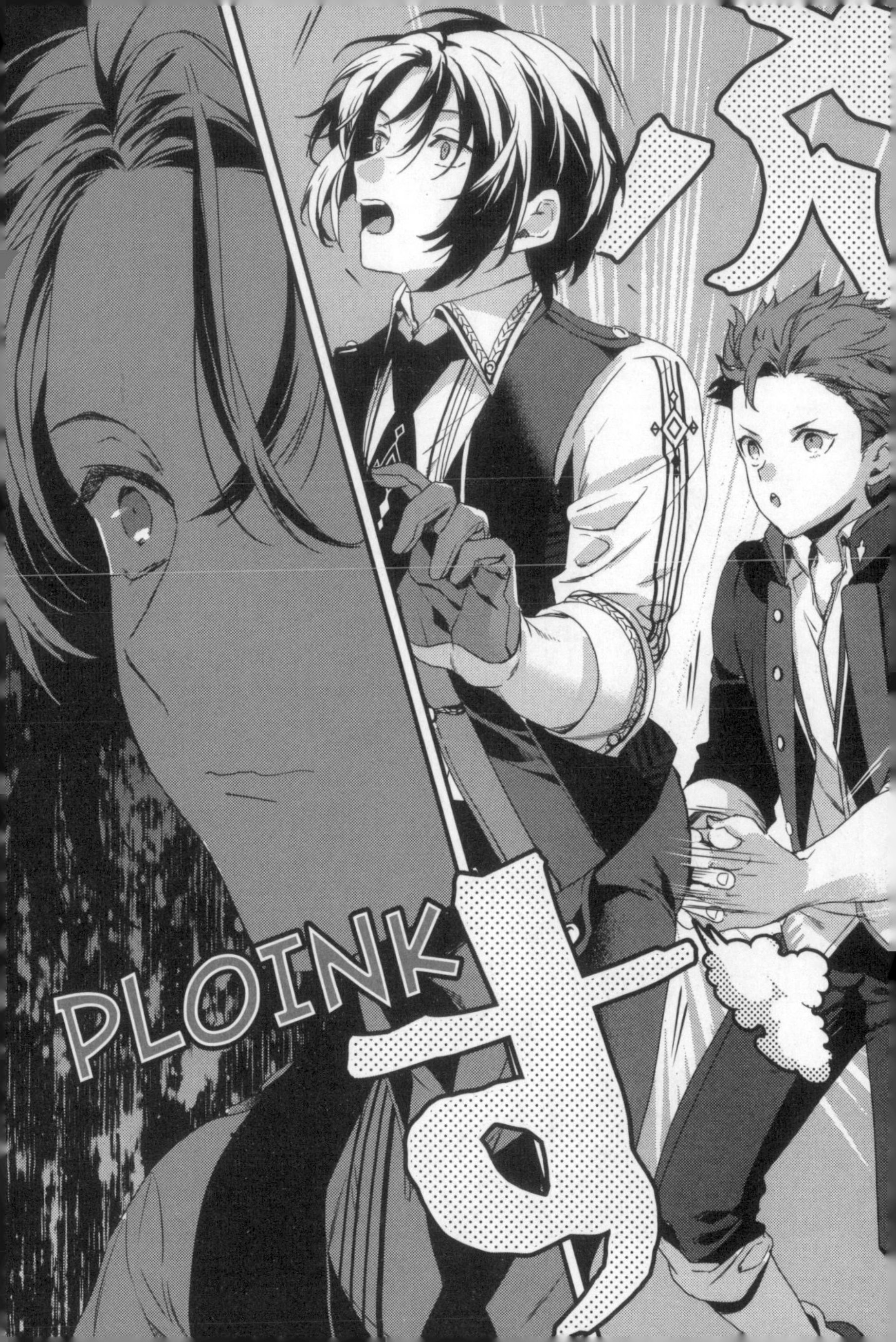
PLOINK

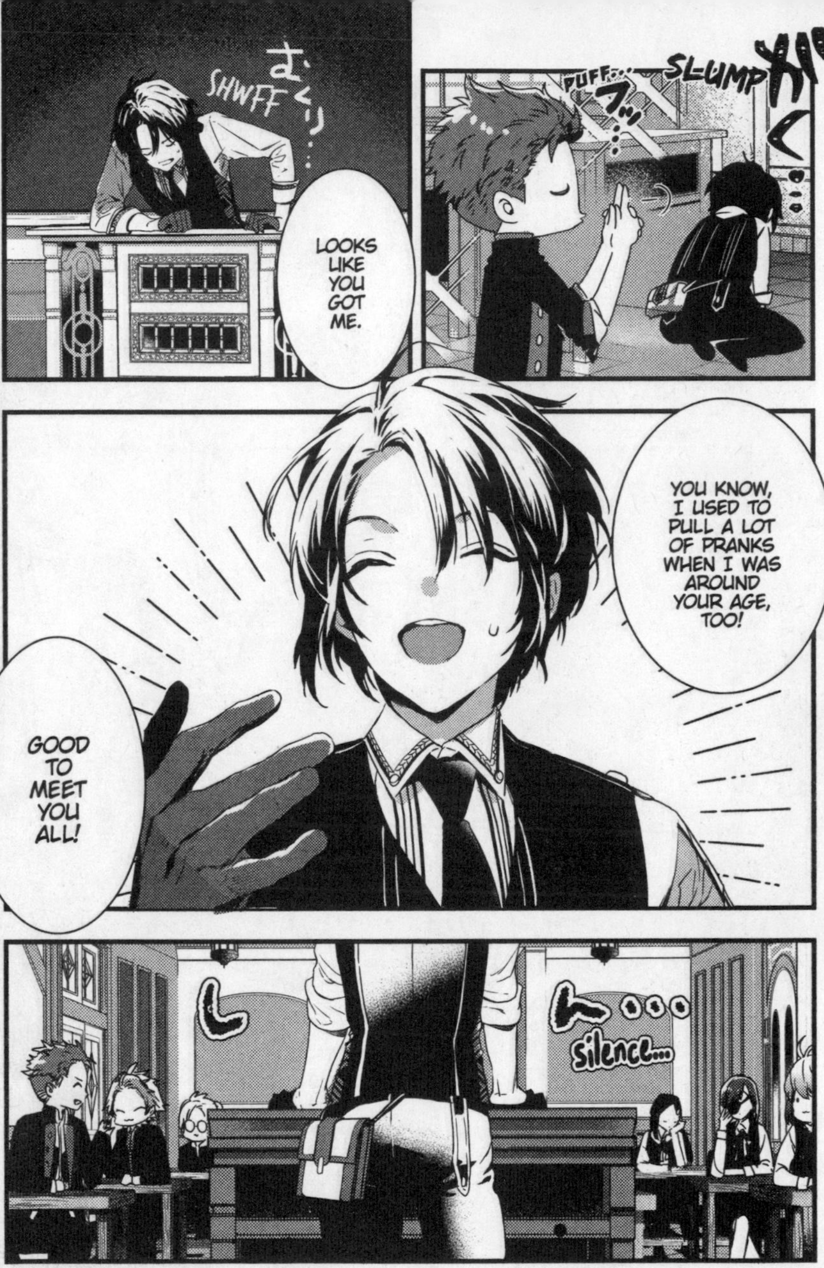
PUFF...
SLUMP
SHWFF
むくり
LOOKS LIKE YOU GOT ME.
YOU KNOW, I USED TO PULL A LOT OF PRANKS WHEN I WAS AROUND YOUR AGE, TOO!
GOOD TO MEET YOU ALL!
silence...

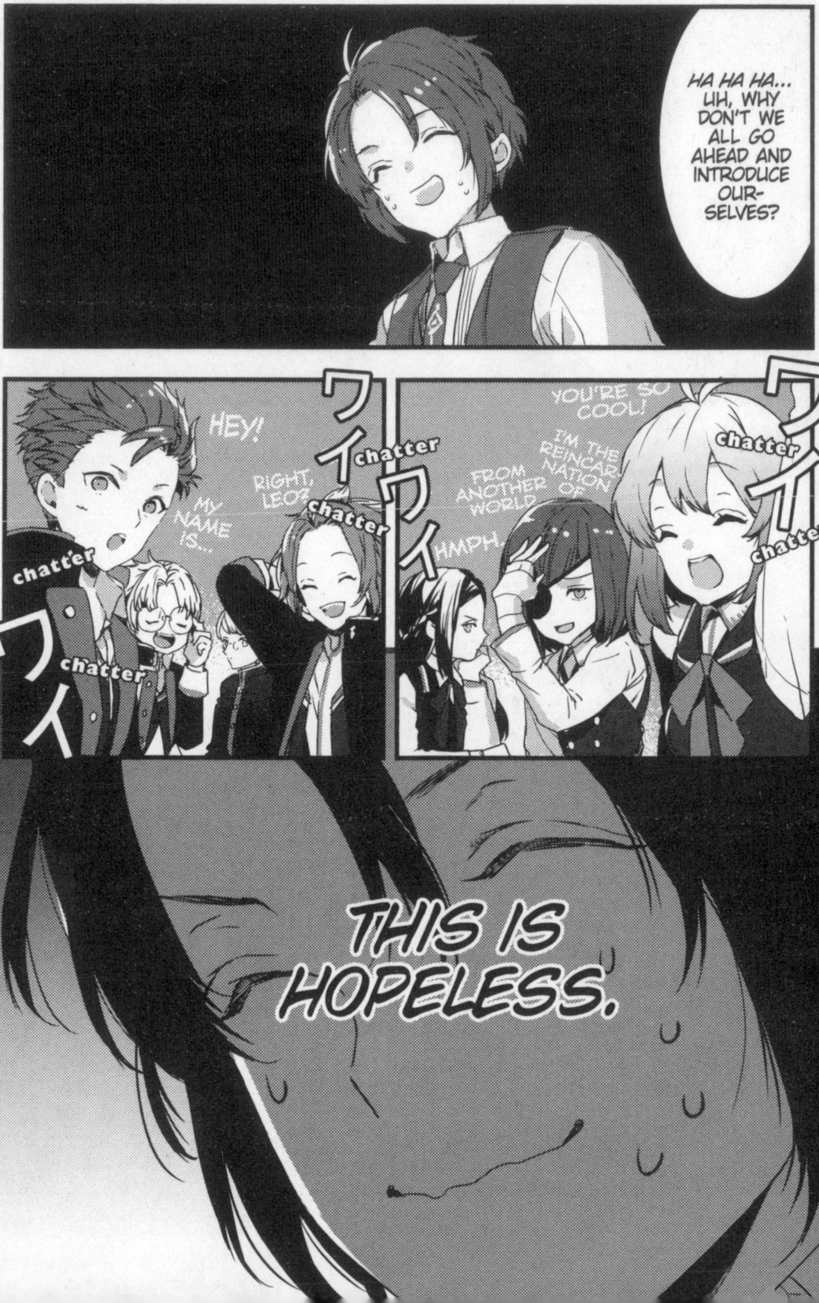

HA HA HA... UH, WHY DON'T WE ALL GO AHEAD AND INTRODUCE OUR-SELVES?
ワイ
chatter
YOU'RE SO COOL!
I'M THE REINCARNATION FROM ANOTHER WORLD OF
HMPH.
chatter
ワイワイ
chatter
HEY!
RIGHT, LEO?
chatter
MY NAME IS...
chatter
ワイ
chatter
THIS IS HOPELESS.

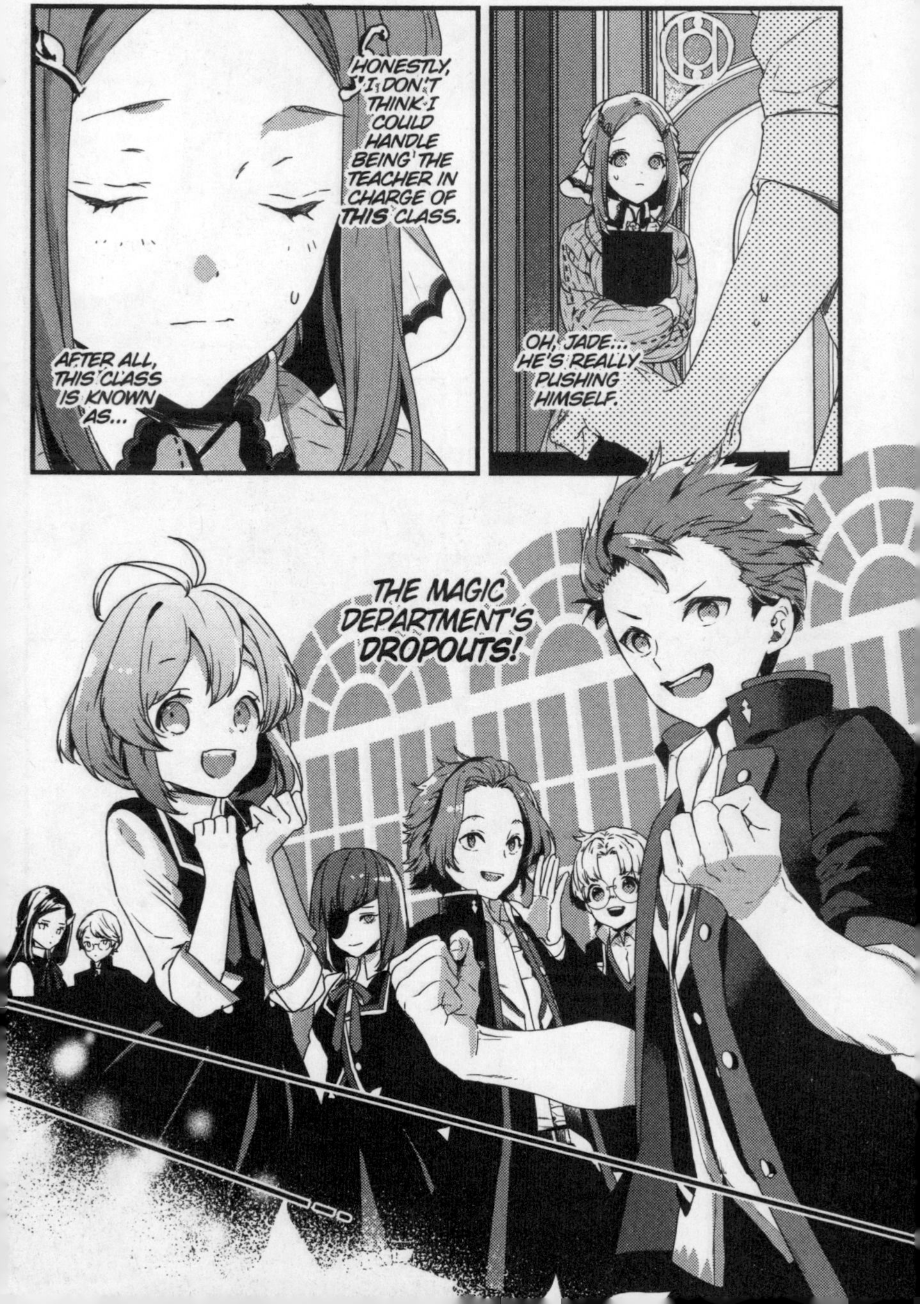
OH, JADE... HE'S REALLY PUSHING HIMSELF.
HONESTLY, I DON'T THINK I COULD HANDLE BEING THE TEACHER IN CHARGE OF THIS CLASS.
AFTER ALL, THIS CLASS IS KNOWN AS...
THE MAGIC DEPARTMENT'S DROPOUTS!

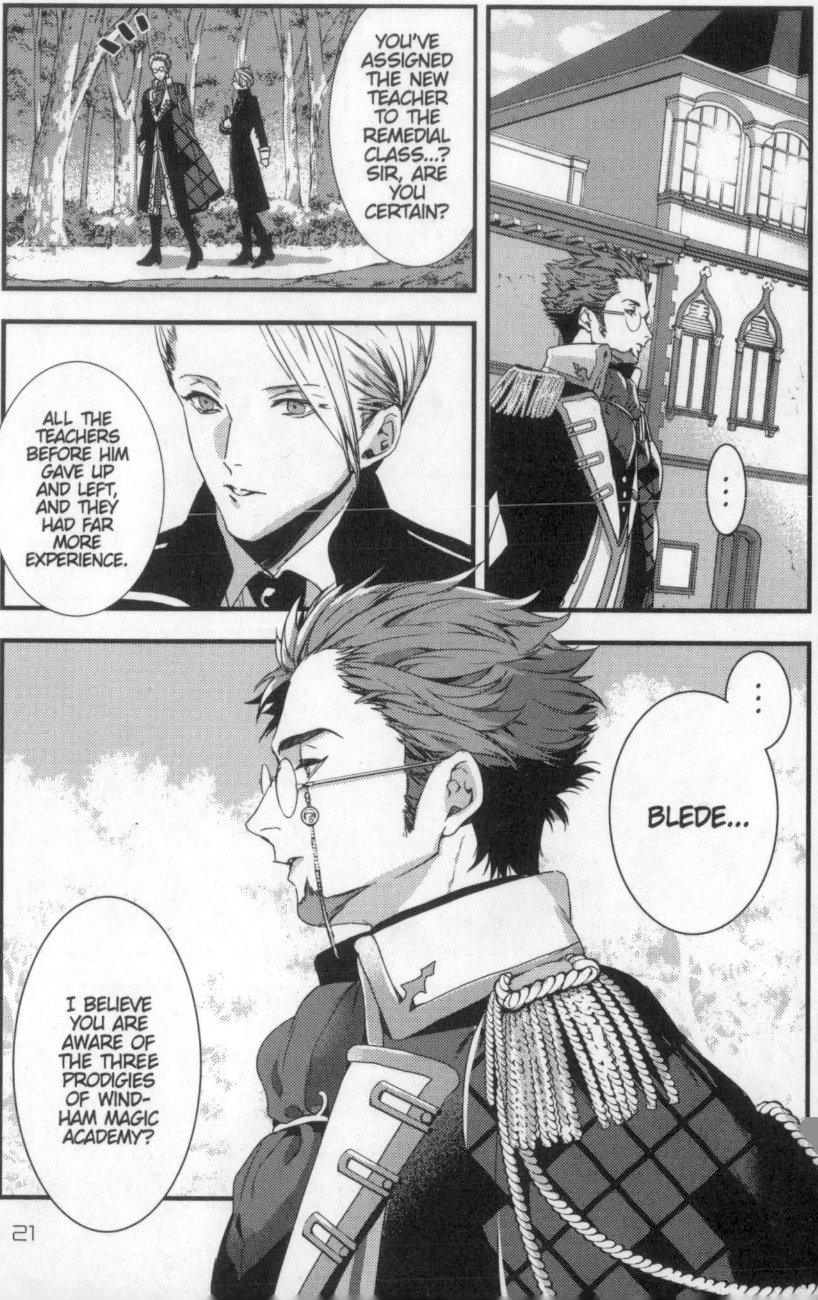
...
YOU'VE ASSIGNED THE NEW TEACHER TO THE REMEDIAL CLASS...? SIR, ARE YOU CERTAIN?
ALL THE TEACHERS BEFORE HIM GAVE UP AND LEFT, AND THEY HAD FAR MORE EXPERIENCE.
...
BLEDE...
I BELIEVE YOU ARE AWARE OF THE THREE PRODIGIES OF WIND-HAM MAGIC ACADEMY?

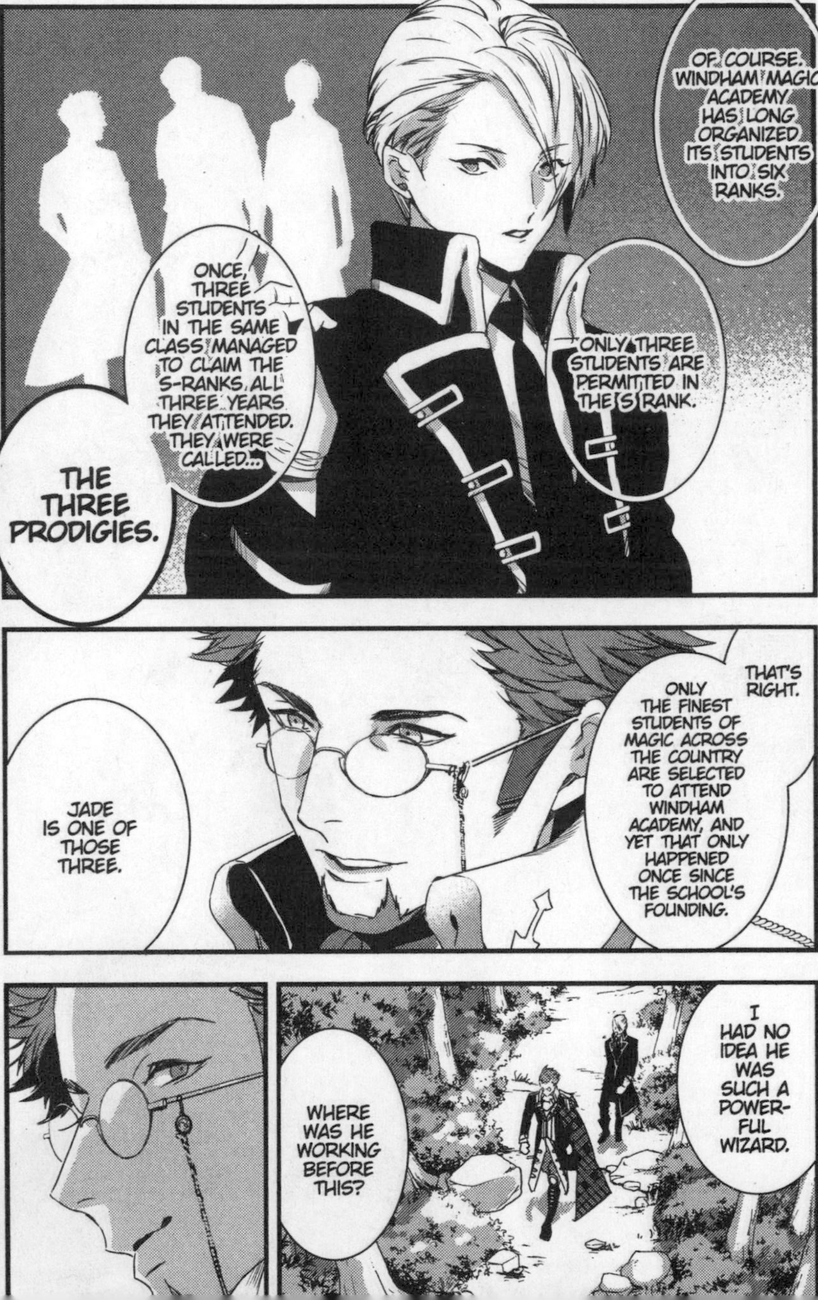
OF COURSE. WINDHAM MAGIC ACADEMY HAS LONG ORGANIZED ITS STUDENTS INTO SIX RANKS.
ONLY THREE STUDENTS ARE PERMITTED IN THE S RANK.
ONCE, THREE STUDENTS IN THE SAME CLASS MANAGED TO CLAIM THE S-RANKS ALL THREE YEARS THEY ATTENDED. THEY WERE CALLED...
THE THREE PRODIGIES.
THAT'S RIGHT.
ONLY THE FINEST STUDENTS OF MAGIC ACROSS THE COUNTRY ARE SELECTED TO ATTEND WINDHAM ACADEMY, AND YET THAT ONLY HAPPENED ONCE SINCE THE SCHOOL'S FOUNDING.
JADE IS ONE OF THOSE THREE.
I HAD NO IDEA HE WAS SUCH A POWER-FUL WIZARD.
WHERE WAS HE WORKING BEFORE THIS?

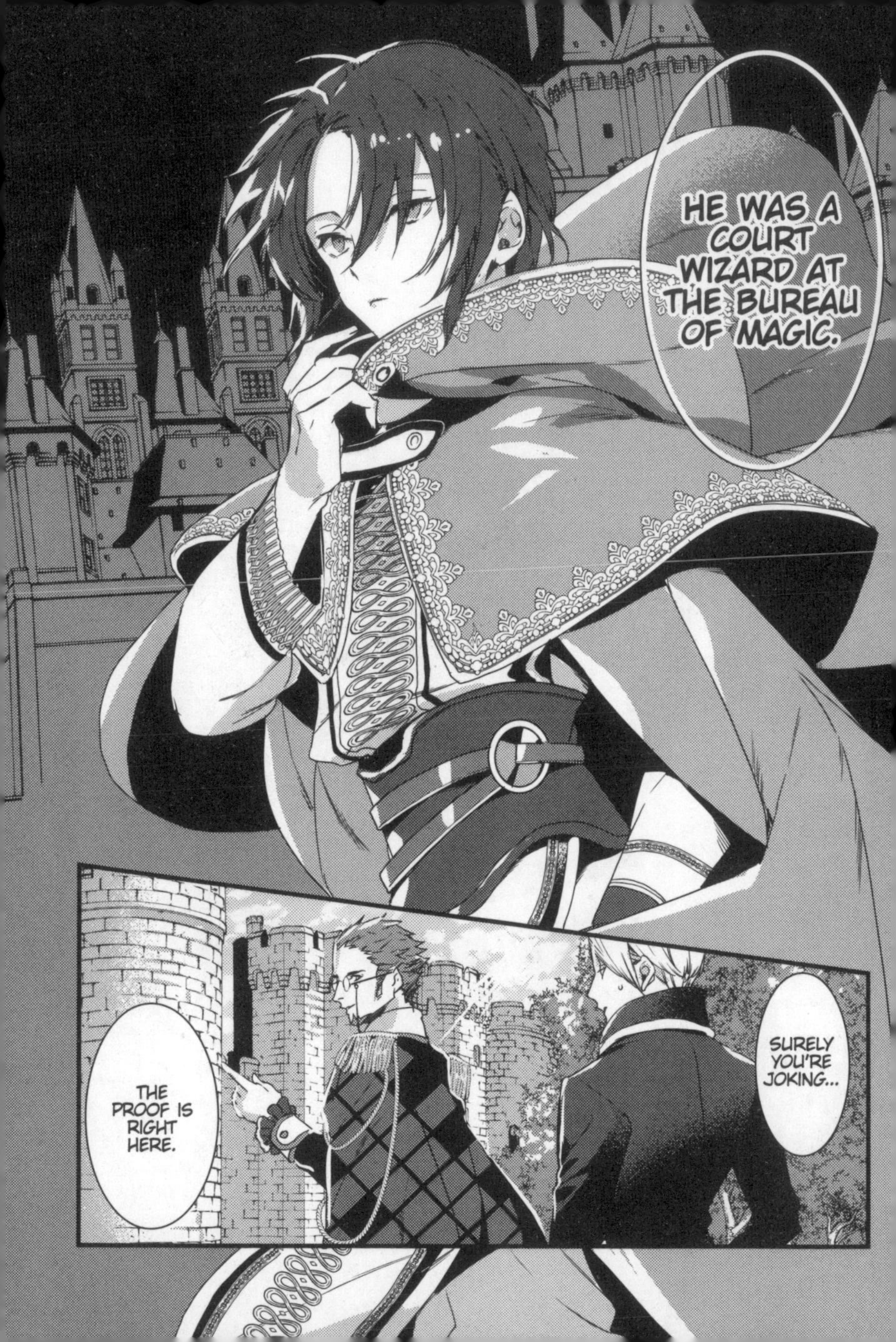
HE WAS A COURT WIZARD AT THE BUREAU OF MAGIC.
SURELY YOU'RE JOKING...
THE PROOF IS RIGHT HERE.

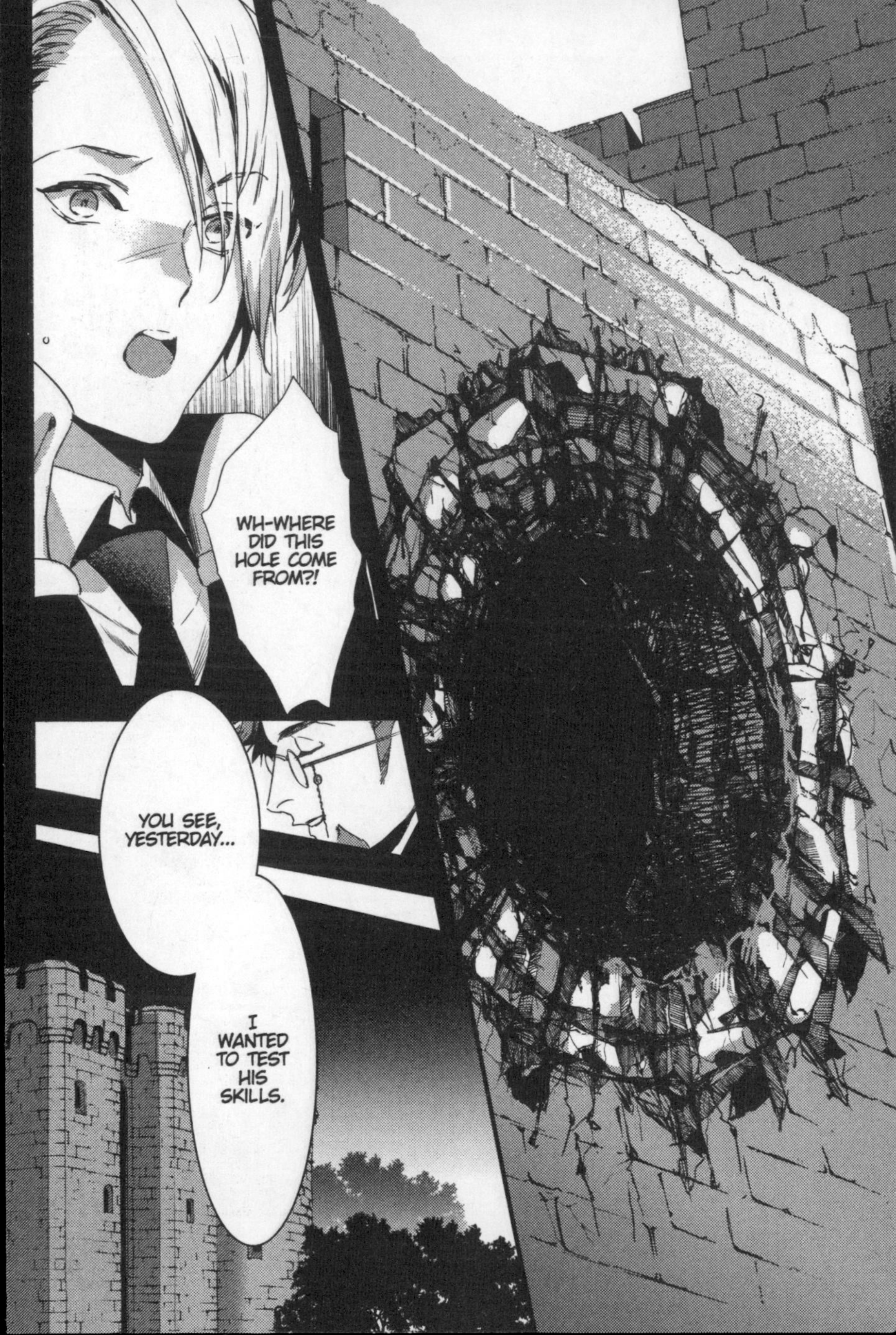
WH-WHERE DID THIS HOLE COME FROM?!
YOU SEE, YESTERDAY...
I WANTED TO TEST HIS SKILLS.

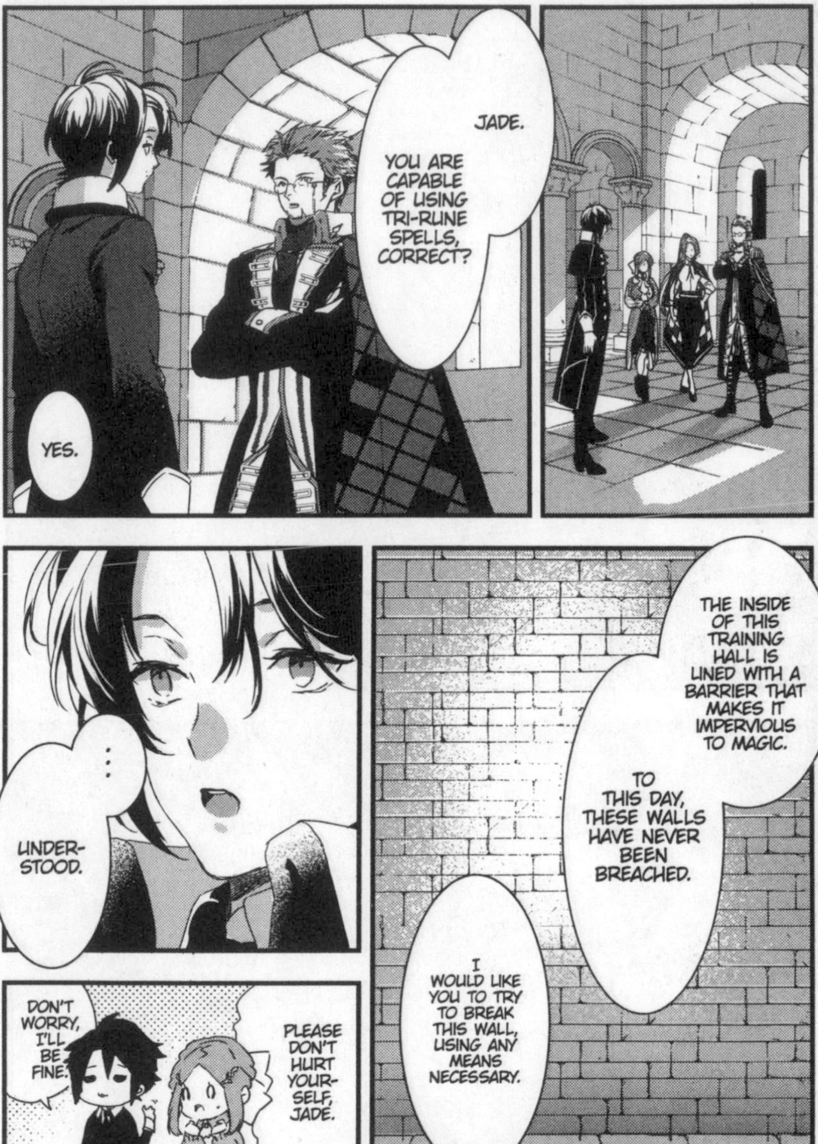
JADE.
YOU ARE CAPABLE OF USING TRI-RUNE SPELLS, CORRECT?
YES.
THE INSIDE OF THIS TRAINING HALL IS LINED WITH A BARRIER THAT MAKES IT IMPERVIOUS TO MAGIC.
TO THIS DAY, THESE WALLS HAVE NEVER BEEN BREACHED.
I WOULD LIKE YOU TO TRY TO BREAK THIS WALL, USING ANY MEANS NECESSARY.
...
UNDER-STOOD.
PLEASE DON'T HURT YOUR-SELF, JADE.
DON'T WORRY, I'LL BE FINE.

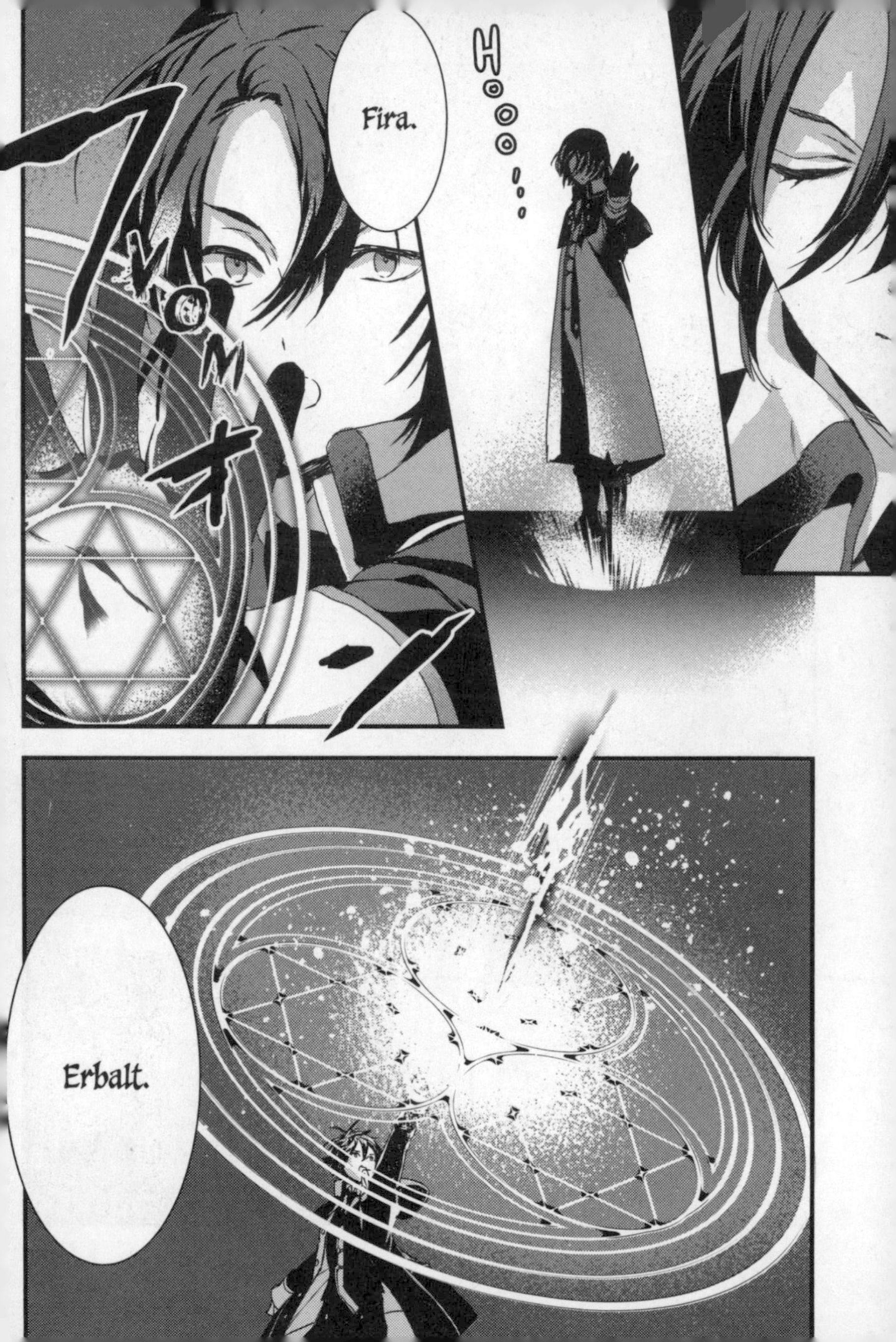
HOOOO...
Fira.
VOM
Erbalt.

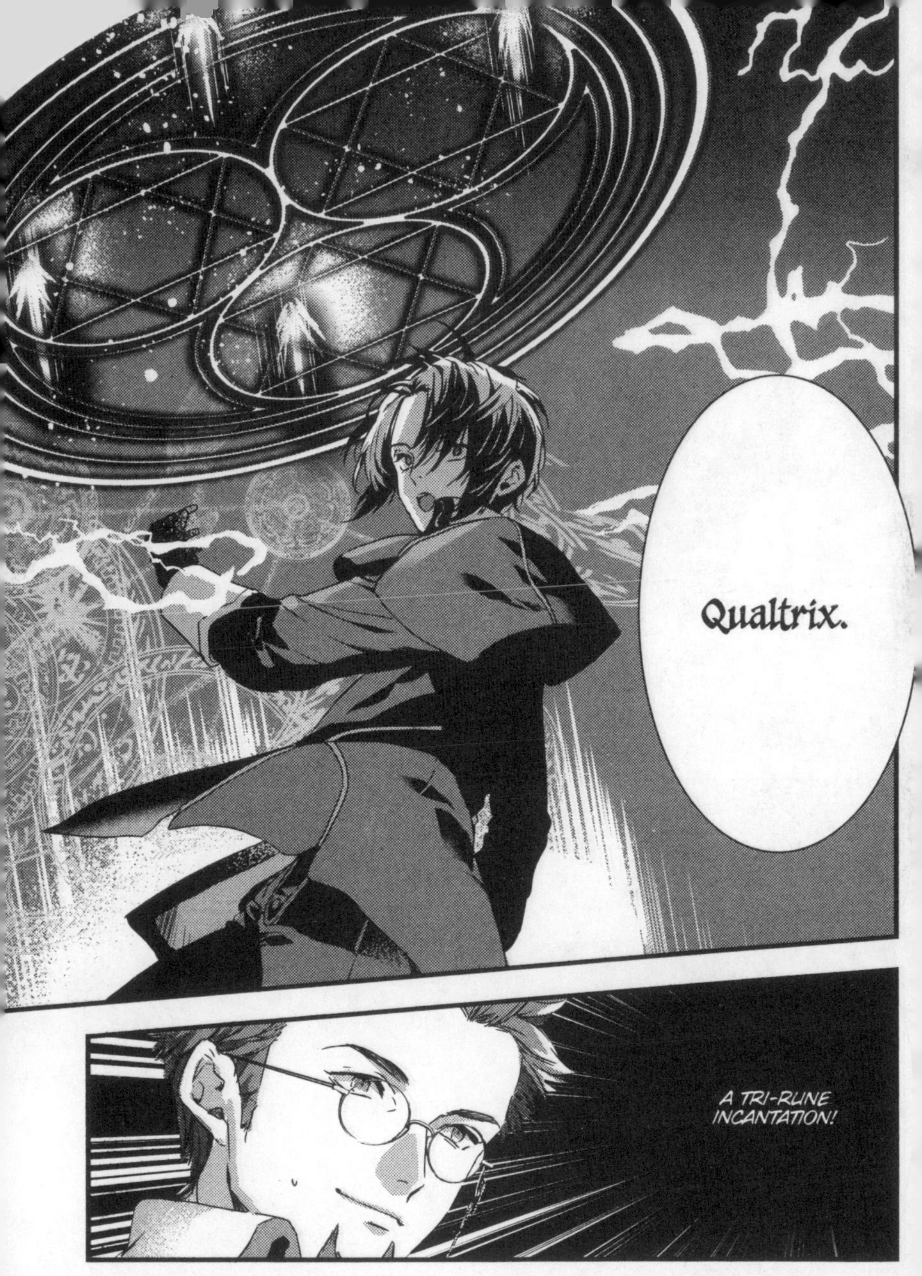
Qualtrix.
A TRI-RUNE INCANTATION!

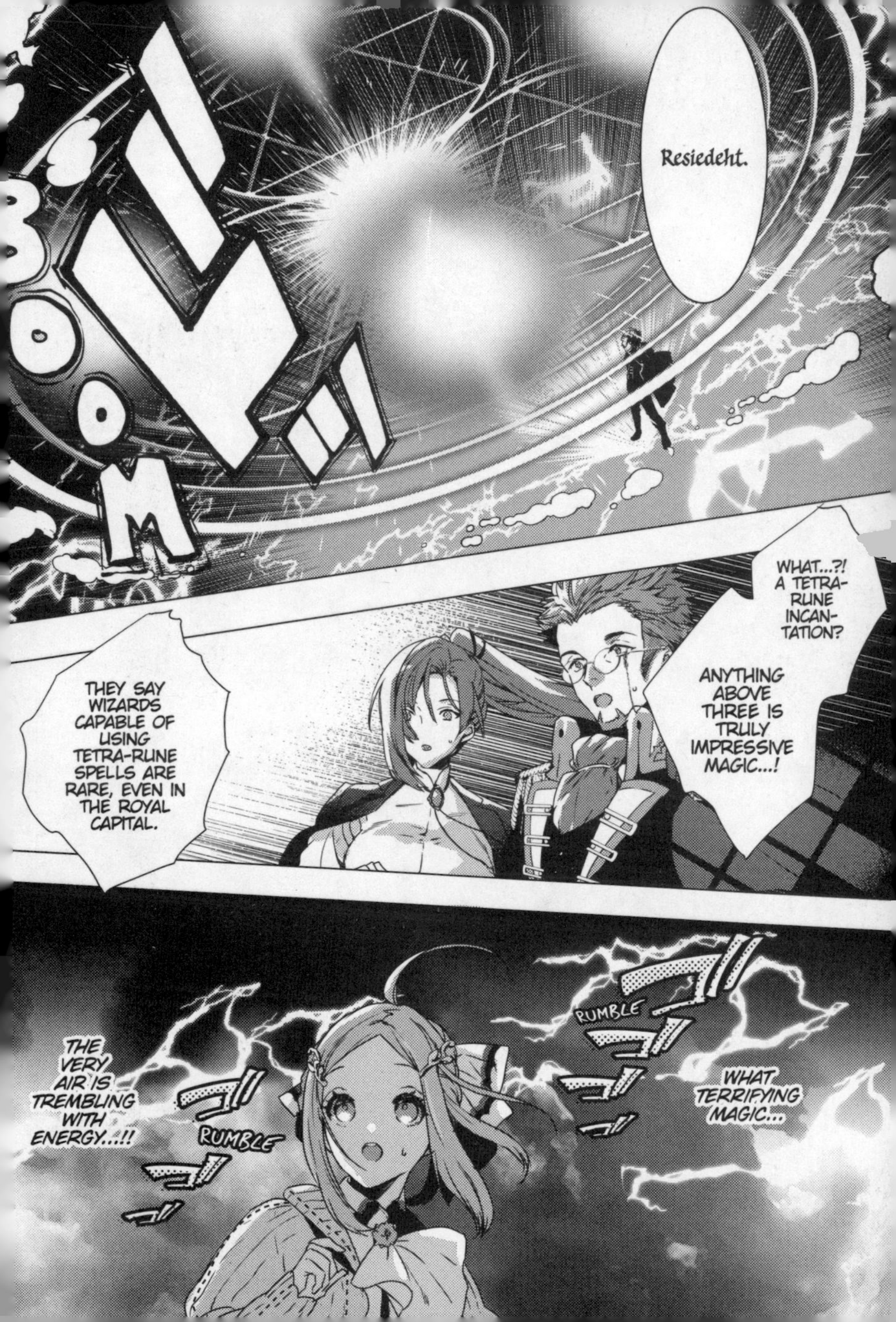
Resiedeht.
BOOM
WHAT...?! A TETRA-RUNE INCANTATION?
ANYTHING ABOVE THREE IS TRULY IMPRESSIVE MAGIC...!
THEY SAY WIZARDS CAPABLE OF USING TETRA-RUNE SPELLS ARE RARE, EVEN IN THE ROYAL CAPITAL.
RUMBLE
WHAT TERRIFYING MAGIC...
RUMBLE
THE VERY AIR IS TREMBLING WITH ENERGY...!!

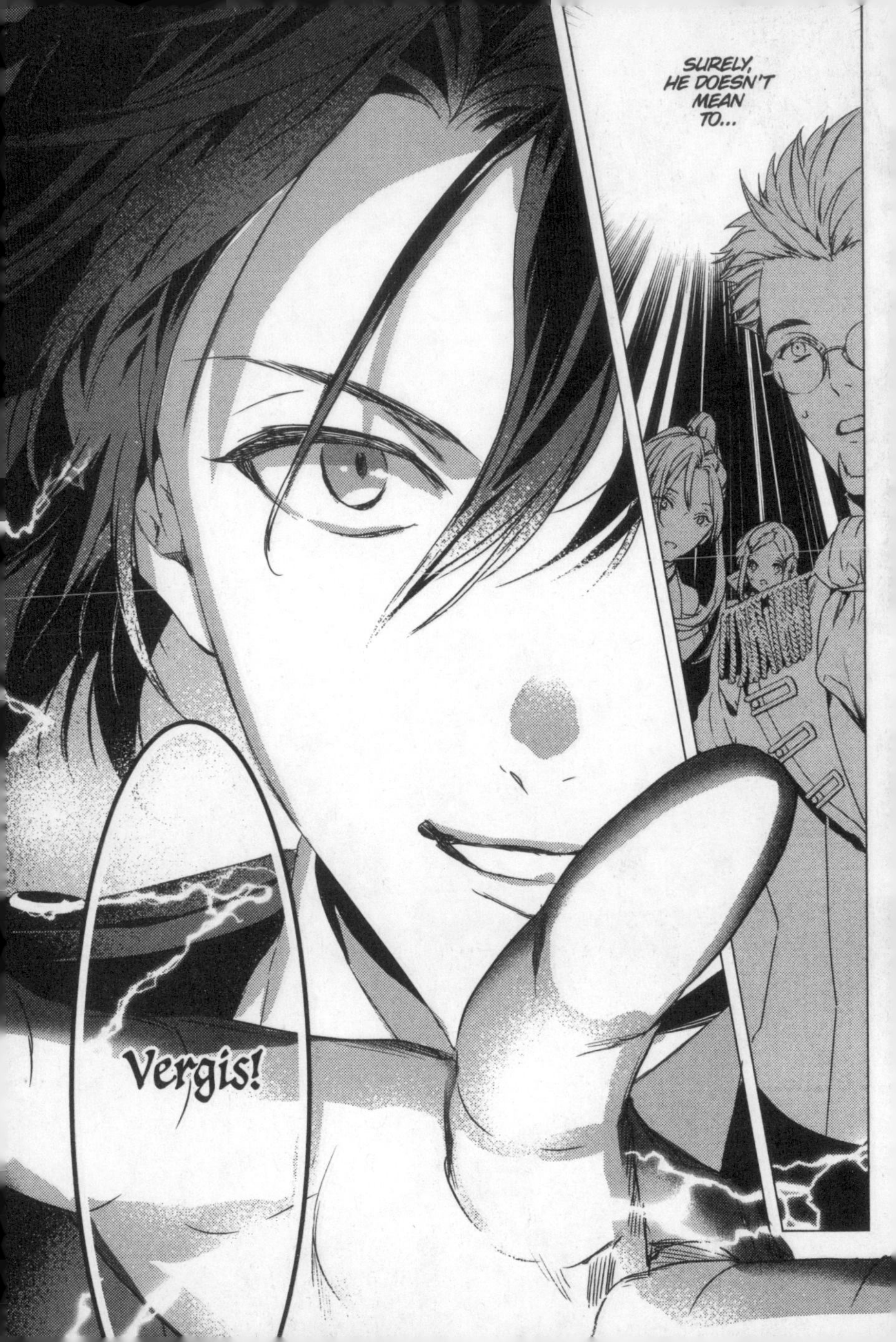
SURELY, HE DOESN'T MEAN TO...
Vergis!

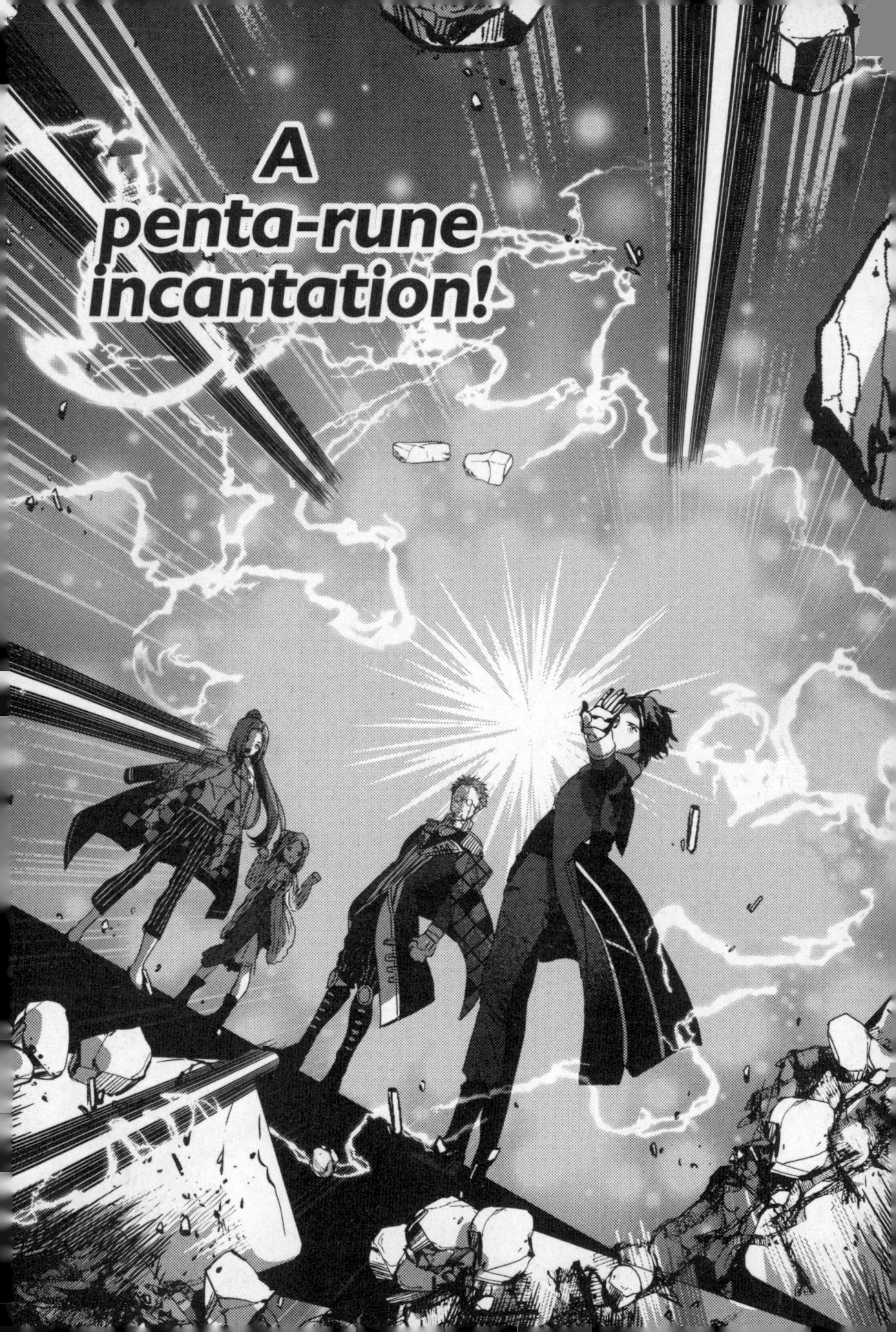
A penta-rune incantation!

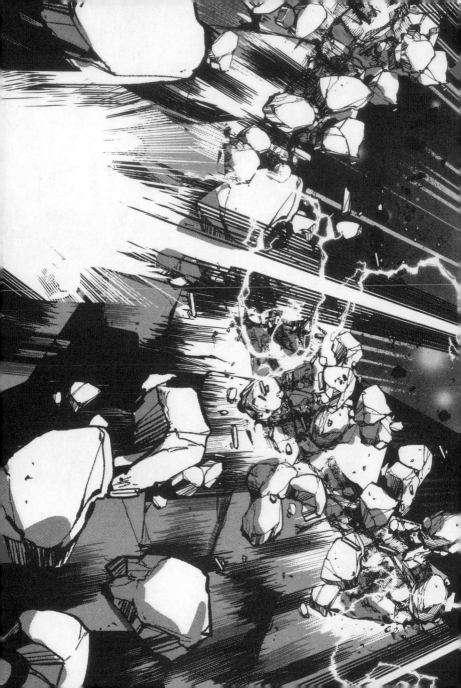

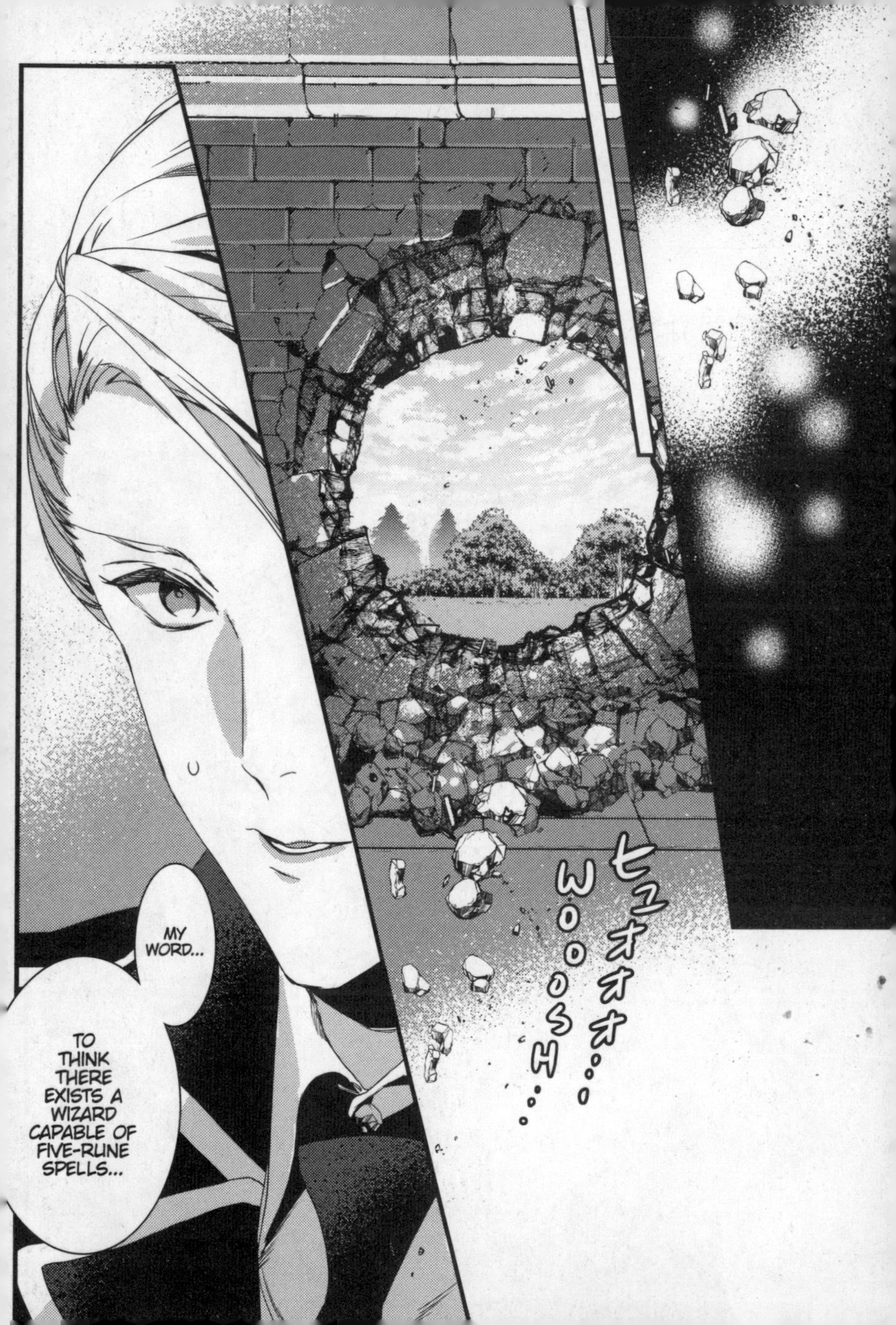
ヒュオオオ…
WOOOOSH…
MY WORD...
TO THINK THERE EXISTS A WIZARD CAPABLE OF FIVE-RUNE SPELLS...

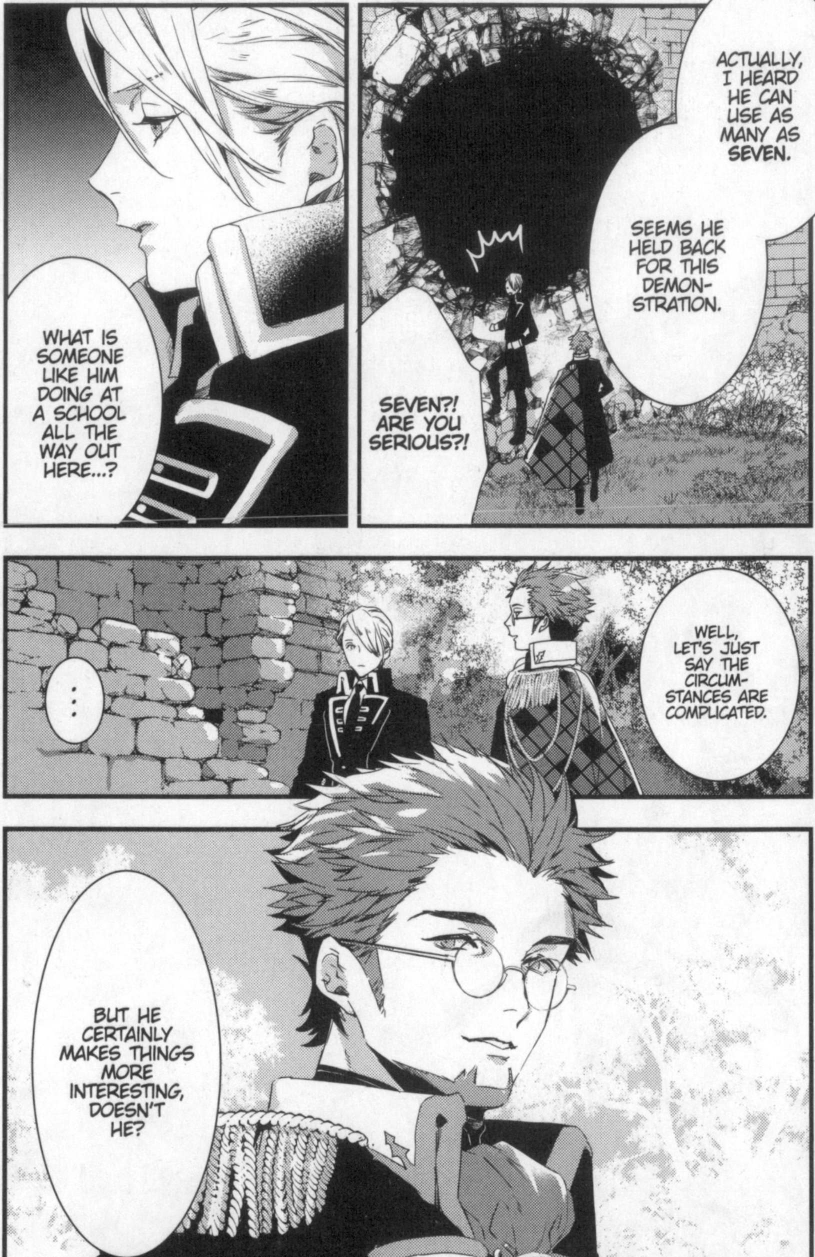
ACTUALLY, I HEARD HE CAN USE AS MANY AS SEVEN.
SEEMS HE HELD BACK FOR THIS DEMON-STRATION.
SEVEN?! ARE YOU SERIOUS?!
WHAT IS SOMEONE LIKE HIM DOING AT A SCHOOL ALL THE WAY OUT HERE...?
WELL, LET'S JUST SAY THE CIRCUM-STANCES ARE COMPLICATED.
...
BUT HE CERTAINLY MAKES THINGS MORE INTERESTING, DOESN'T HE?

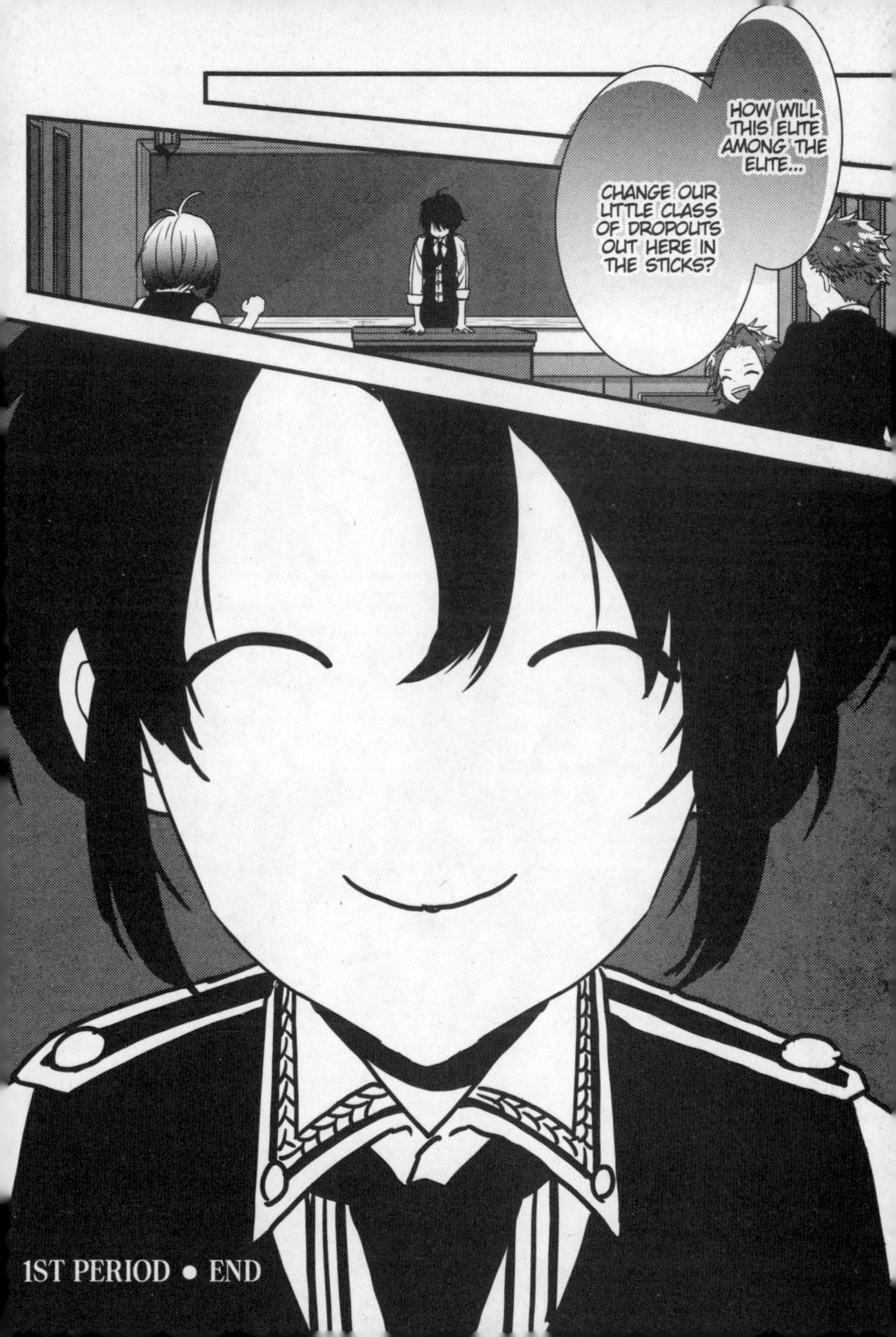
HOW WILL THIS ELITE AMONG THE ELITE...
CHANGE OUR LITTLE CLASS OF DROPOUTS OUT HERE IN THE STICKS?
1ST PERIOD • END

I Got

FIRED

as a
Court Wizard
so Now I'm Moving
to the Country
to Become a
Magic Teacher

I Got Fired as a
COURT WIZARD
so Now I'm Moving to the Country to Become a
MAGIC TEACHER

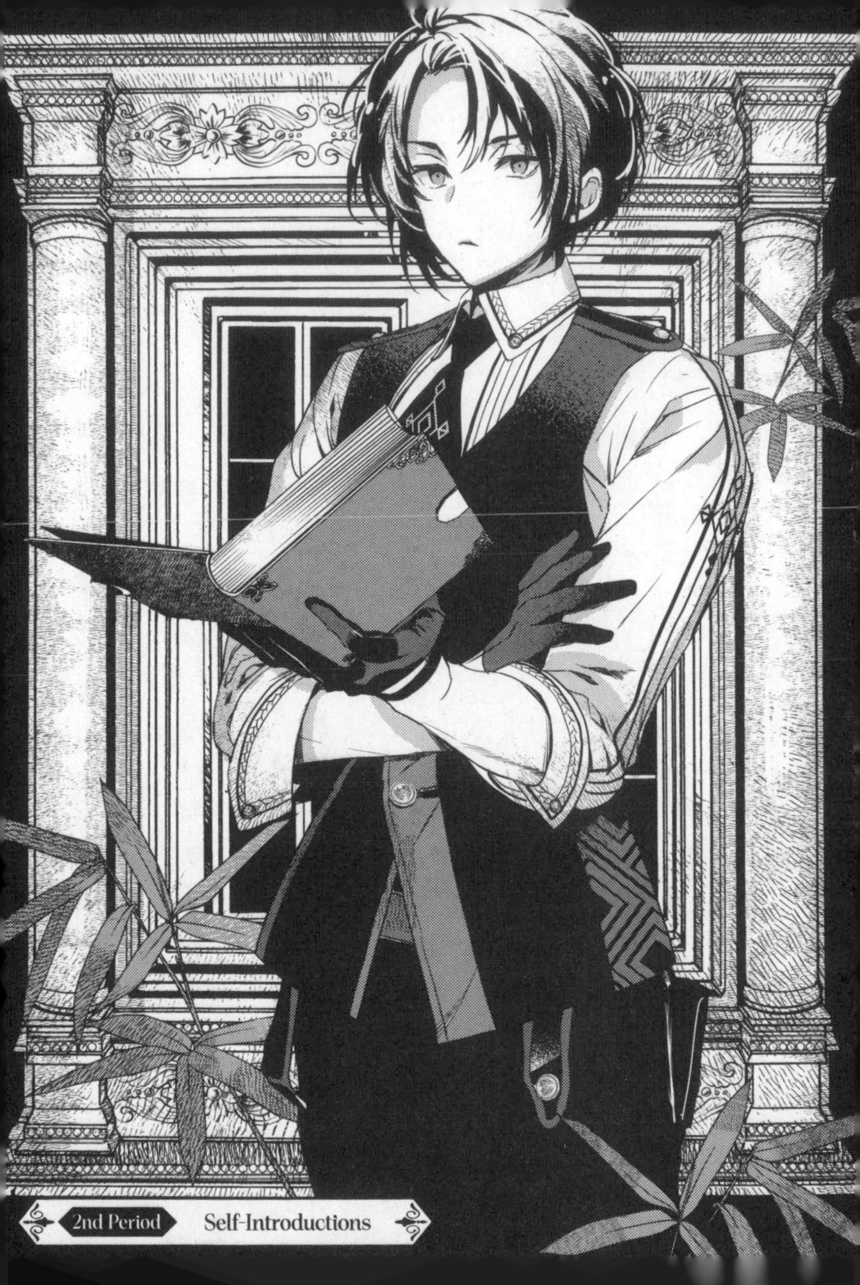

2nd Period Self-Introductions

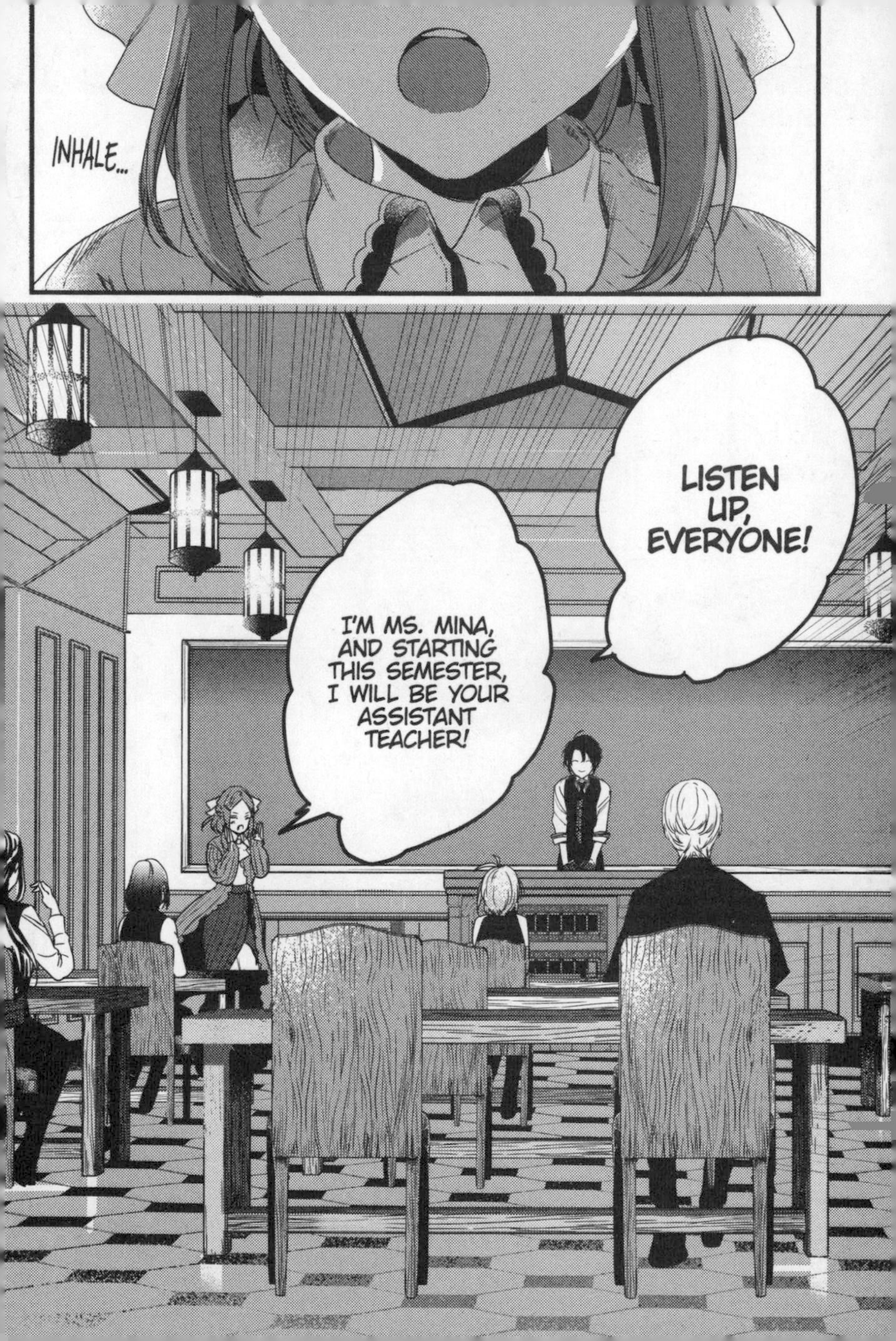
INHALE...
LISTEN UP, EVERYONE!
I'M MS. MINA, AND STARTING THIS SEMESTER, I WILL BE YOUR ASSISTANT TEACHER!

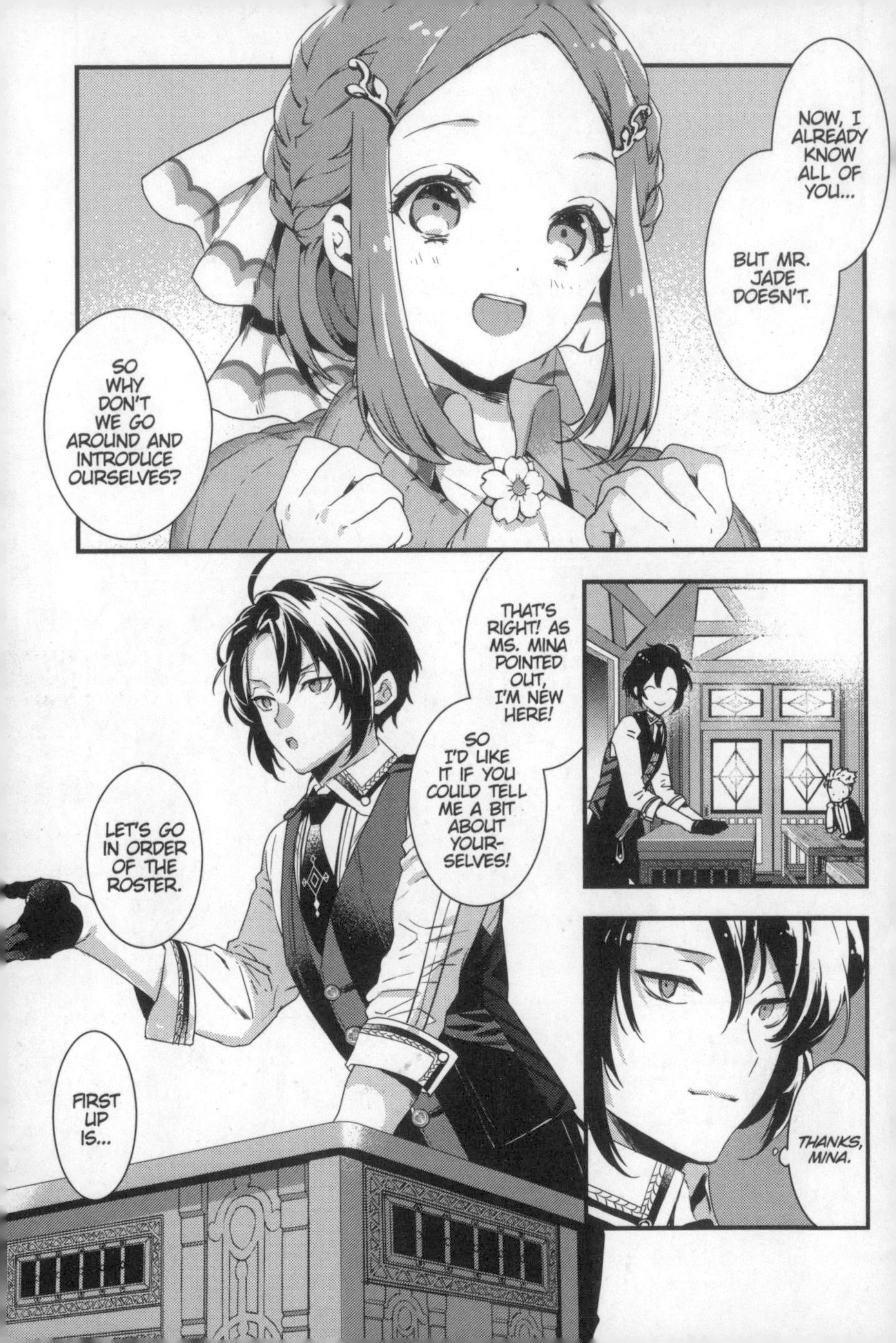
NOW, I ALREADY KNOW ALL OF YOU...
BUT MR. JADE DOESN'T.
SO WHY DON'T WE GO AROUND AND INTRODUCE OURSELVES?
THANKS, MINA.
THAT'S RIGHT! AS MS. MINA POINTED OUT, I'M NEW HERE!
SO I'D LIKE IT IF YOU COULD TELL ME A BIT ABOUT YOUR-SELVES!
LET'S GO IN ORDER OF THE ROSTER.
FIRST UP IS...

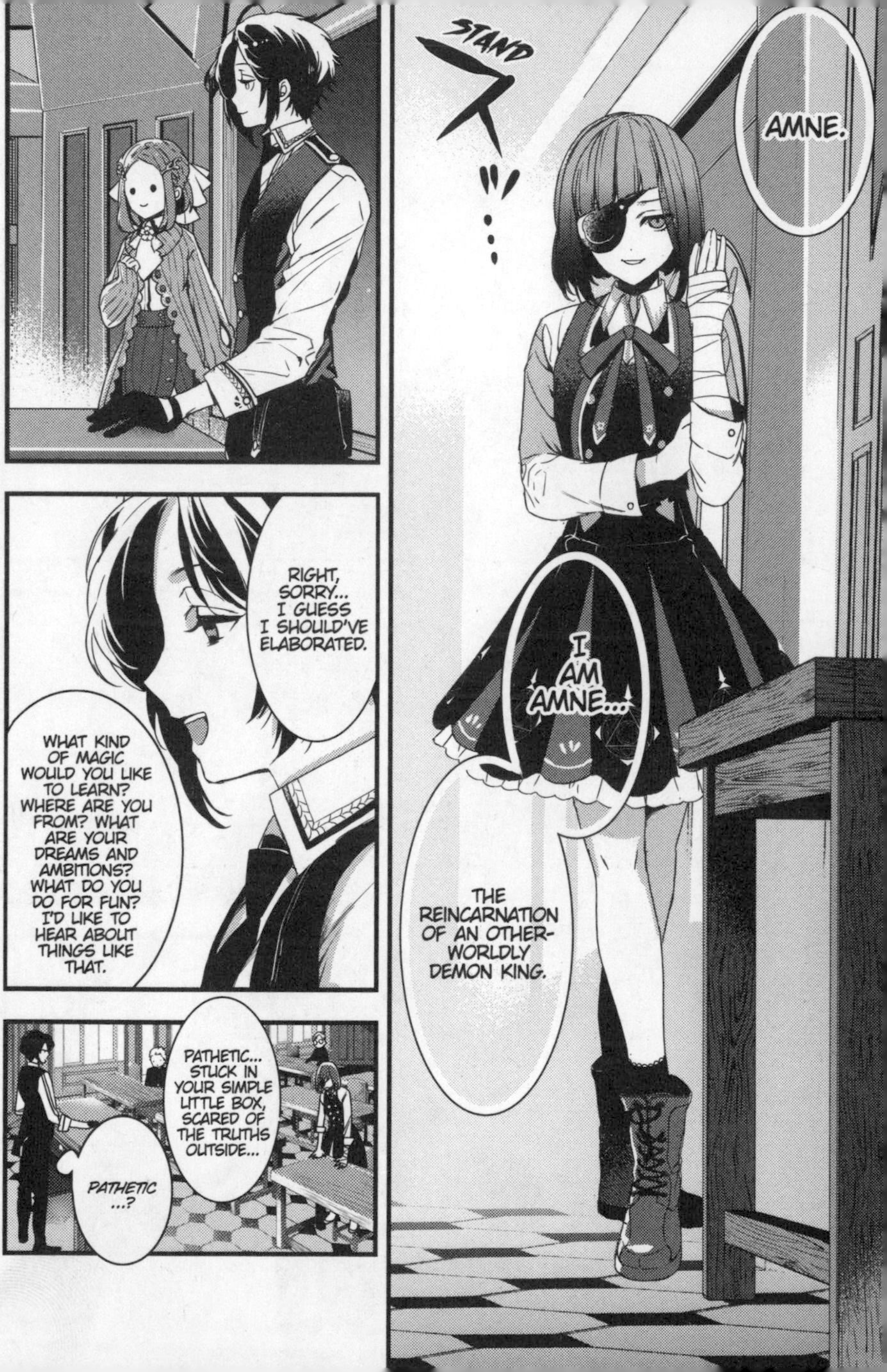
AMNE.
STAND
I AM AMNE...
THE REINCARNATION OF AN OTHER-WORLDLY DEMON KING.
RIGHT, SORRY... I GUESS I SHOULD'VE ELABORATED.
WHAT KIND OF MAGIC WOULD YOU LIKE TO LEARN? WHERE ARE YOU FROM? WHAT ARE YOUR DREAMS AND AMBITIONS? WHAT DO YOU DO FOR FUN? I'D LIKE TO HEAR ABOUT THINGS LIKE THAT.
PATHETIC... STUCK IN YOUR SIMPLE LITTLE BOX, SCARED OF THE TRUTHS OUTSIDE...
PATHETIC ...?

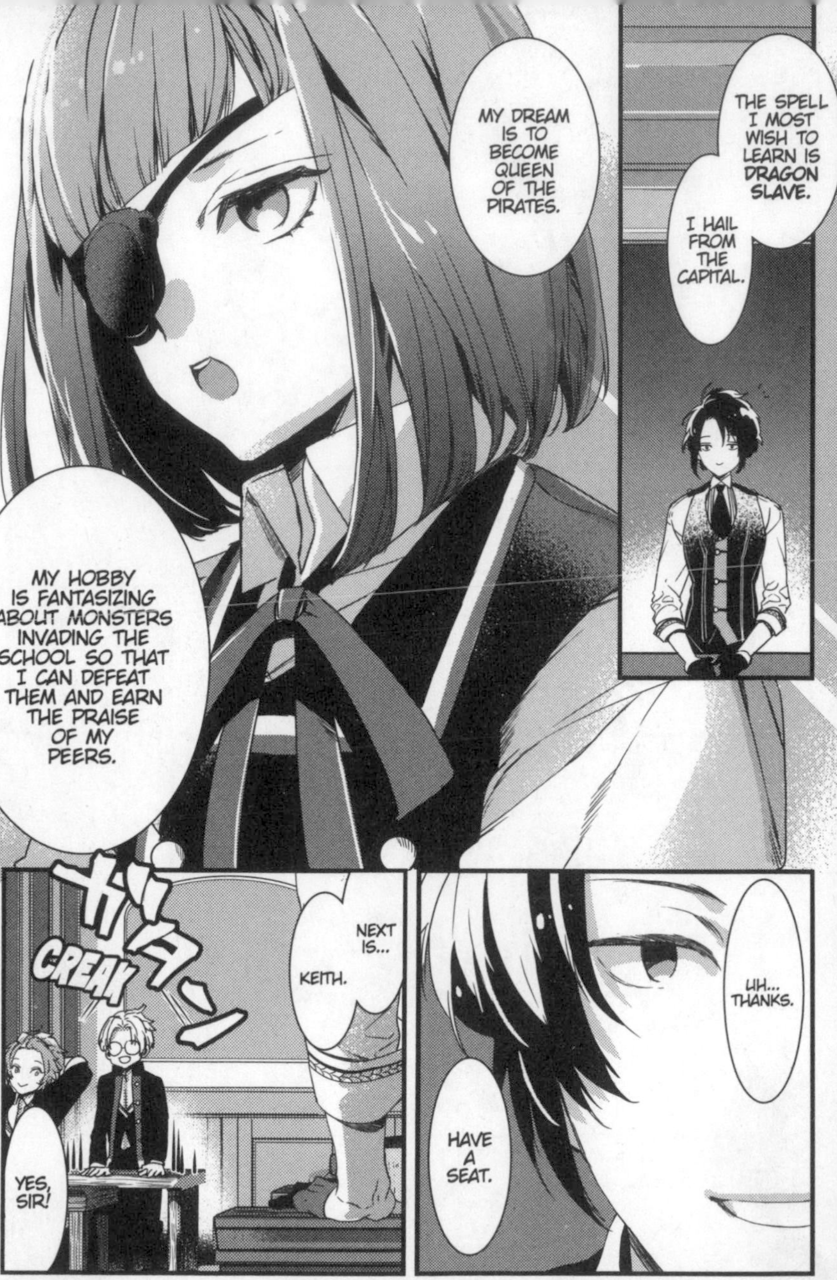
THE SPELL I MOST WISH TO LEARN IS DRAGON SLAVE.
I HAIL FROM THE CAPITAL.
MY DREAM IS TO BECOME QUEEN OF THE PIRATES.
MY HOBBY IS FANTASIZING ABOUT MONSTERS INVADING THE SCHOOL SO THAT I CAN DEFEAT THEM AND EARN THE PRAISE OF MY PEERS.
UH... THANKS.
HAVE A SEAT.
NEXT IS...
KEITH.
CREAK
YES, SIR!

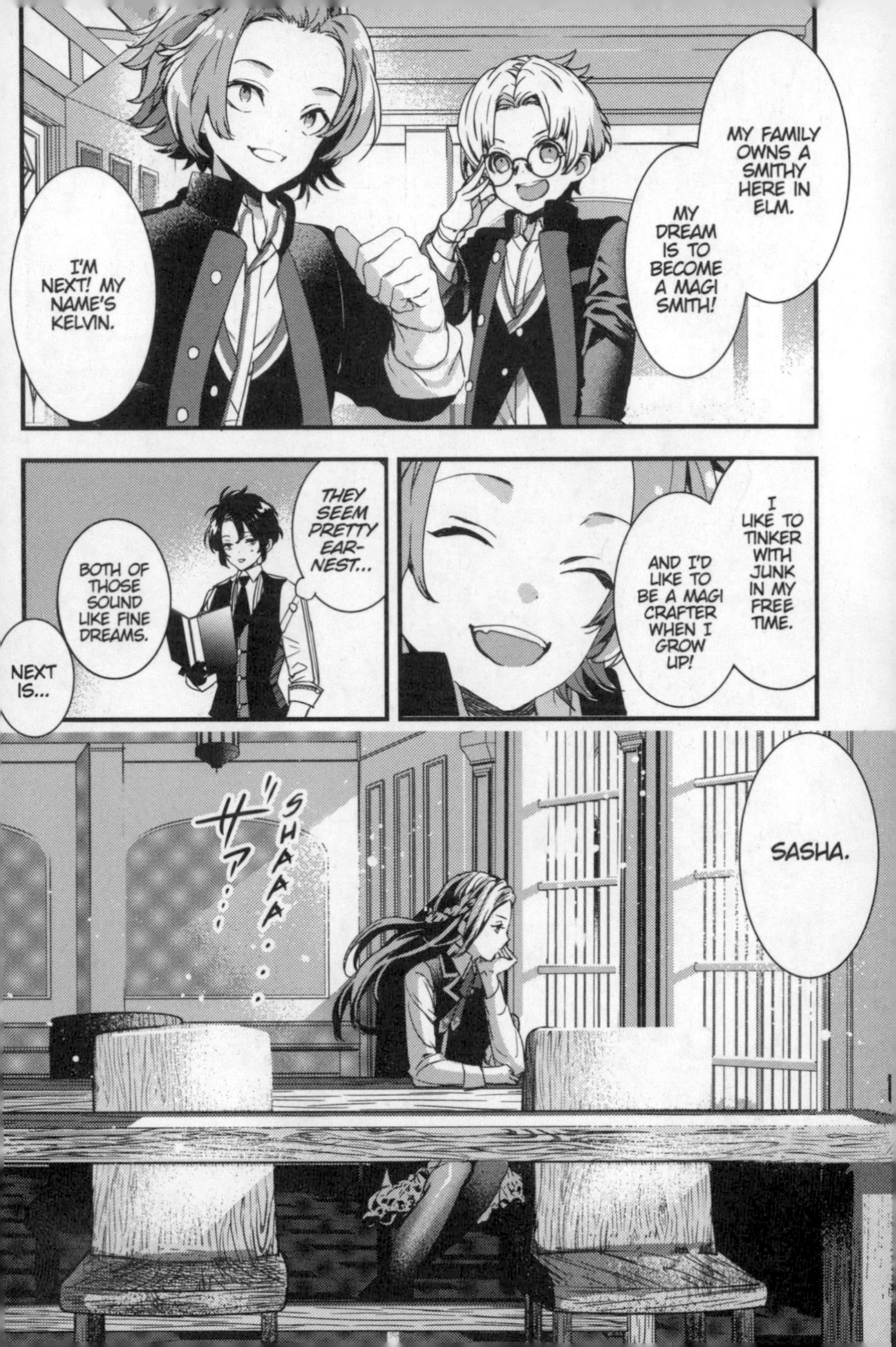
MY FAMILY OWNS A SMITHY HERE IN ELM.
MY DREAM IS TO BECOME A MAGI SMITH!
I'M NEXT! MY NAME'S KELVIN.
I LIKE TO TINKER WITH JUNK IN MY FREE TIME.
AND I'D LIKE TO BE A MAGI CRAFTER WHEN I GROW UP!
THEY SEEM PRETTY EAR-NEST...
BOTH OF THOSE SOUND LIKE FINE DREAMS.
NEXT IS...
SASHA.
SHAAAA...

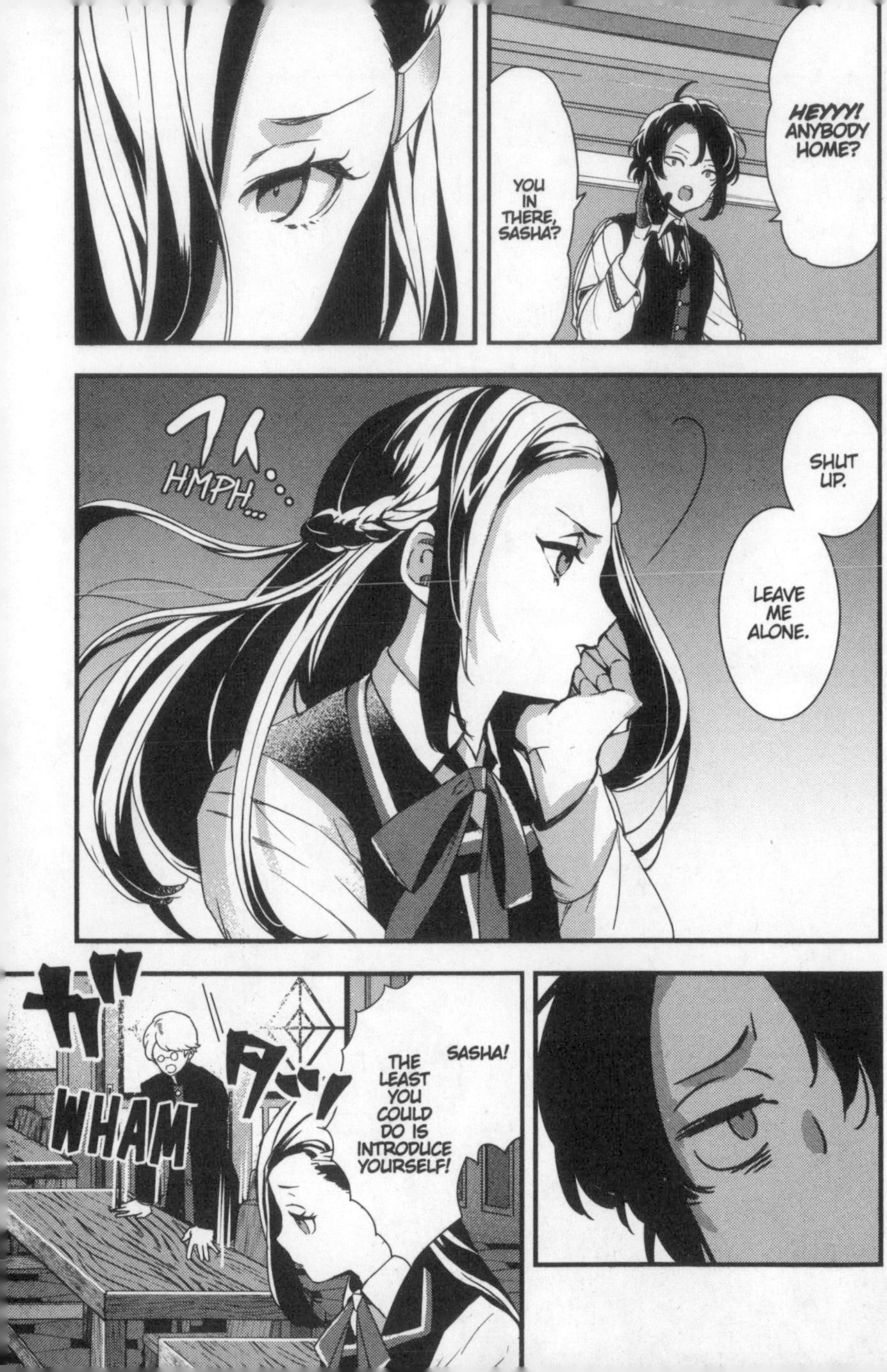
HEYYY! ANYBODY HOME?
YOU IN THERE, SASHA?
SHUT UP.
LEAVE ME ALONE.
HMPH...
SASHA!
THE LEAST YOU COULD DO IS INTRODUCE YOURSELF!
WHAM

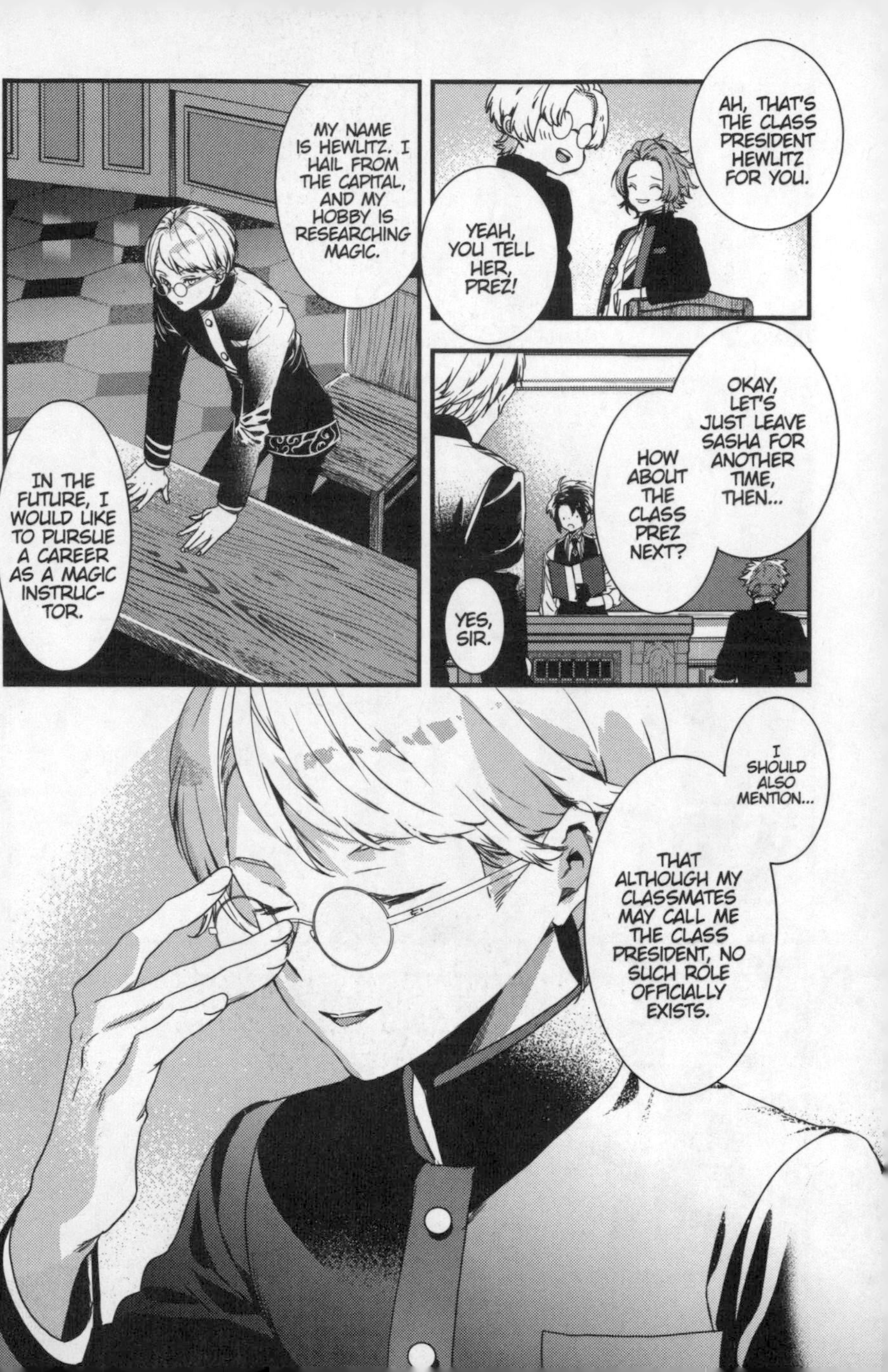
AH, THAT'S THE CLASS PRESIDENT HEWLITZ FOR YOU.
YEAH, YOU TELL HER, PREZ!
OKAY, LET'S JUST LEAVE SASHA FOR ANOTHER TIME, THEN...
HOW ABOUT THE CLASS PREZ NEXT?
YES, SIR.
MY NAME IS HEWLITZ. I HAIL FROM THE CAPITAL, AND MY HOBBY IS RESEARCHING MAGIC.
IN THE FUTURE, I WOULD LIKE TO PURSUE A CAREER AS A MAGIC INSTRUC-TOR.
I SHOULD ALSO MENTION...
THAT ALTHOUGH MY CLASSMATES MAY CALL ME THE CLASS PRESIDENT, NO SUCH ROLE OFFICIALLY EXISTS.

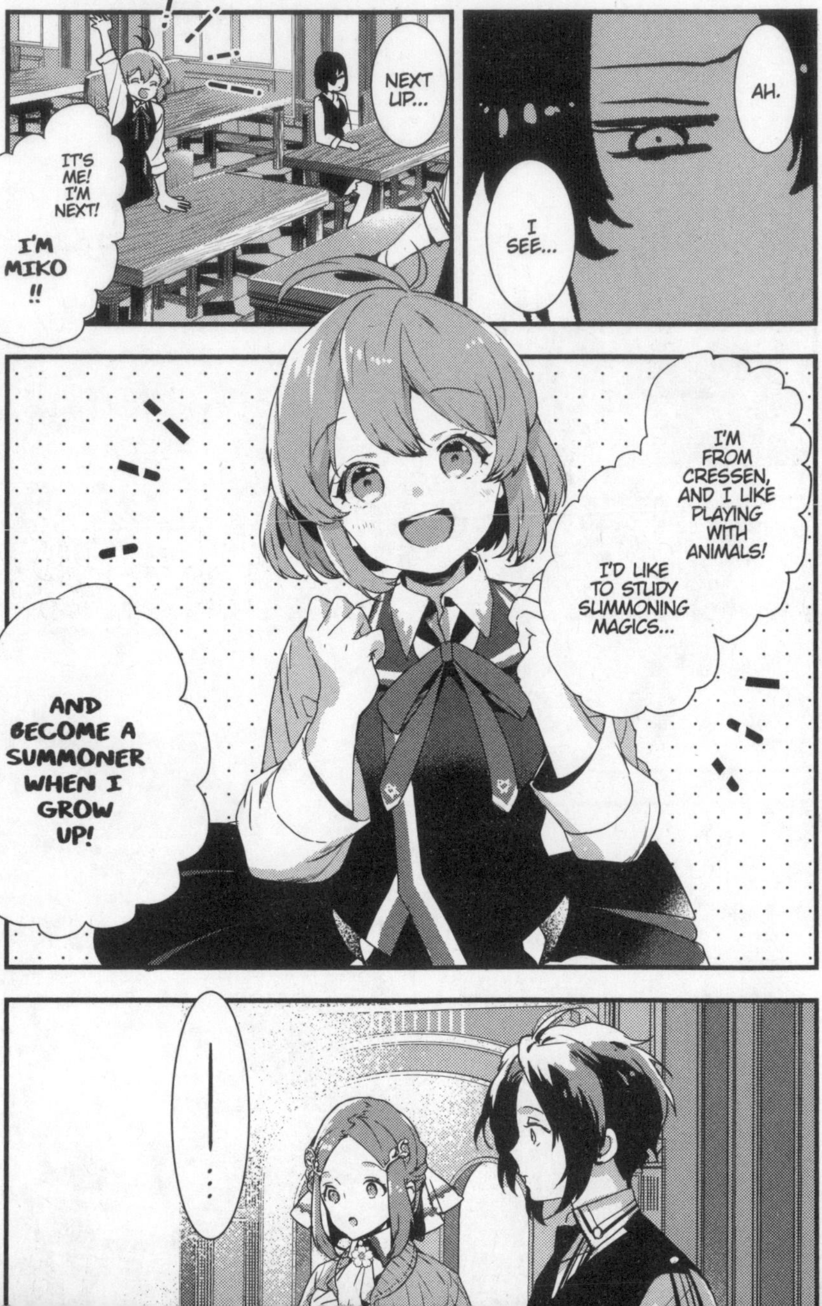
AH.
I SEE...
NEXT UP...
IT'S ME! I'M NEXT!
I'M MIKO !!
I'M FROM CRESSEN, AND I LIKE PLAYING WITH ANIMALS!
I'D LIKE TO STUDY SUMMONING MAGICS...
AND BECOME A SUMMONER WHEN I GROW UP!
—...

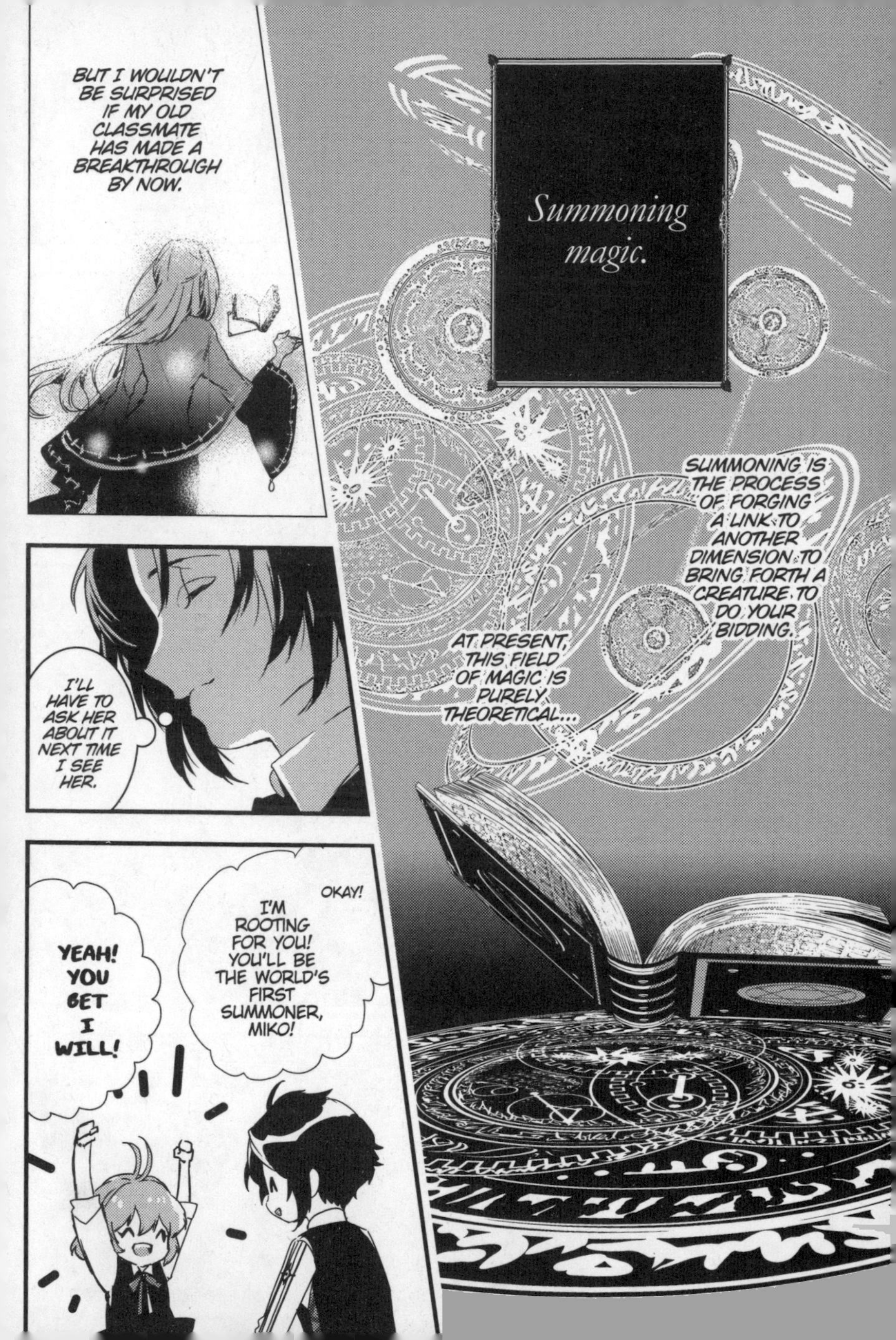
Summoning magic.
SUMMONING IS THE PROCESS OF FORGING A LINK TO ANOTHER DIMENSION TO BRING FORTH A CREATURE TO DO YOUR BIDDING.
AT PRESENT, THIS FIELD OF MAGIC IS PURELY THEORETICAL...
BUT I WOULDN'T BE SURPRISED IF MY OLD CLASSMATE HAS MADE A BREAKTHROUGH BY NOW.
I'LL HAVE TO ASK HER ABOUT IT NEXT TIME I SEE HER.
OKAY!
I'M ROOTING FOR YOU! YOU'LL BE THE WORLD'S FIRST SUMMONER, MIKO!
YEAH! YOU GET I WILL!

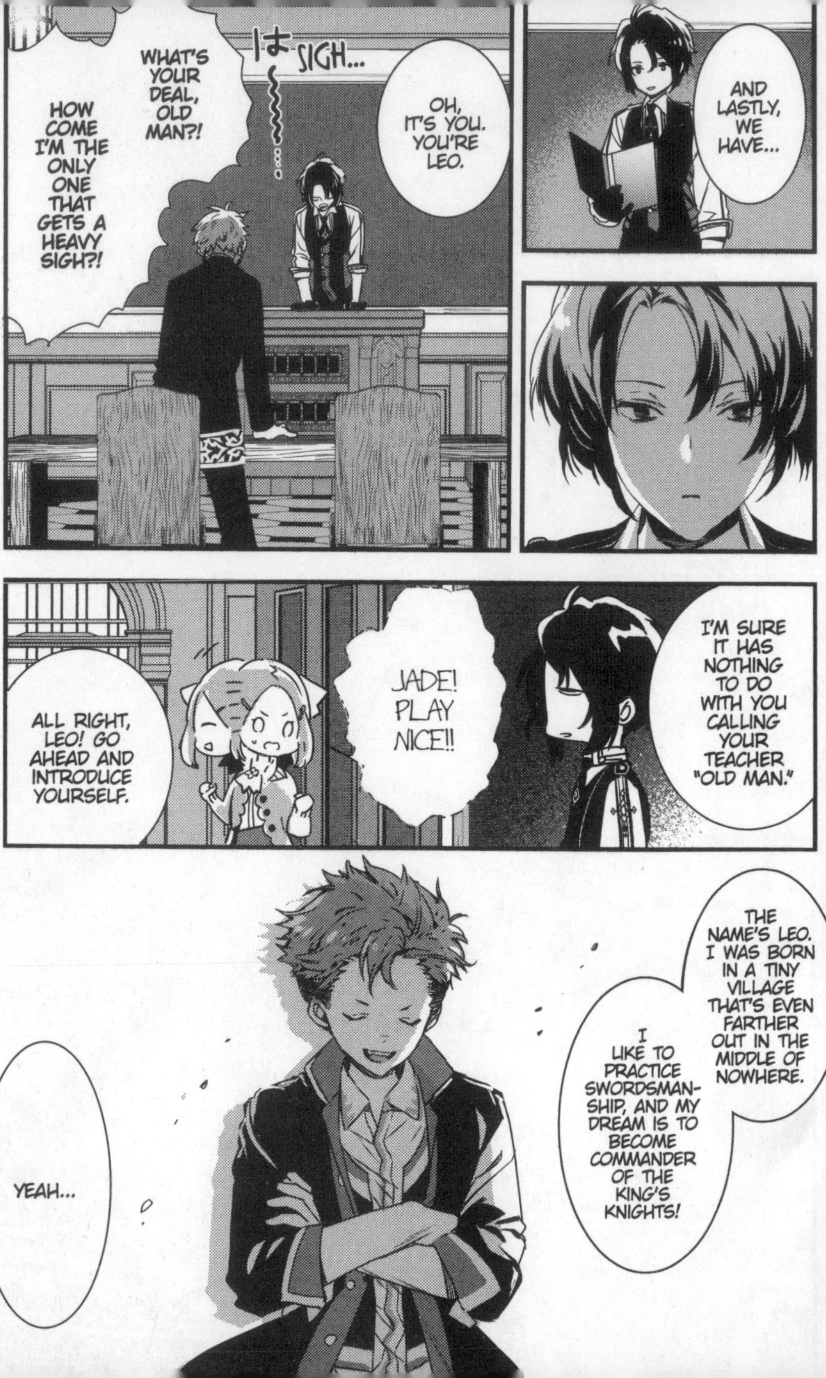
AND LASTLY, WE HAVE...
OH, IT'S YOU. YOU'RE LEO.
は SIGH...
WHAT'S YOUR DEAL, OLD MAN?!
HOW COME I'M THE ONLY ONE THAT GETS A HEAVY SIGH?!
I'M SURE IT HAS NOTHING TO DO WITH YOU CALLING YOUR TEACHER "OLD MAN."
JADE! PLAY NICE!!
ALL RIGHT, LEO! GO AHEAD AND INTRODUCE YOURSELF.
THE NAME'S LEO. I WAS BORN IN A TINY VILLAGE THAT'S EVEN FARTHER OUT IN THE MIDDLE OF NOWHERE.
I LIKE TO PRACTICE SWORDSMANSHIP, AND MY DREAM IS TO BECOME COMMANDER OF THE KING'S KNIGHTS!
YEAH...

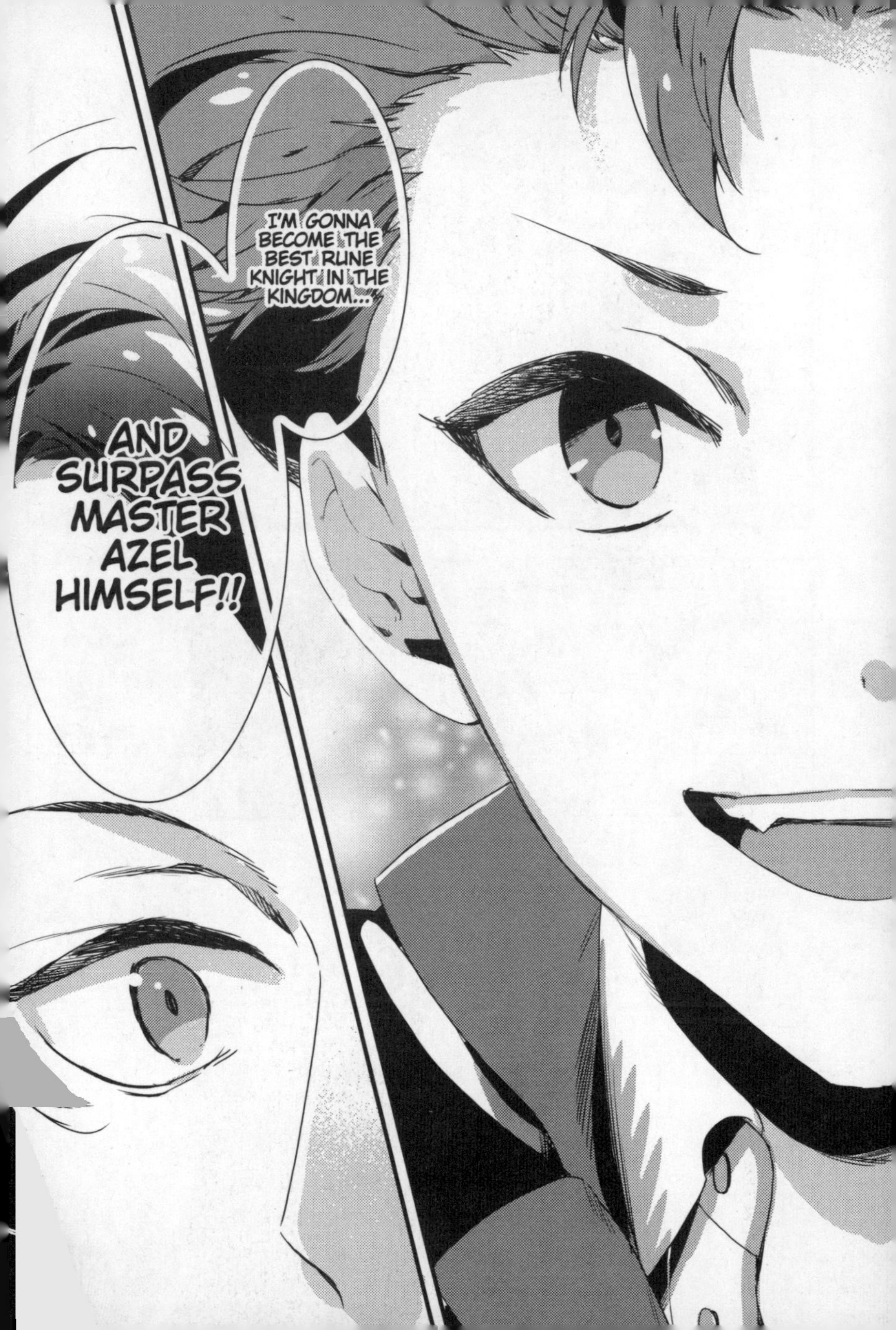
I'M GONNA BECOME THE BEST RUNE KNIGHT IN THE KINGDOM...
AND SURPASS MASTER AZEL HIMSELF!!

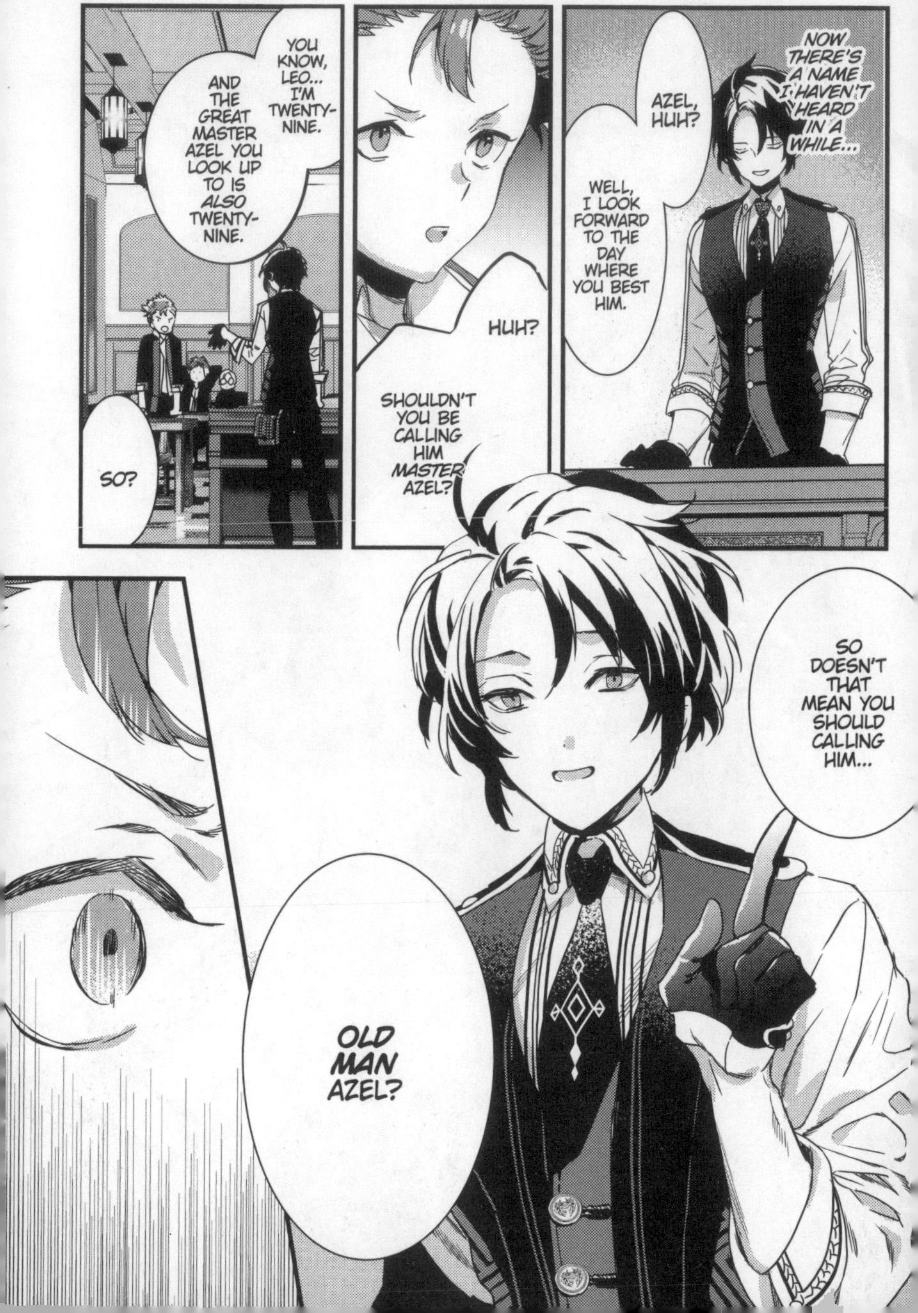
NOW THERE'S A NAME I HAVEN'T HEARD IN A WHILE...
AZEL, HUH?
WELL, I LOOK FORWARD TO THE DAY WHERE YOU BEST HIM.
HUH?
SHOULDN'T YOU BE CALLING HIM *MASTER* AZEL?
YOU KNOW, LEO... I'M TWENTY-NINE.
AND THE GREAT MASTER AZEL YOU LOOK UP TO IS *ALSO* TWENTY-NINE.
SO?
SO DOESN'T THAT MEAN YOU SHOULD CALLING HIM...
OLD MAN AZEL?

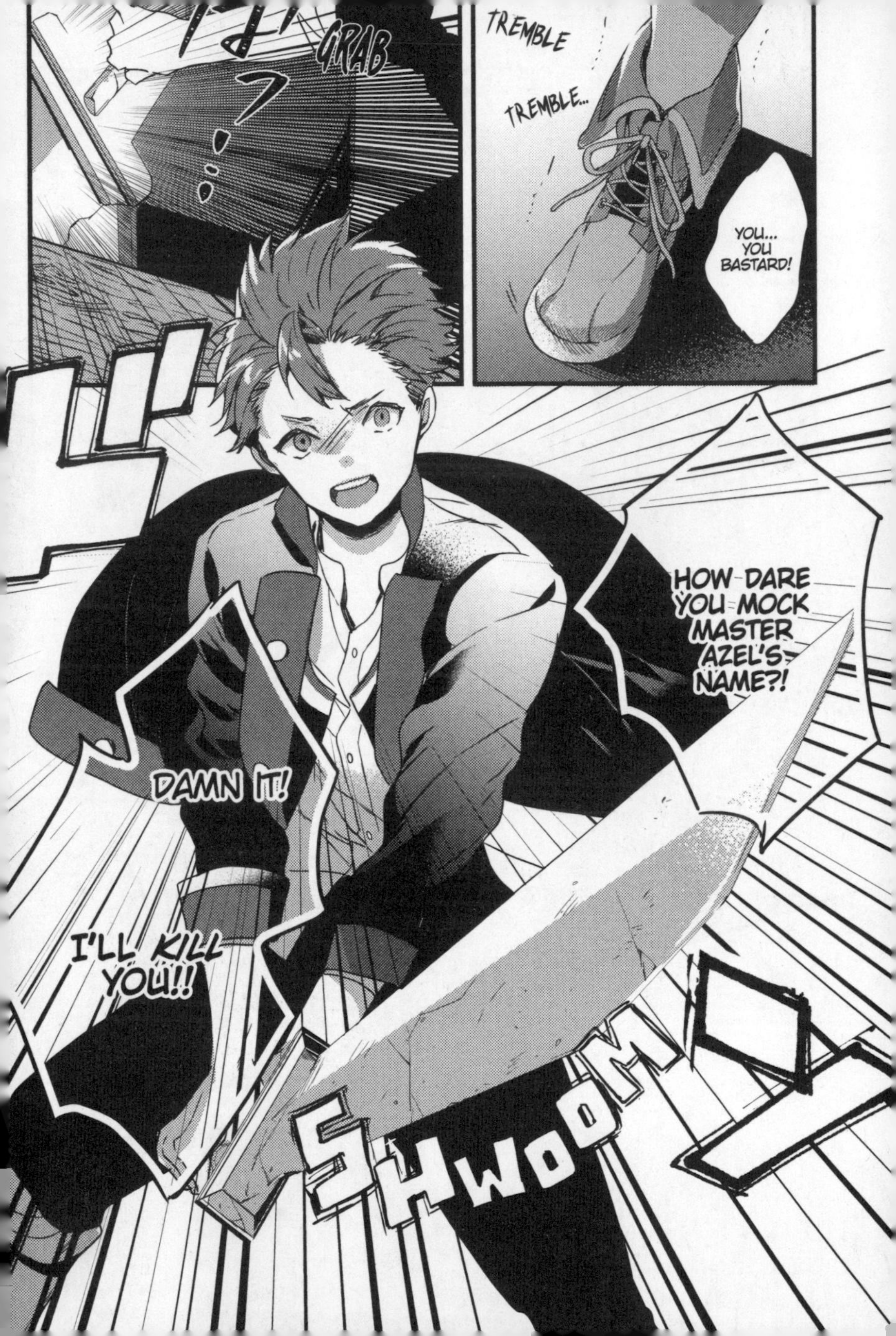
TREMBLE
TREMBLE...
YOU... YOU BASTARD!
GRAB
HOW DARE YOU MOCK MASTER AZEL'S NAME?!
DAMN IT!
I'LL KILL YOU!!
SHWOOM

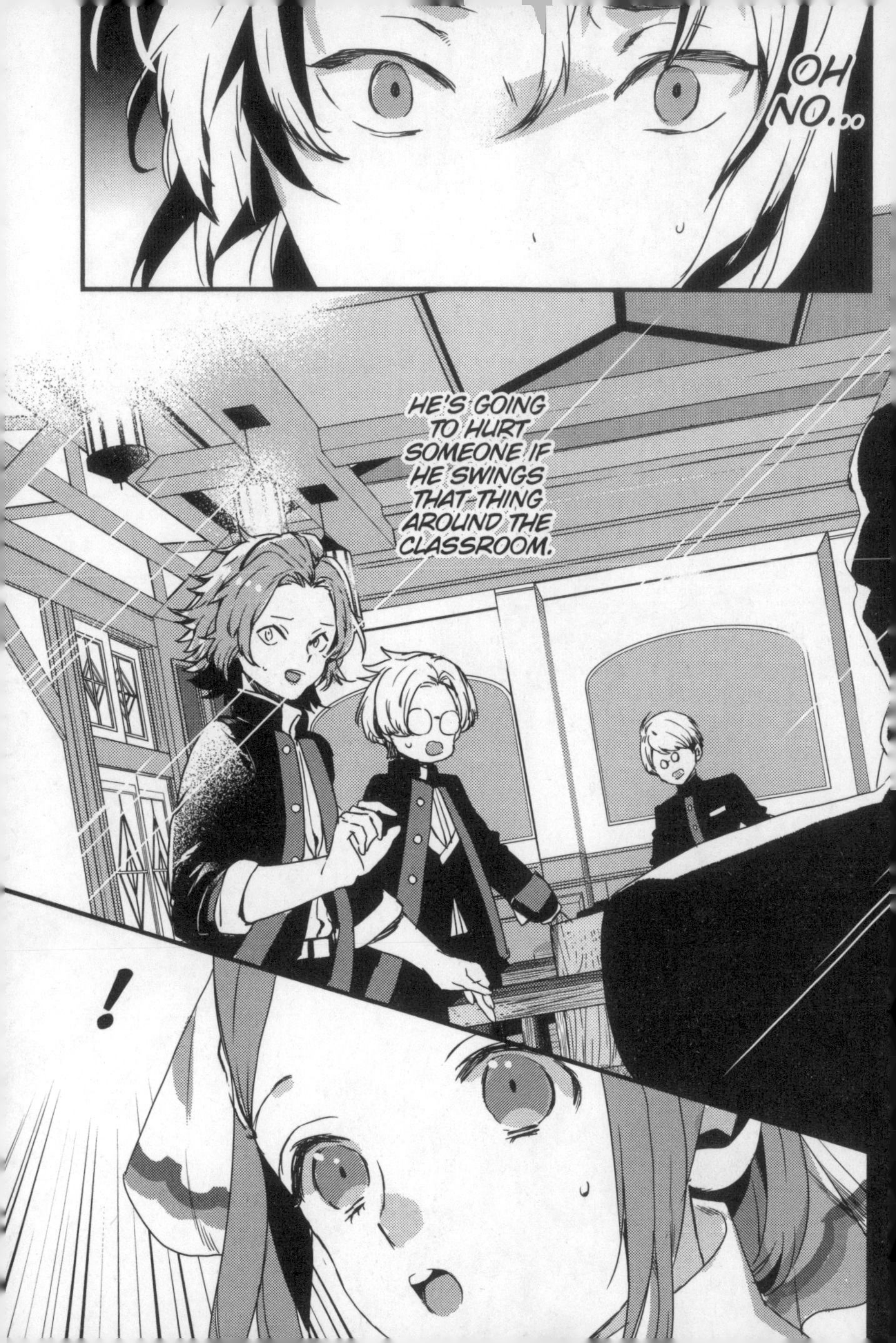
OH NO...
HE'S GOING TO HURT SOMEONE IF HE SWINGS THAT THING AROUND THE CLASSROOM.
!

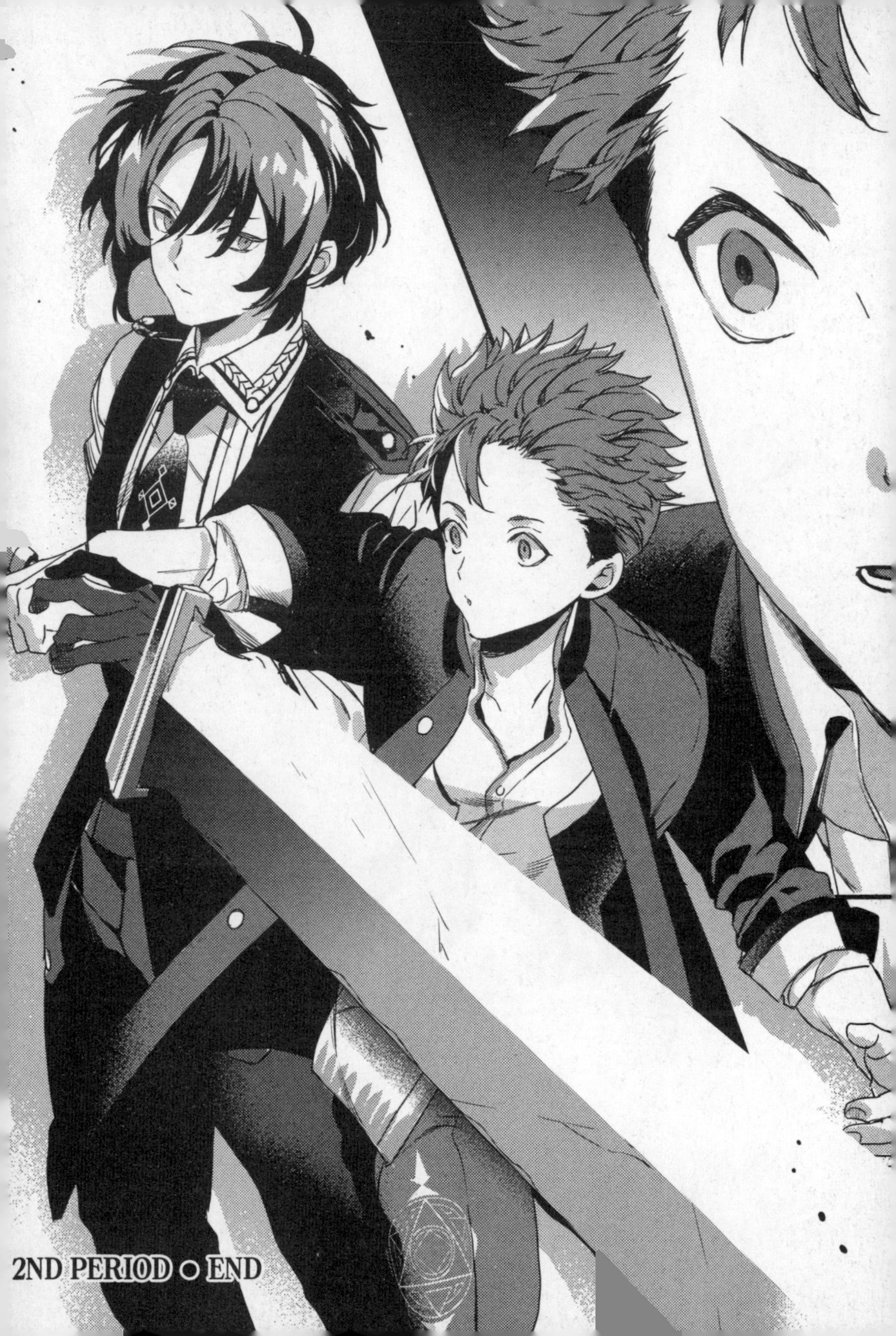
2ND PERIOD ○ END

I Got

FIRED

as a
Court Wizard
so Now I'm Moving
to the Country
to Become a
Magic Teacher

I Got Fired as a
COURT WIZARD
so Now I'm Moving to the Country to Become a
MAGIC TEACHER

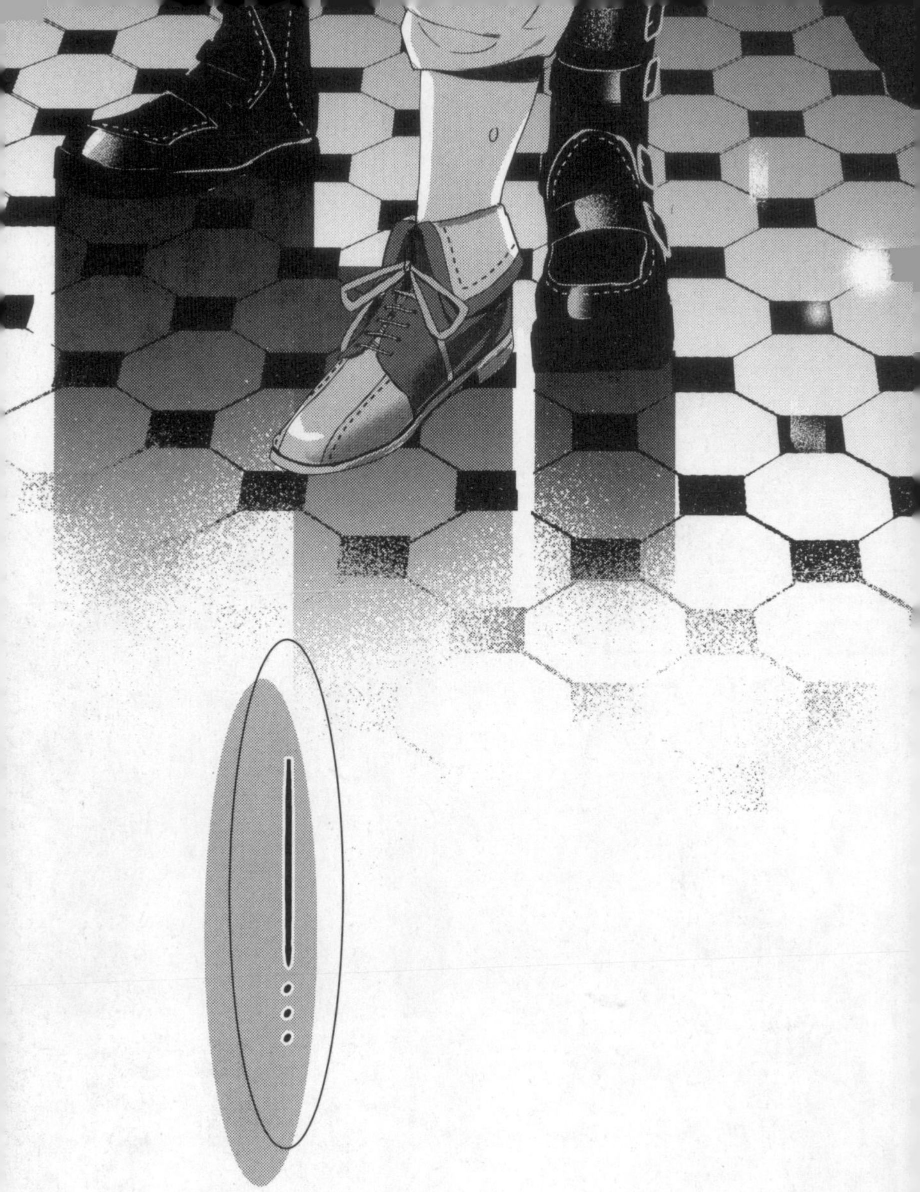

3rd Period — The True Potential of the Remedial Class

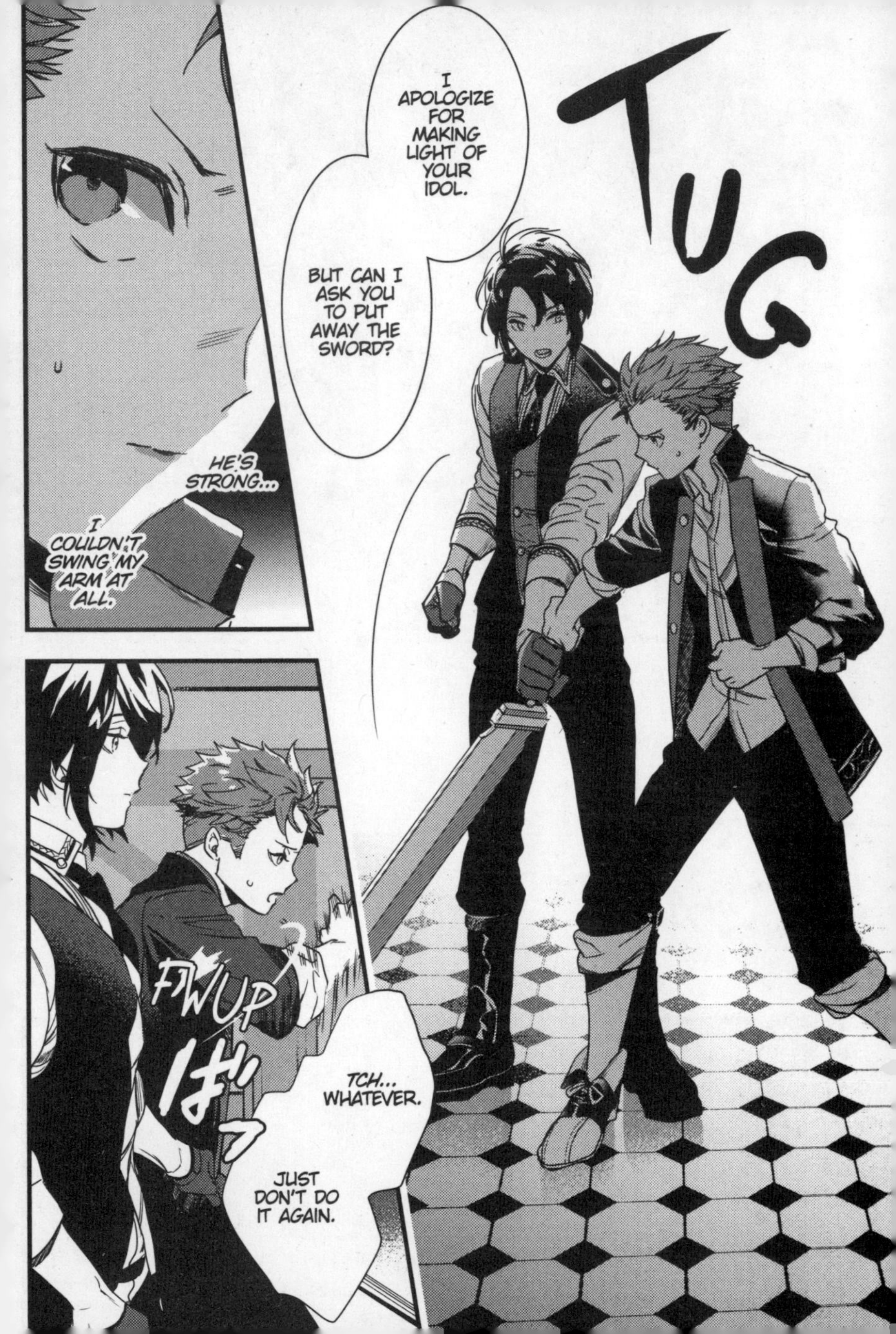
TUG
I APOLOGIZE FOR MAKING LIGHT OF YOUR IDOL.
BUT CAN I ASK YOU TO PUT AWAY THE SWORD?
HE'S STRONG...
I COULDN'T SWING MY ARM AT ALL.
FWUP
ばっ
TCH... WHATEVER.
JUST DON'T DO IT AGAIN.

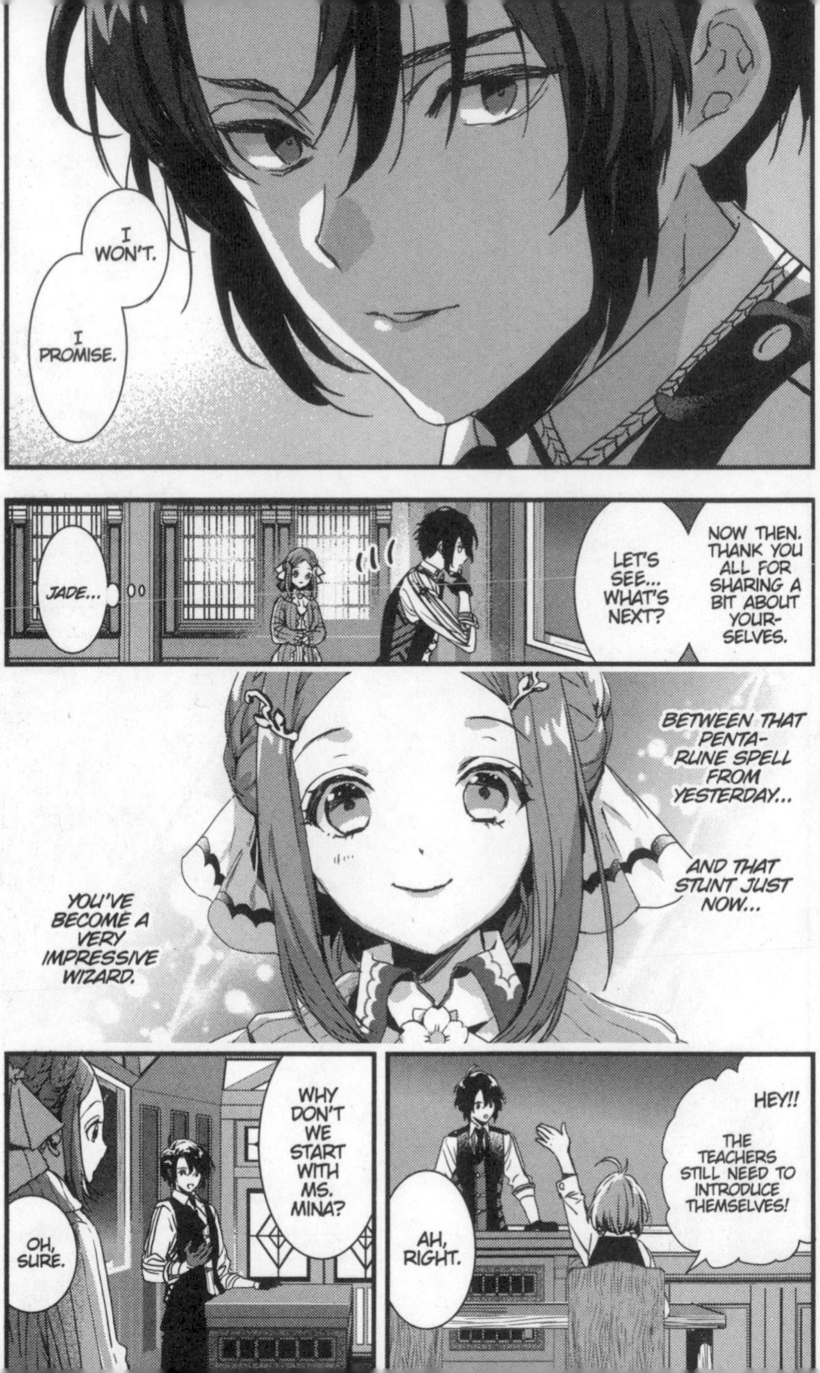
I WON'T.
I PROMISE.
NOW THEN. THANK YOU ALL FOR SHARING A BIT ABOUT YOURSELVES.
LET'S SEE... WHAT'S NEXT?
JADE...
BETWEEN THAT PENTA-RUNE SPELL FROM YESTERDAY...
AND THAT STUNT JUST NOW...
YOU'VE BECOME A VERY IMPRESSIVE WIZARD.
HEY!!
THE TEACHERS STILL NEED TO INTRODUCE THEMSELVES!
AH, RIGHT.
WHY DON'T WE START WITH MS. MINA?
OH, SURE.

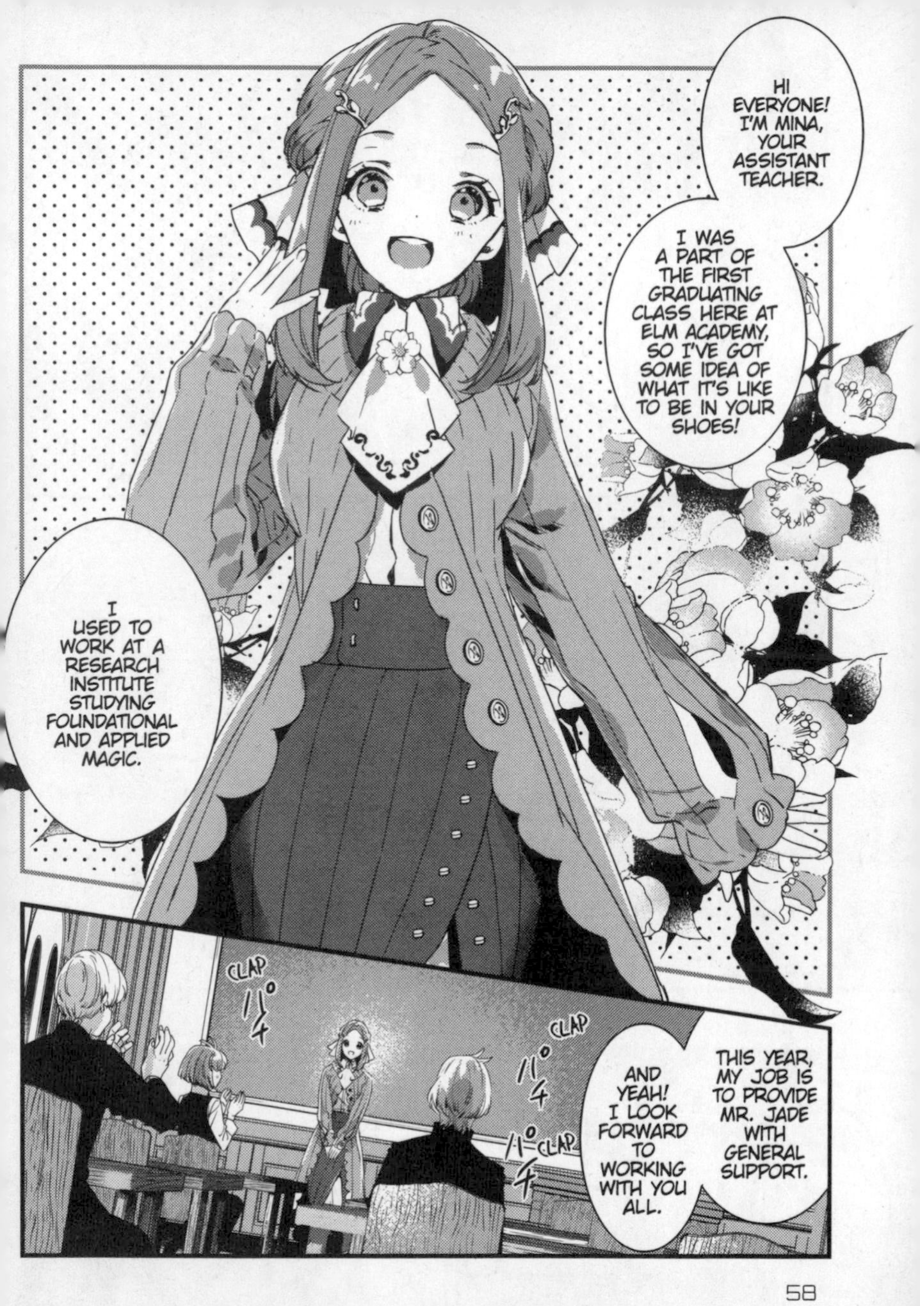
HI EVERYONE! I'M MINA, YOUR ASSISTANT TEACHER.
I WAS A PART OF THE FIRST GRADUATING CLASS HERE AT ELM ACADEMY, SO I'VE GOT SOME IDEA OF WHAT IT'S LIKE TO BE IN YOUR SHOES!
I USED TO WORK AT A RESEARCH INSTITUTE STUDYING FOUNDATIONAL AND APPLIED MAGIC.
THIS YEAR, MY JOB IS TO PROVIDE MR. JADE WITH GENERAL SUPPORT.
AND YEAH! I LOOK FORWARD TO WORKING WITH YOU ALL.
CLAP
CLAP
CLAP

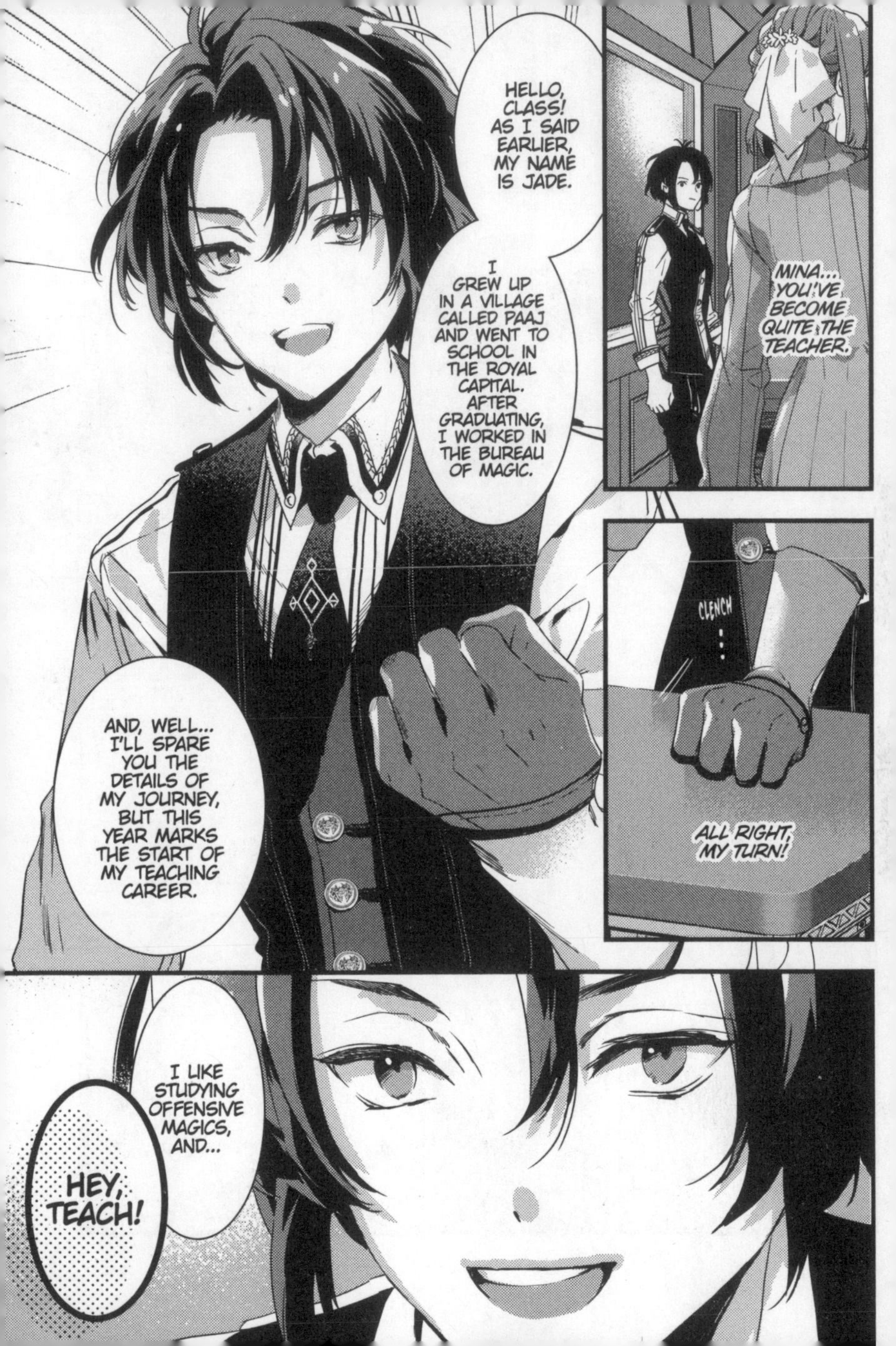
MINA... YOU'VE BECOME QUITE THE TEACHER.
CLENCH
...
ALL RIGHT, MY TURN!
HELLO, CLASS! AS I SAID EARLIER, MY NAME IS JADE.
I GREW UP IN A VILLAGE CALLED PAAJ AND WENT TO SCHOOL IN THE ROYAL CAPITAL. AFTER GRADUATING, I WORKED IN THE BUREAU OF MAGIC.
AND, WELL... I'LL SPARE YOU THE DETAILS OF MY JOURNEY, BUT THIS YEAR MARKS THE START OF MY TEACHING CAREER.
I LIKE STUDYING OFFENSIVE MAGICS, AND...
HEY, TEACH!

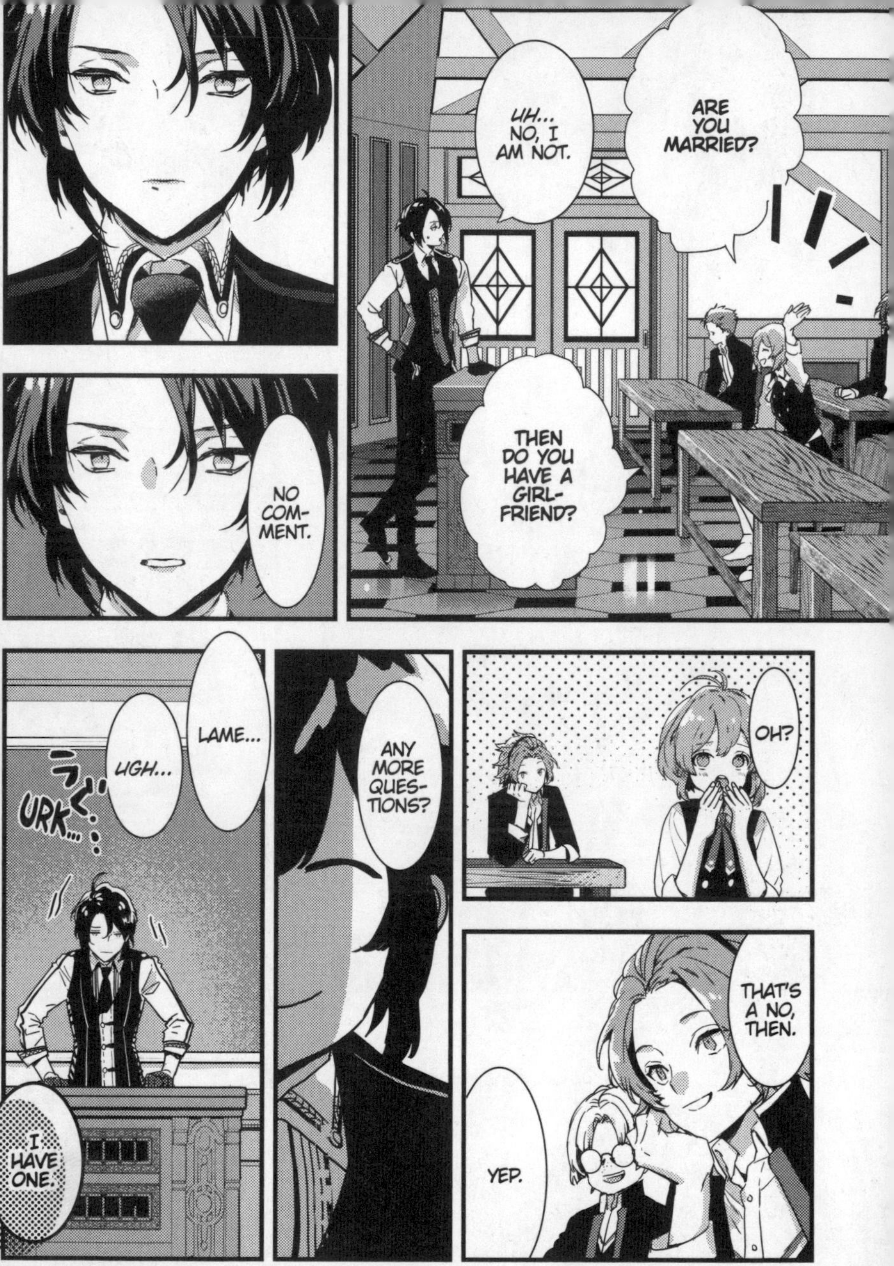
ARE YOU MARRIED?
UH... NO, I AM NOT.
THEN DO YOU HAVE A GIRL-FRIEND?
NO COM-MENT.
OH?
THAT'S A NO, THEN.
YEP.
ANY MORE QUES-TIONS?
LAME...
UGH...
URK...
I HAVE ONE.

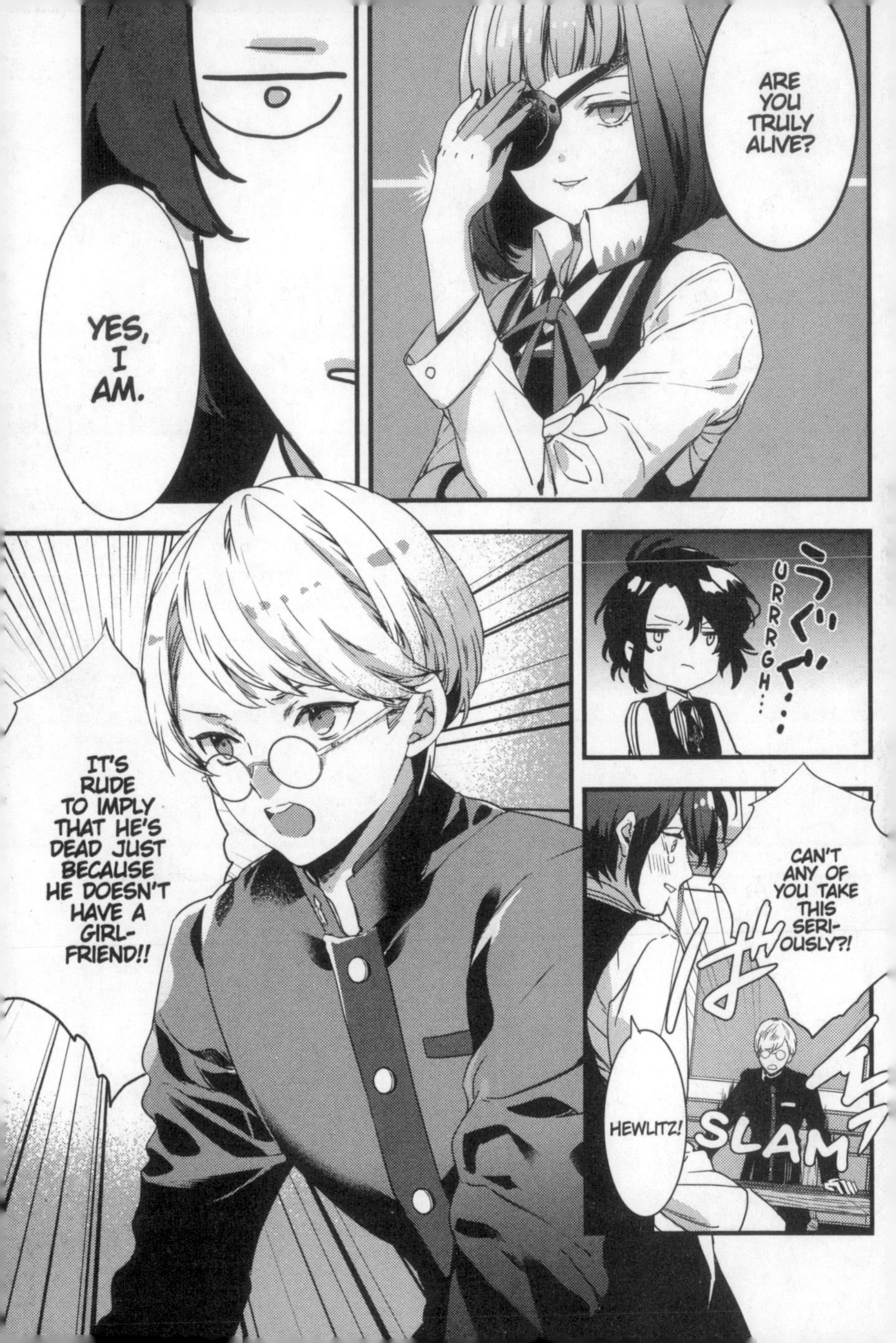
ARE YOU TRULY ALIVE?
YES, I AM.
うぐぐ… URRRGH…
CAN'T ANY OF YOU TAKE THIS SERI-OUSLY?!
HEWLITZ!
SLAM
IT'S RUDE TO IMPLY THAT HE'S DEAD JUST BECAUSE HE DOESN'T HAVE A GIRL-FRIEND!!

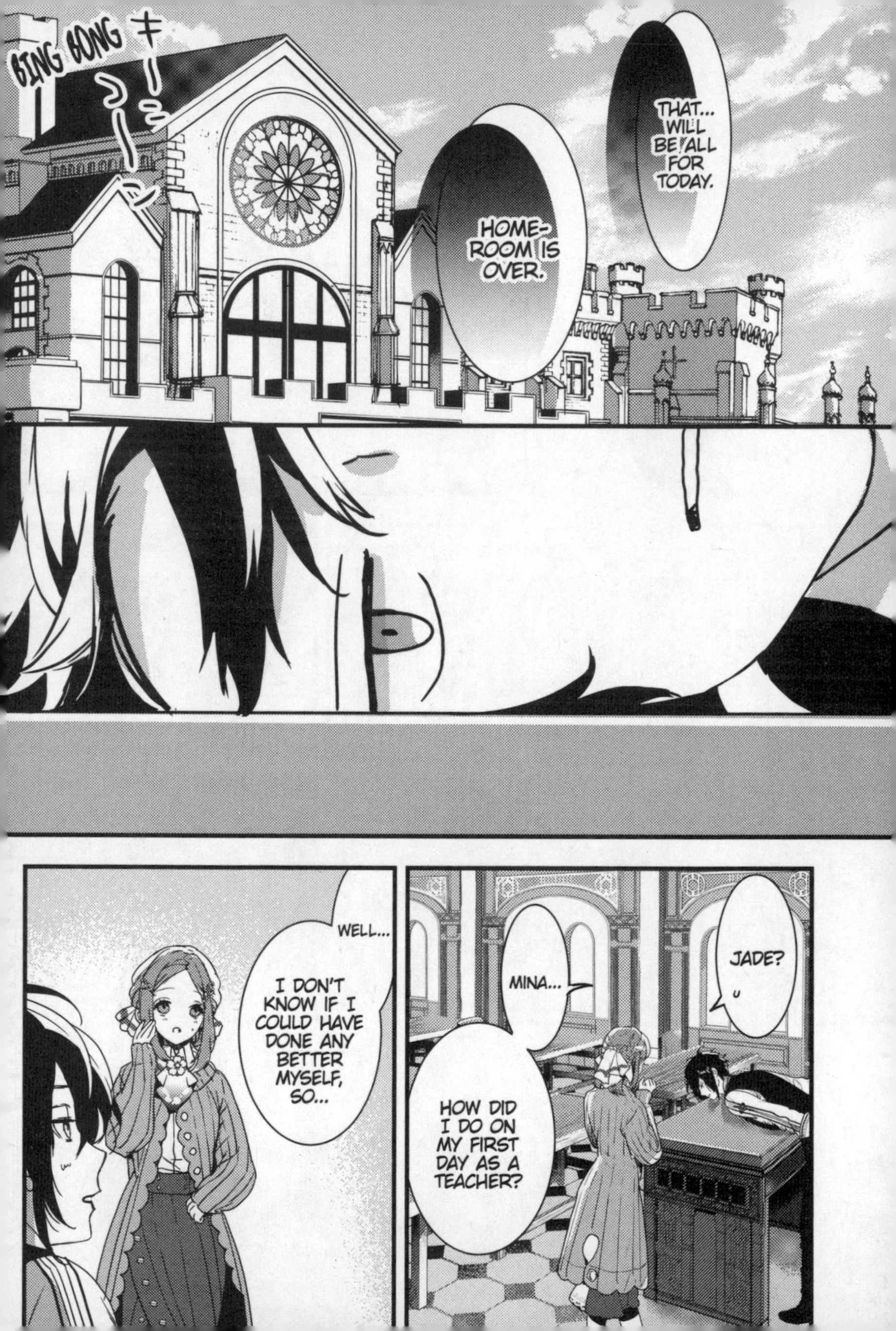
THAT... WILL BE ALL FOR TODAY.
HOME-ROOM IS OVER.
BING BONG
JADE?
MINA...
HOW DID I DO ON MY FIRST DAY AS A TEACHER?
WELL...
I DON'T KNOW IF I COULD HAVE DONE ANY BETTER MYSELF, SO...

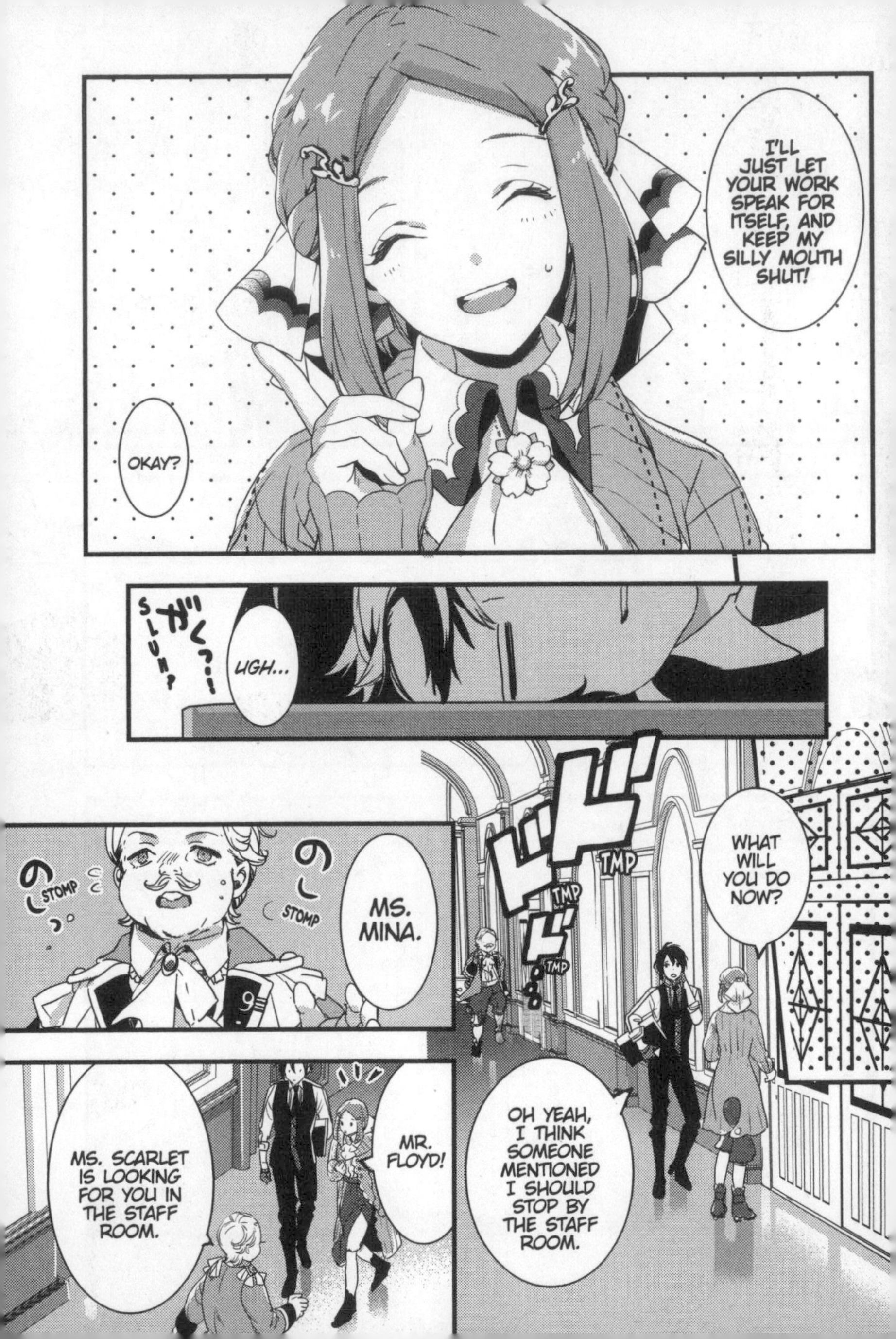
I'LL JUST LET YOUR WORK SPEAK FOR ITSELF, AND KEEP MY SILLY MOUTH SHUT!
OKAY?
がくっ
SLUMP
UGH...
WHAT WILL YOU DO NOW?
ドドド
TMP TMP TMP
OH YEAH, I THINK SOMEONE MENTIONED I SHOULD STOP BY THE STAFF ROOM.
のしのし
STOMP STOMP
MS. MINA.
MR. FLOYD!
MS. SCARLET IS LOOKING FOR YOU IN THE STAFF ROOM.

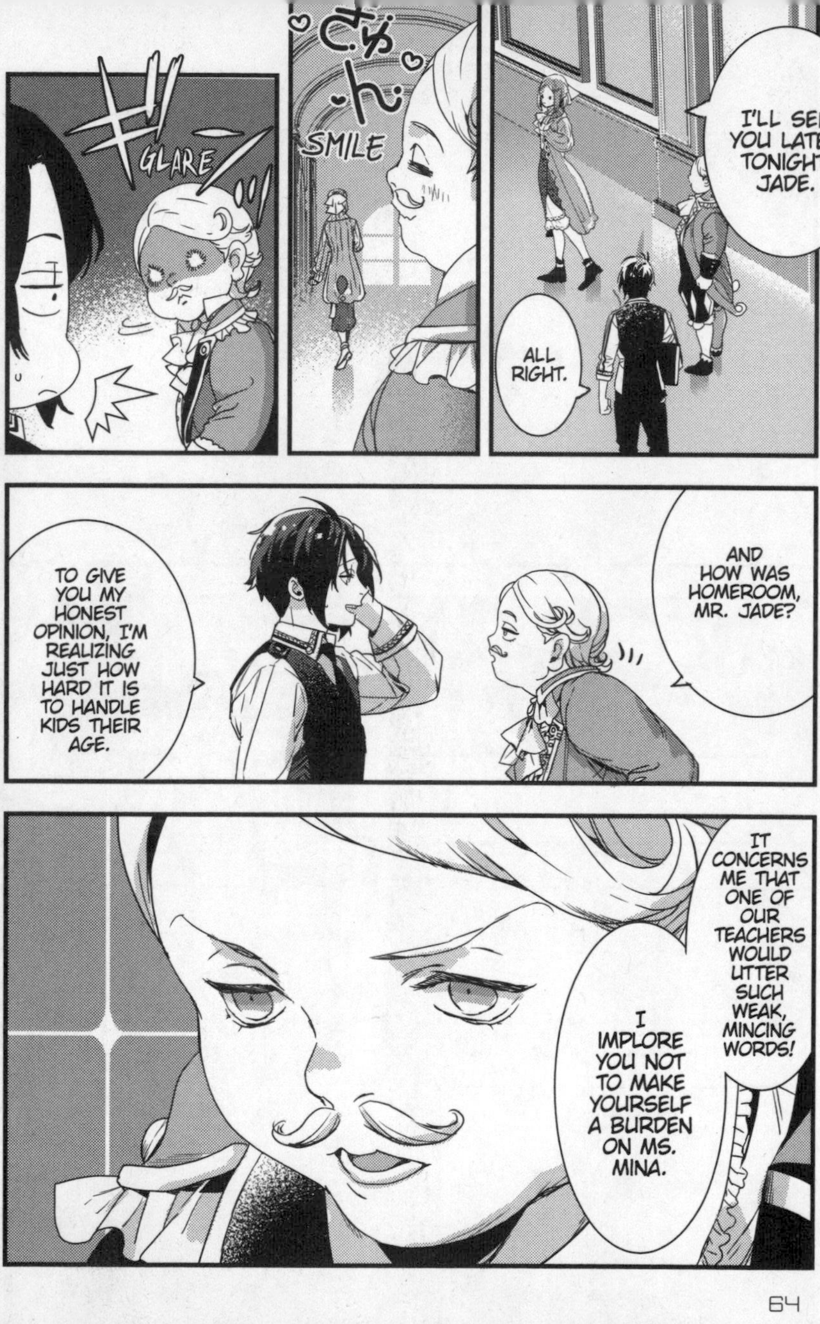
I'LL SEE YOU LATER TONIGHT, JADE.
ALL RIGHT.
SMILE
GLARE
AND HOW WAS HOMEROOM, MR. JADE?
TO GIVE YOU MY HONEST OPINION, I'M REALIZING JUST HOW HARD IT IS TO HANDLE KIDS THEIR AGE.
IT CONCERNS ME THAT ONE OF OUR TEACHERS WOULD UTTER SUCH WEAK, MINCING WORDS!
I IMPLORE YOU NOT TO MAKE YOURSELF A BURDEN ON MS. MINA.

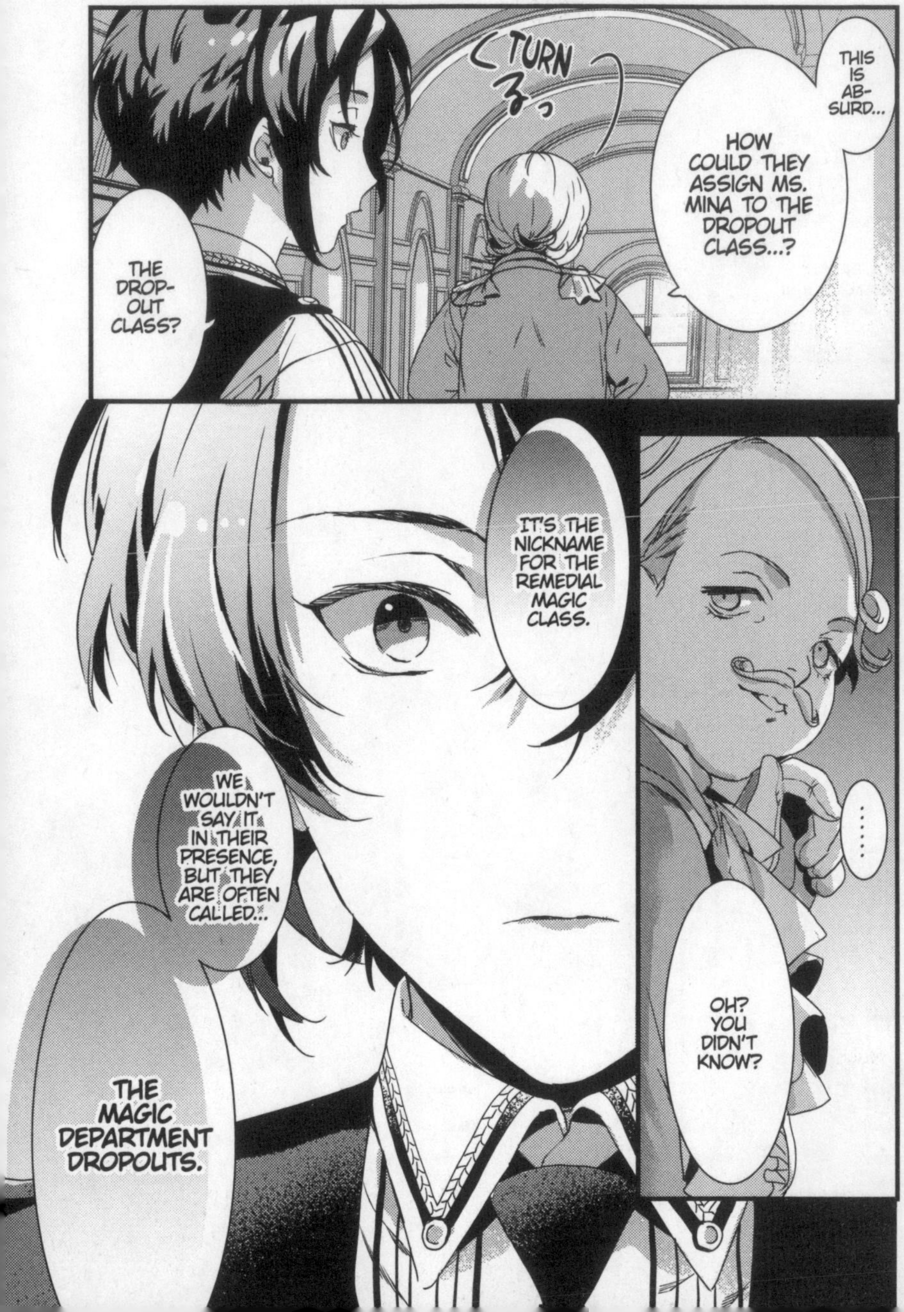
THIS IS ABSURD...
HOW COULD THEY ASSIGN MS. MINA TO THE DROPOUT CLASS...?
TURN
THE DROPOUT CLASS?
......
OH? YOU DIDN'T KNOW?
IT'S THE NICKNAME FOR THE REMEDIAL MAGIC CLASS.
WE WOULDN'T SAY IT IN THEIR PRESENCE, BUT THEY ARE OFTEN CALLED...
THE MAGIC DEPARTMENT DROPOUTS.

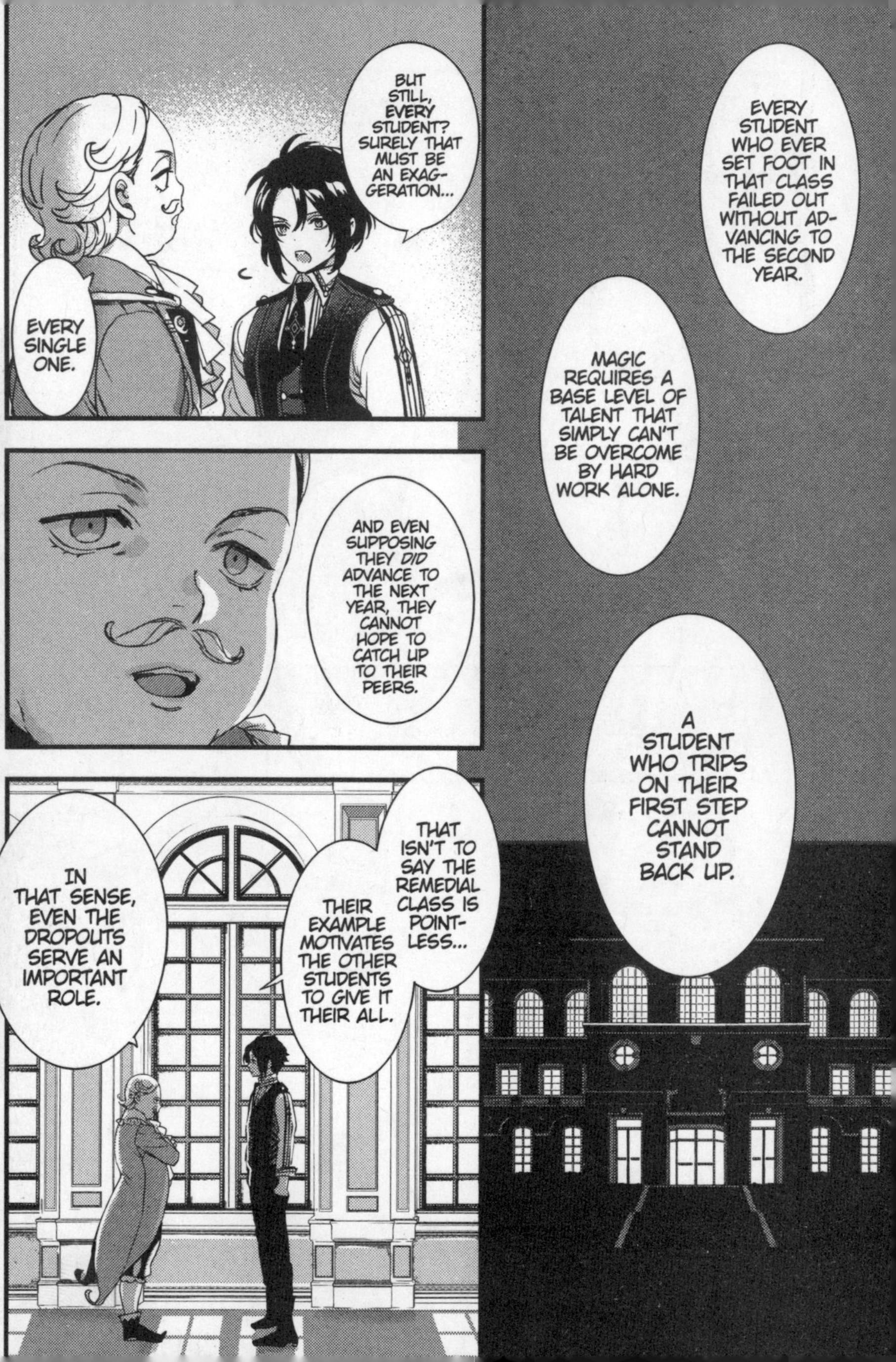
EVERY STUDENT WHO EVER SET FOOT IN THAT CLASS FAILED OUT WITHOUT AD-VANCING TO THE SECOND YEAR.
MAGIC REQUIRES A BASE LEVEL OF TALENT THAT SIMPLY CAN'T BE OVERCOME BY HARD WORK ALONE.
A STUDENT WHO TRIPS ON THEIR FIRST STEP CANNOT STAND BACK UP.
BUT STILL, EVERY STUDENT? SURELY THAT MUST BE AN EXAG-GERATION...
EVERY SINGLE ONE.
AND EVEN SUPPOSING THEY *DID* ADVANCE TO THE NEXT YEAR, THEY CANNOT HOPE TO CATCH UP TO THEIR PEERS.
THAT ISN'T TO SAY THE REMEDIAL CLASS IS POINT-LESS...
THEIR EXAMPLE MOTIVATES THE OTHER STUDENTS TO GIVE IT THEIR ALL.
IN THAT SENSE, EVEN THE DROPOUTS SERVE AN IMPORTANT ROLE.

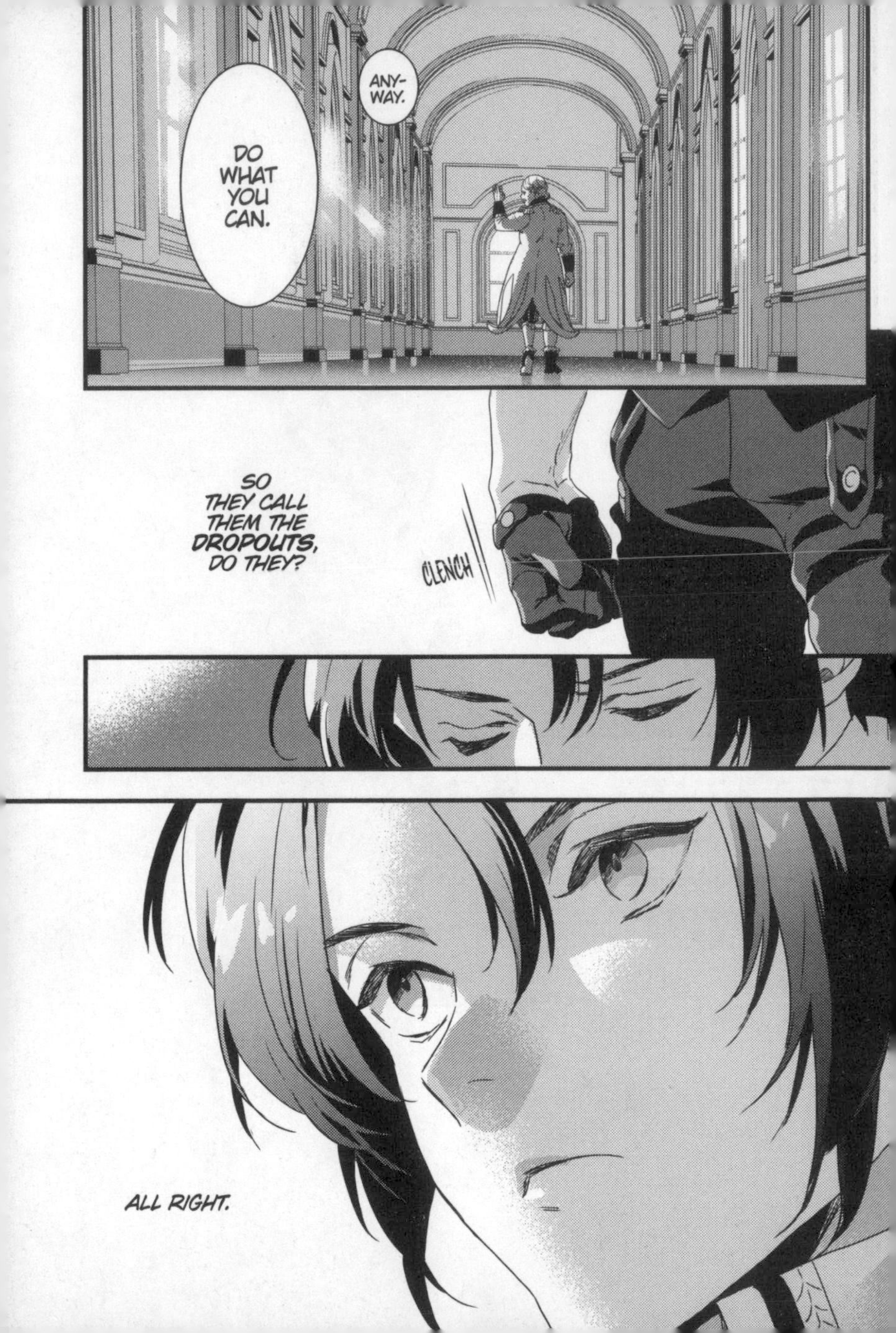
ANY-WAY.
DO WHAT YOU CAN.
SO THEY CALL THEM THE DROPOUTS, DO THEY?
CLENCH
ALL RIGHT.

I'LL TEACH THOSE KIDS TO USE THE MAGIC THEY ASPIRE TO...
AND THEN...
I'LL HELP MAKE THEIR DREAMS A REALITY!!

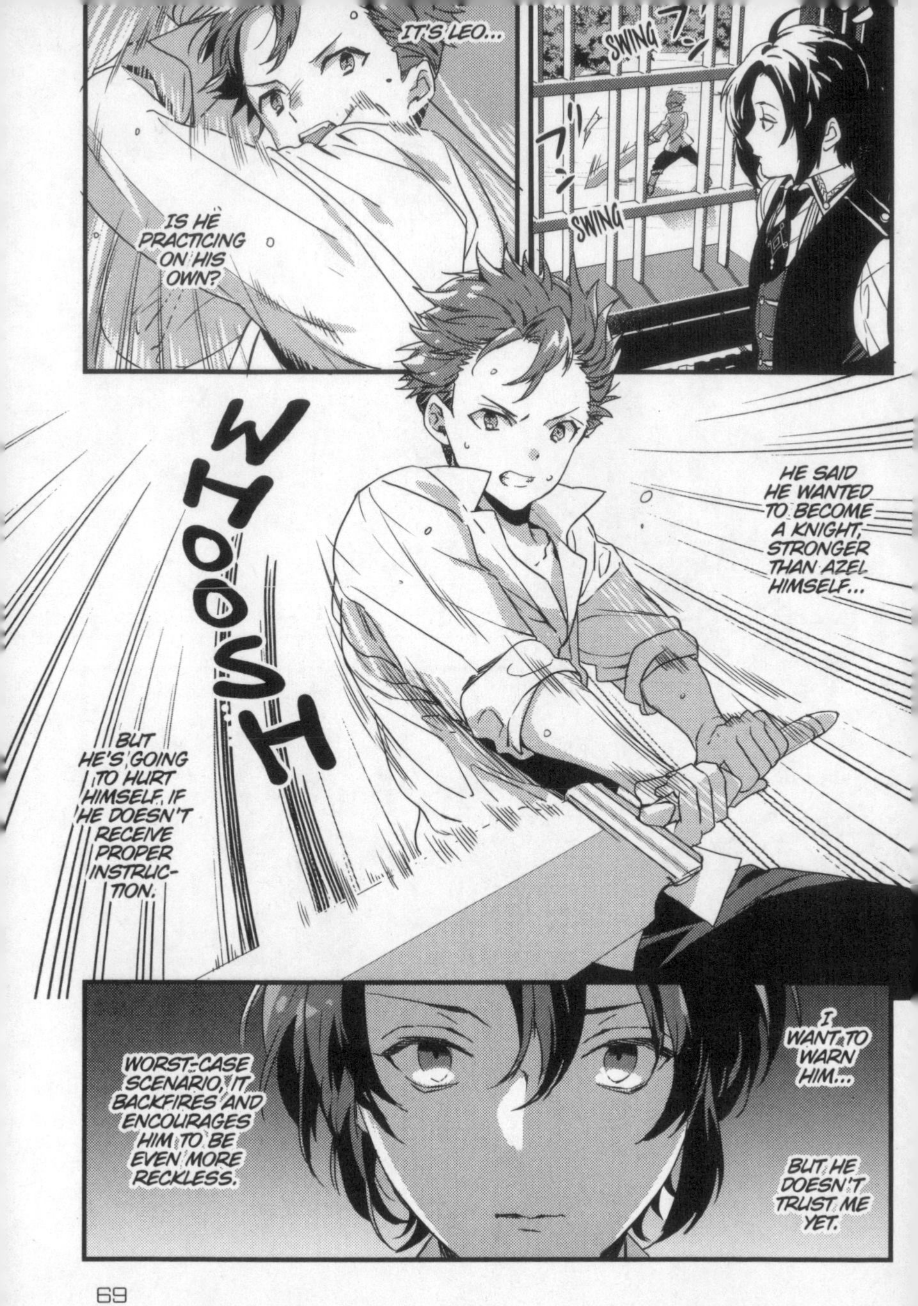
SWING
SWING
IT'S LEO...
IS HE PRACTICING ON HIS OWN?
WHOOSH
HE SAID HE WANTED TO BECOME A KNIGHT, STRONGER THAN AZEL HIMSELF...
BUT HE'S GOING TO HURT HIMSELF IF HE DOESN'T RECEIVE PROPER INSTRUCTION.
I WANT TO WARN HIM...
BUT HE DOESN'T TRUST ME YET.
WORST-CASE SCENARIO, IT BACKFIRES AND ENCOURAGES HIM TO BE EVEN MORE RECKLESS.

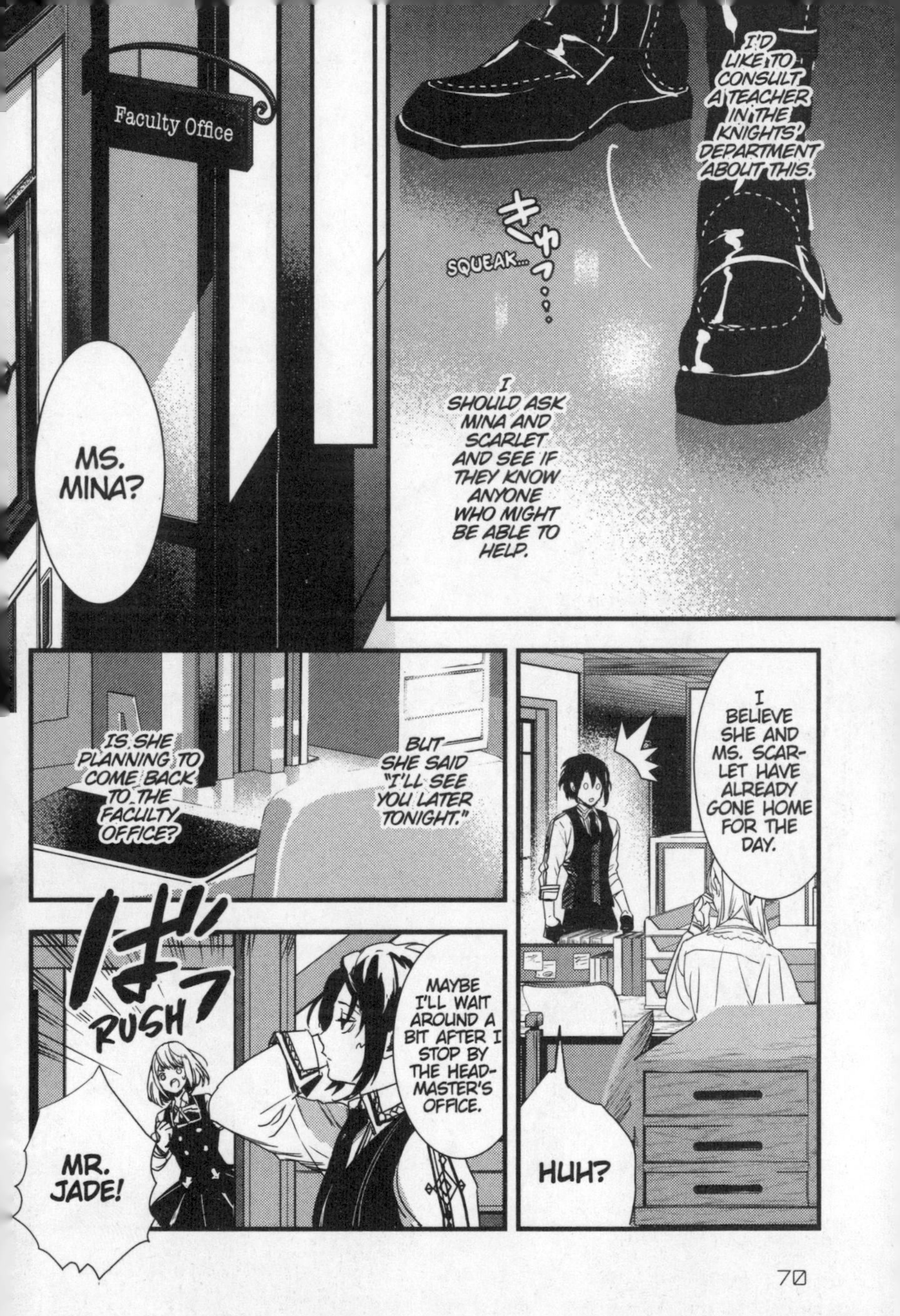
I'D LIKE TO CONSULT A TEACHER IN THE KNIGHTS' DEPARTMENT ABOUT THIS.
SQUEAK...
I SHOULD ASK MINA AND SCARLET AND SEE IF THEY KNOW ANYONE WHO MIGHT BE ABLE TO HELP.
Faculty Office
MS. MINA?
I BELIEVE SHE AND MS. SCARLET HAVE ALREADY GONE HOME FOR THE DAY.
HUH?
BUT SHE SAID "I'LL SEE YOU LATER TONIGHT."
IS SHE PLANNING TO COME BACK TO THE FACULTY OFFICE?
MAYBE I'LL WAIT AROUND A BIT AFTER I STOP BY THE HEADMASTER'S OFFICE.
RUSH
MR. JADE!

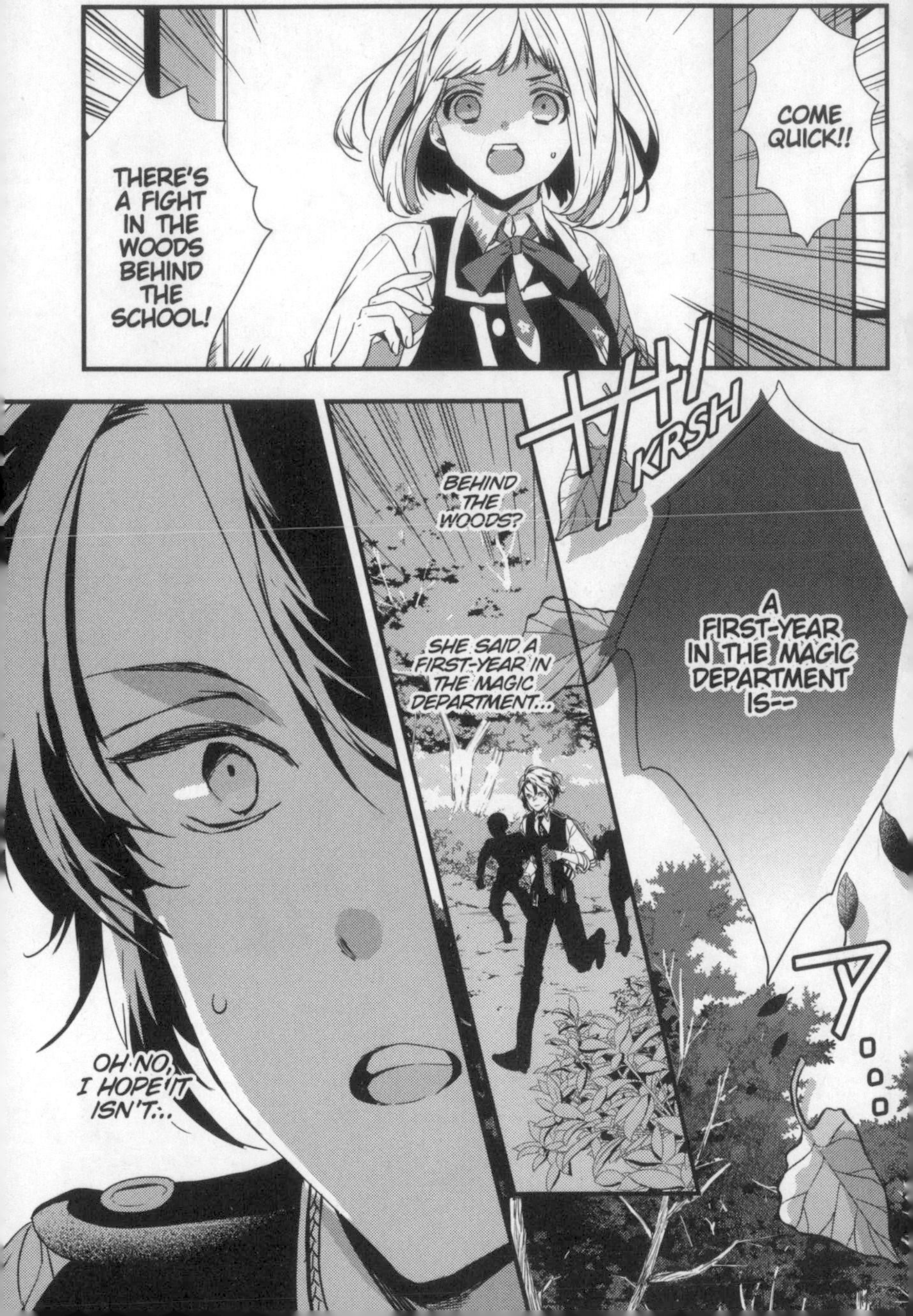
COME QUICK!!
THERE'S A FIGHT IN THE WOODS BEHIND THE SCHOOL!
KRSH
A FIRST-YEAR IN THE MAGIC DEPARTMENT IS--
BEHIND THE WOODS?
SHE SAID A FIRST-YEAR IN THE MAGIC DEPARTMENT...
OH NO, I HOPE IT ISN'T...

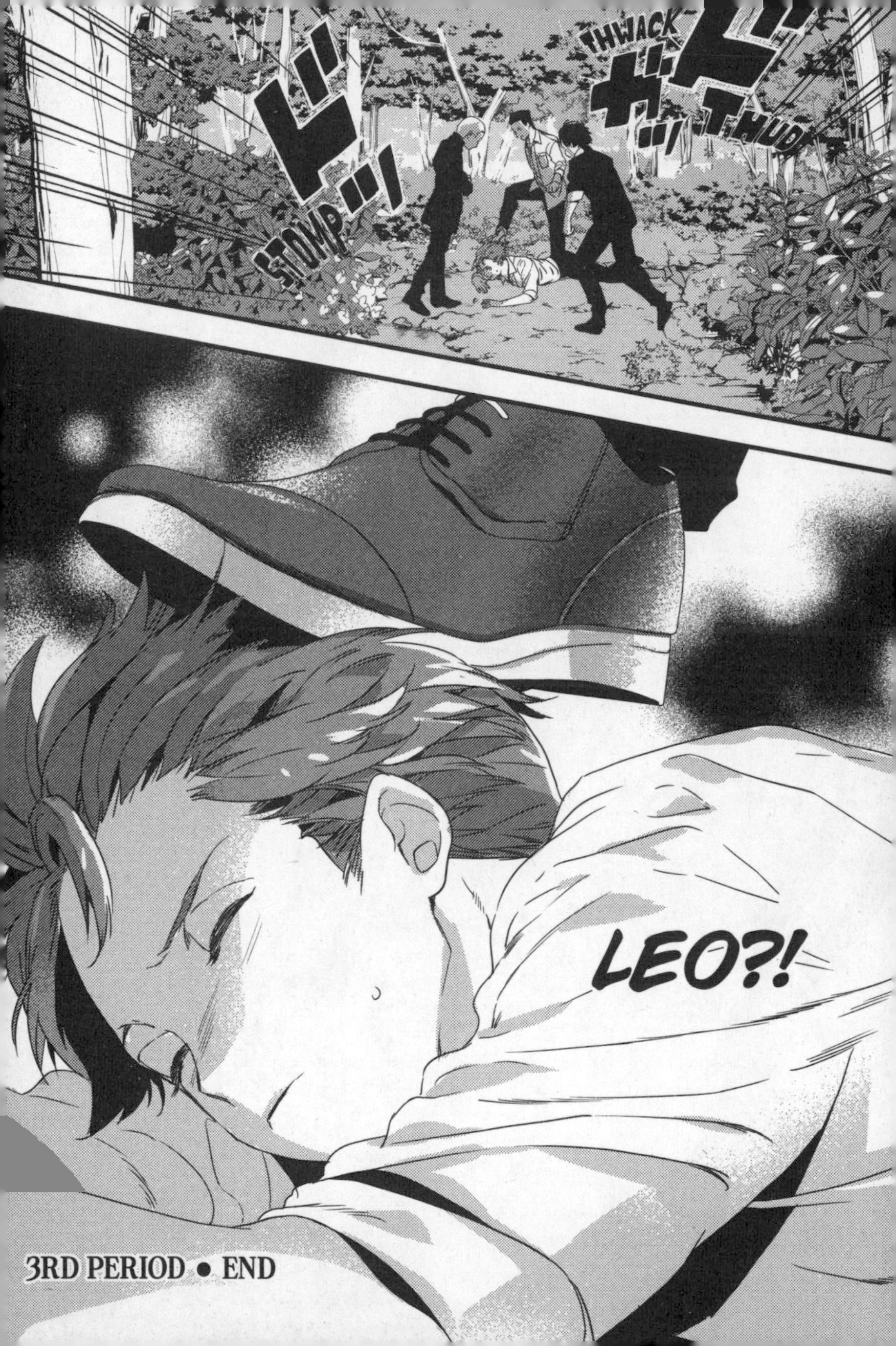
THWACK
THUD
STOMP
LEO?!

3RD PERIOD • END

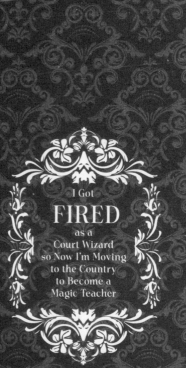

I Got

FIRED

as a
Court Wizard
so Now I'm Moving
to the Country
to Become a
Magic Teacher

I Got Fired as a
COURT WIZARD
so Now I'm Moving to the Country to Become a
MAGIC TEACHER

4th Period
Principled and Proud

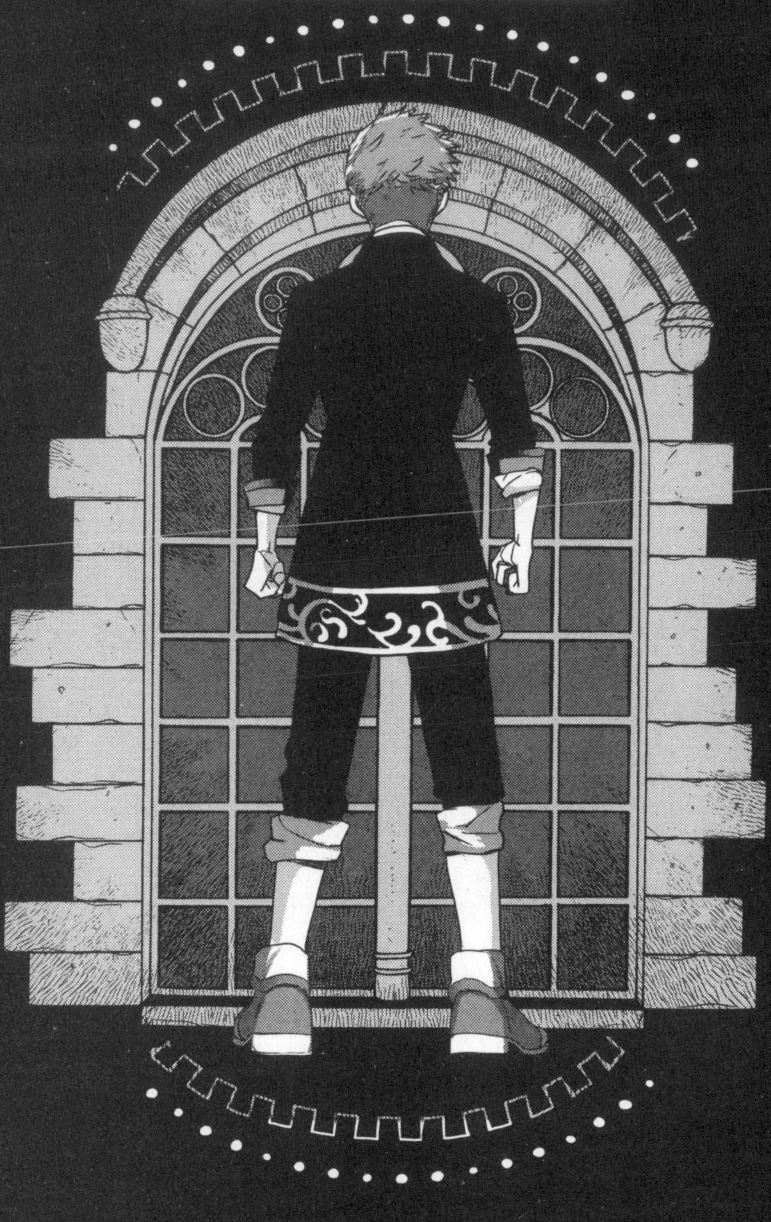

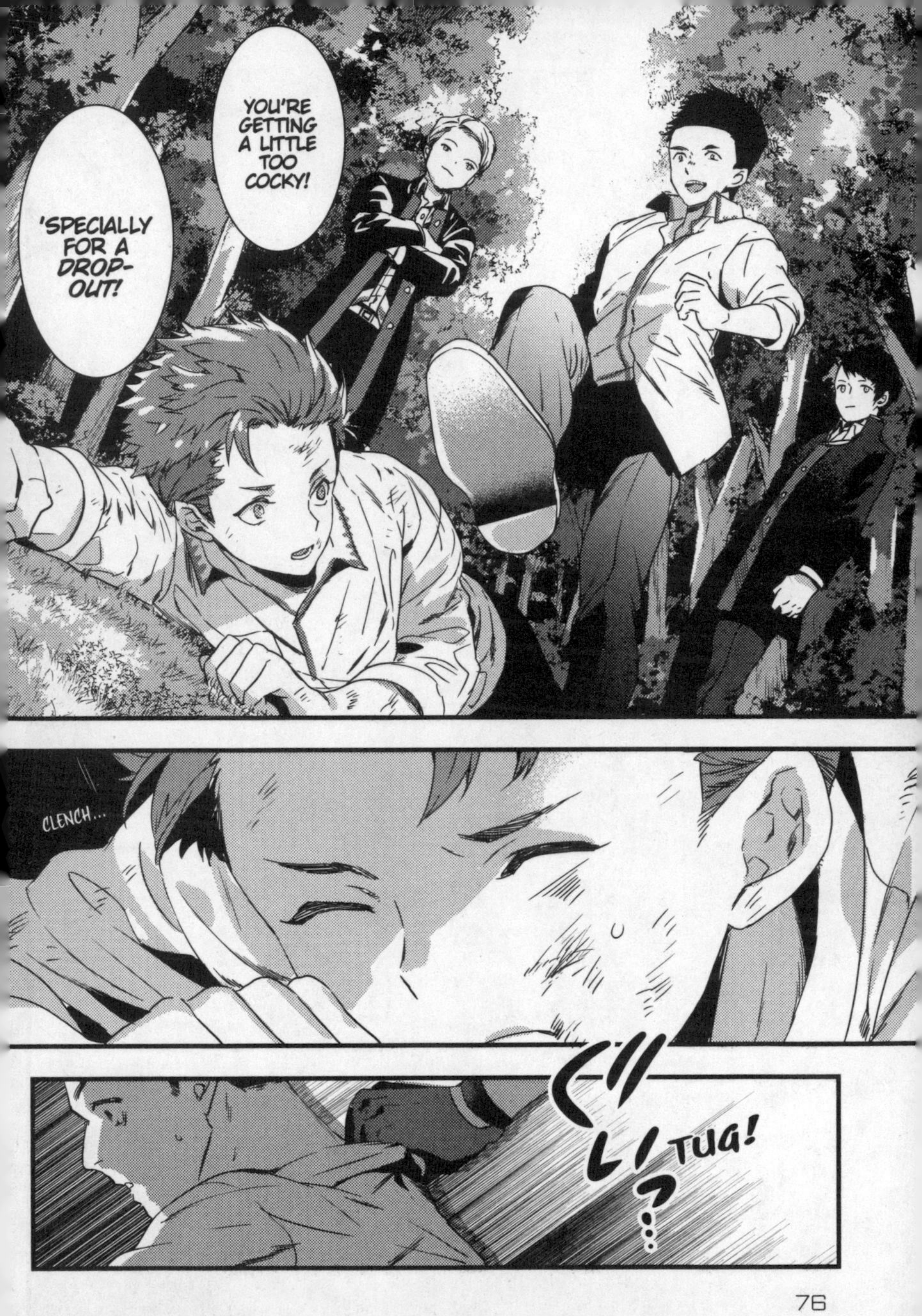
YOU'RE GETTING A LITTLE TOO COCKY!
'SPECIALLY FOR A DROP-OUT!
CLENCH...
ぐい
TUG!
?...

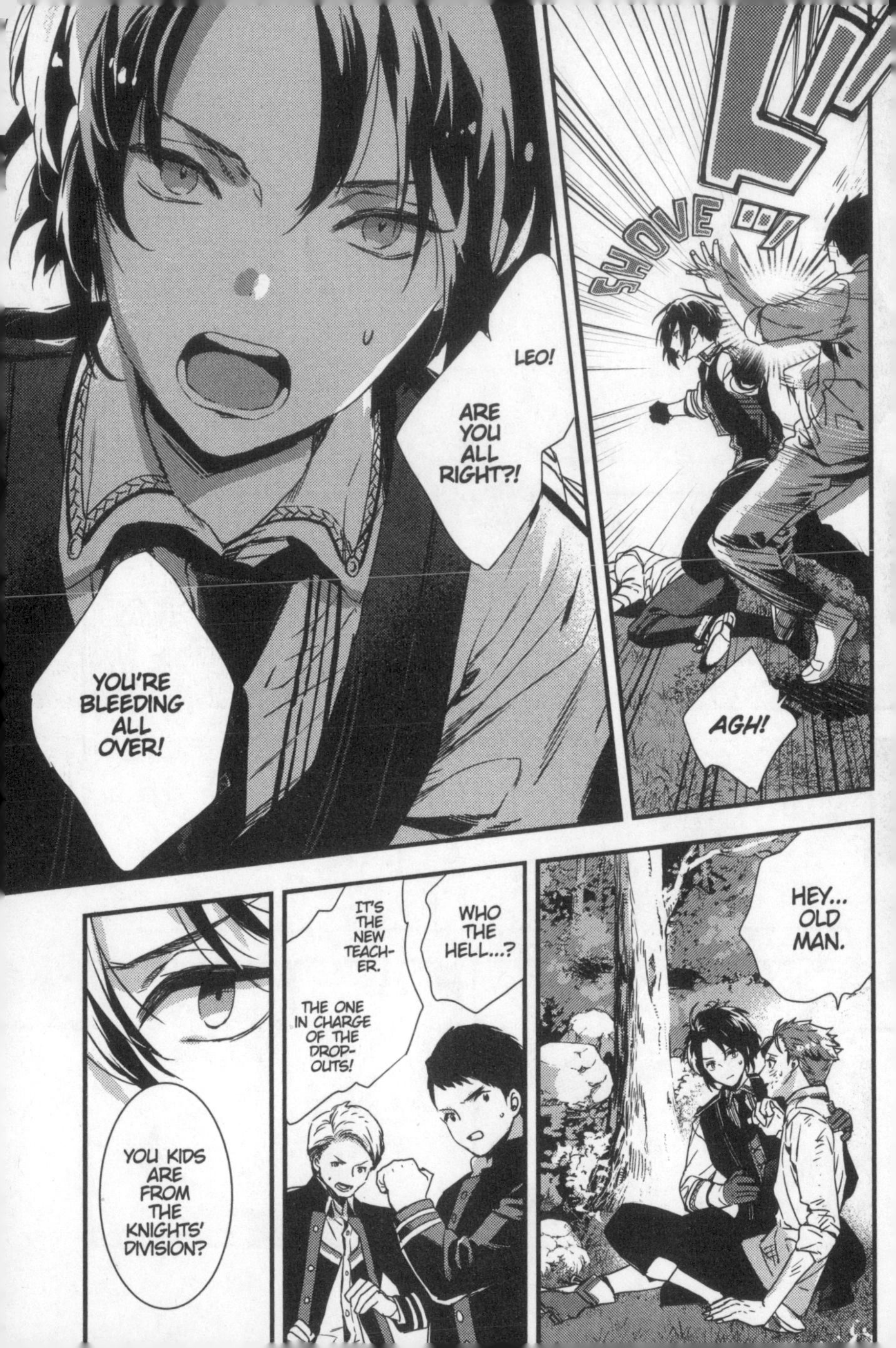
SHOVE
AGH!
LEO!
ARE YOU ALL RIGHT?!
YOU'RE BLEEDING ALL OVER!
HEY... OLD MAN.
WHO THE HELL...?
IT'S THE NEW TEACHER.
THE ONE IN CHARGE OF THE DROPOUTS!
YOU KIDS ARE FROM THE KNIGHTS' DIVISION?

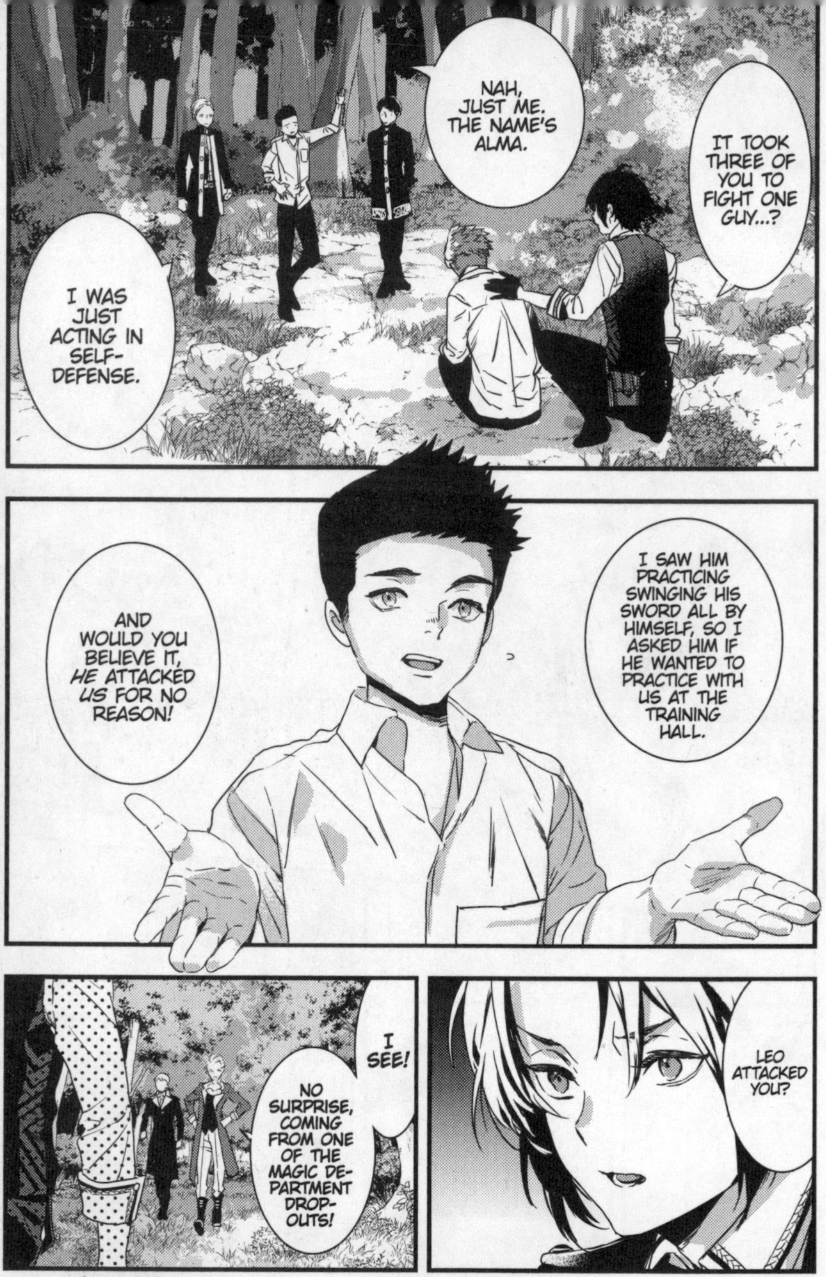
IT TOOK THREE OF YOU TO FIGHT ONE GUY...?
NAH, JUST ME. THE NAME'S ALMA.
I WAS JUST ACTING IN SELF-DEFENSE.
I SAW HIM PRACTICING SWINGING HIS SWORD ALL BY HIMSELF, SO I ASKED HIM IF HE WANTED TO PRACTICE WITH US AT THE TRAINING HALL.
AND WOULD YOU BELIEVE IT, *HE* ATTACKED *US* FOR NO REASON!
LEO ATTACKED YOU?
I SEE!
NO SURPRISE, COMING FROM ONE OF THE MAGIC DEPARTMENT DROPOUTS!

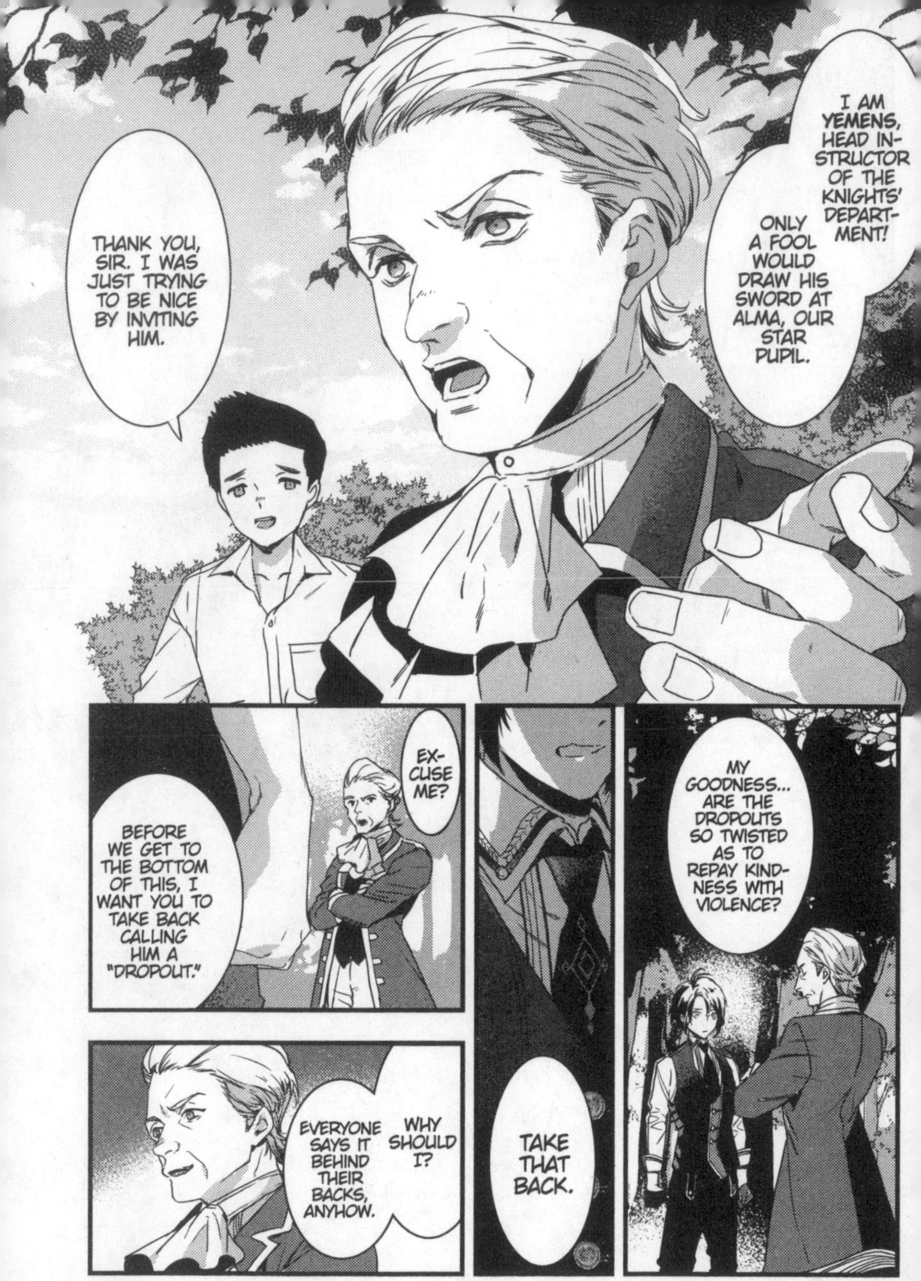
I AM YEMENS, HEAD IN-STRUCTOR OF THE KNIGHTS' DEPART-MENT!
ONLY A FOOL WOULD DRAW HIS SWORD AT ALMA, OUR STAR PUPIL.
THANK YOU, SIR. I WAS JUST TRYING TO BE NICE BY INVITING HIM.
MY GOODNESS... ARE THE DROPOUTS SO TWISTED AS TO REPAY KIND-NESS WITH VIOLENCE?
TAKE THAT BACK.
EX-CUSE ME?
BEFORE WE GET TO THE BOTTOM OF THIS, I WANT YOU TO TAKE BACK CALLING HIM A "DROPOUT."
WHY SHOULD I?
EVERYONE SAYS IT BEHIND THEIR BACKS, ANYHOW.

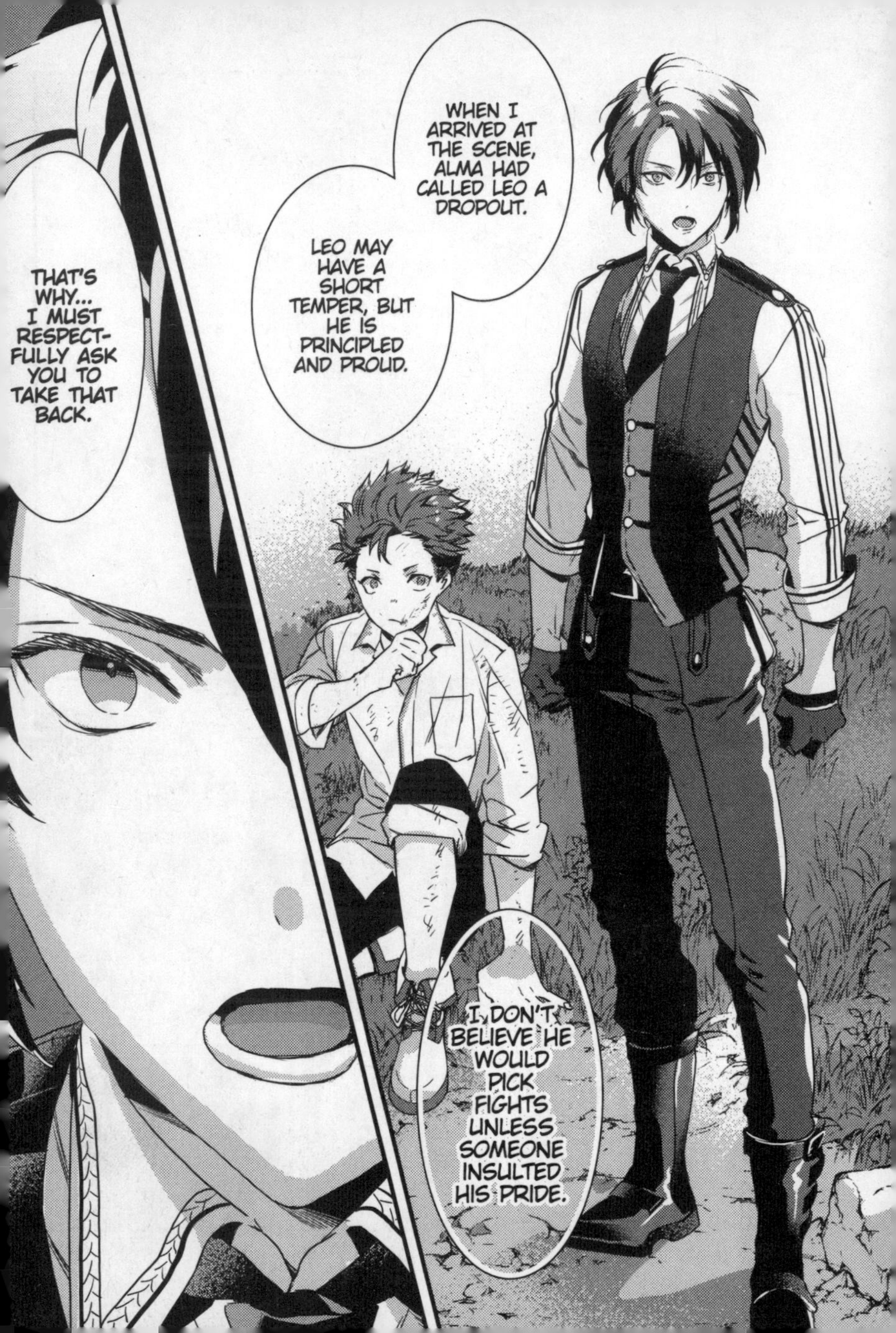
WHEN I ARRIVED AT THE SCENE, ALMA HAD CALLED LEO A DROPOUT.
LEO MAY HAVE A SHORT TEMPER, BUT HE IS PRINCIPLED AND PROUD.
I DON'T BELIEVE HE WOULD PICK FIGHTS UNLESS SOMEONE INSULTED HIS PRIDE.
THAT'S WHY... I MUST RESPECTFULLY ASK YOU TO TAKE THAT BACK.

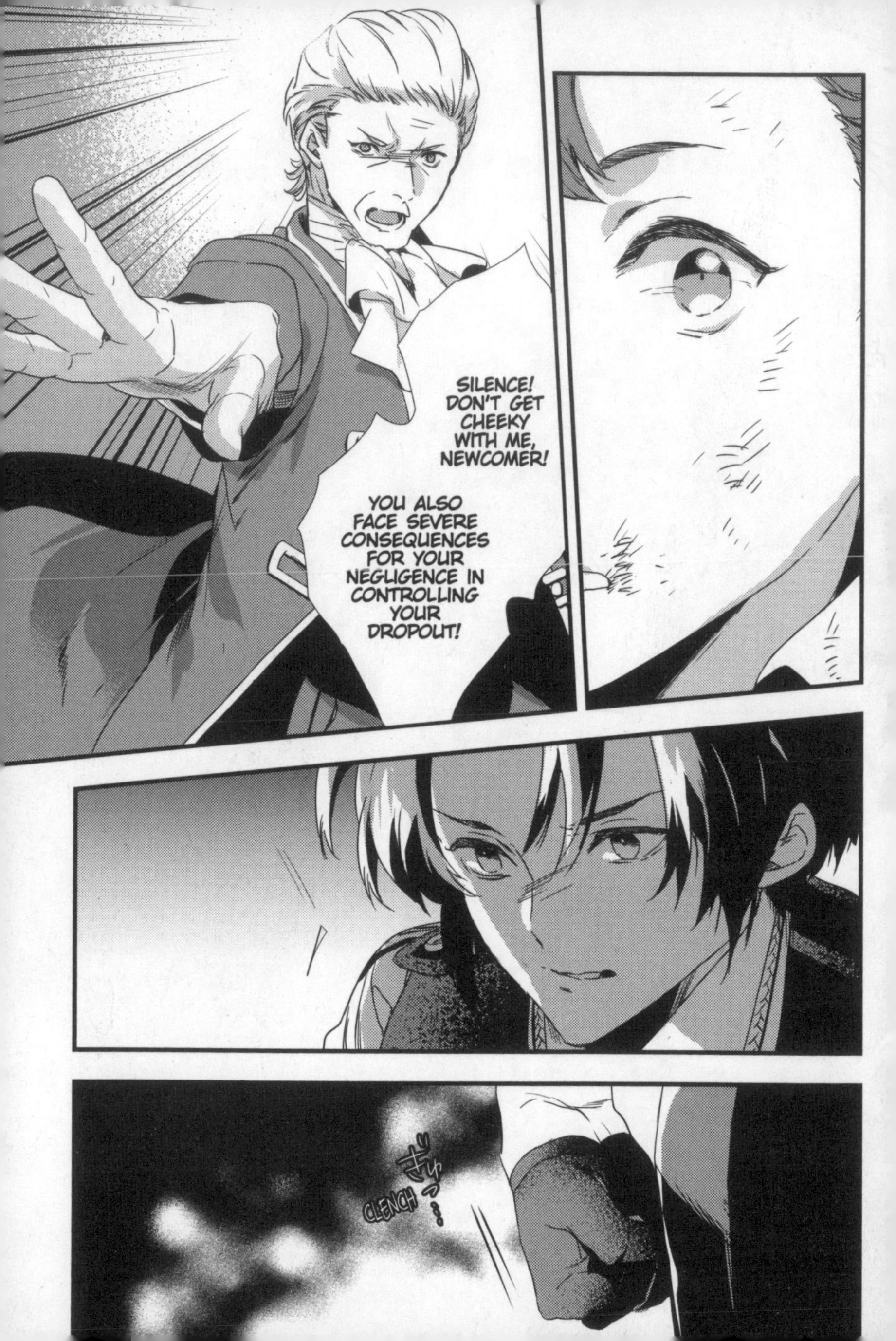
SILENCE! DON'T GET CHEEKY WITH ME, NEWCOMER!
YOU ALSO FACE SEVERE CONSEQUENCES FOR YOUR NEGLIGENCE IN CONTROLLING YOUR DROPOUT!
ぎゅっ…
CLENCH

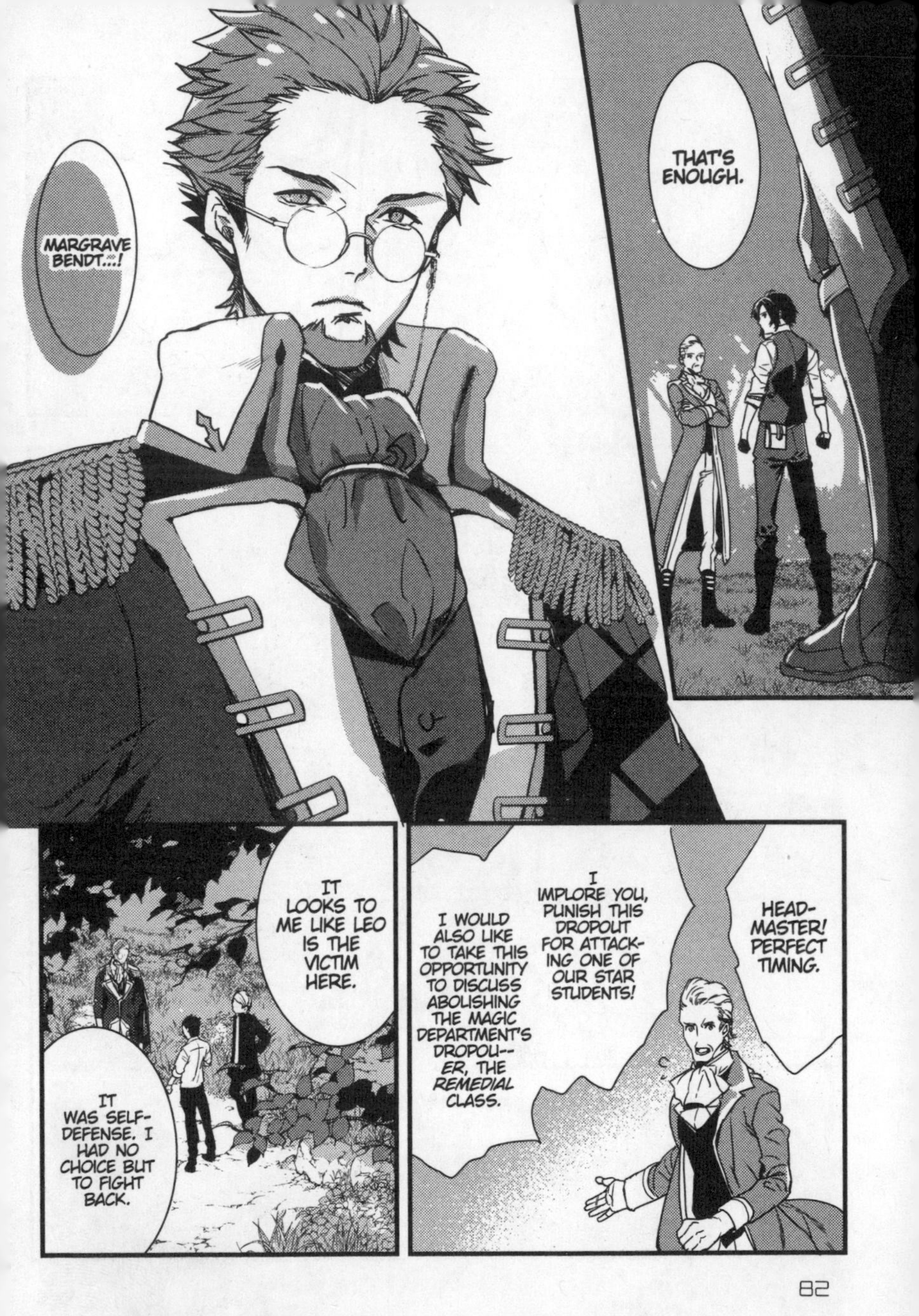
THAT'S ENOUGH.
MARGRAVE BENDT...!
HEADMASTER! PERFECT TIMING.
I IMPLORE YOU, PUNISH THIS DROPOUT FOR ATTACKING ONE OF OUR STAR STUDENTS!
I WOULD ALSO LIKE TO TAKE THIS OPPORTUNITY TO DISCUSS ABOLISHING THE MAGIC DEPARTMENT'S DROPOU-- ER, THE *REMEDIAL* CLASS.
IT LOOKS TO ME LIKE LEO IS THE VICTIM HERE.
IT WAS SELF-DEFENSE. I HAD NO CHOICE BUT TO FIGHT BACK.

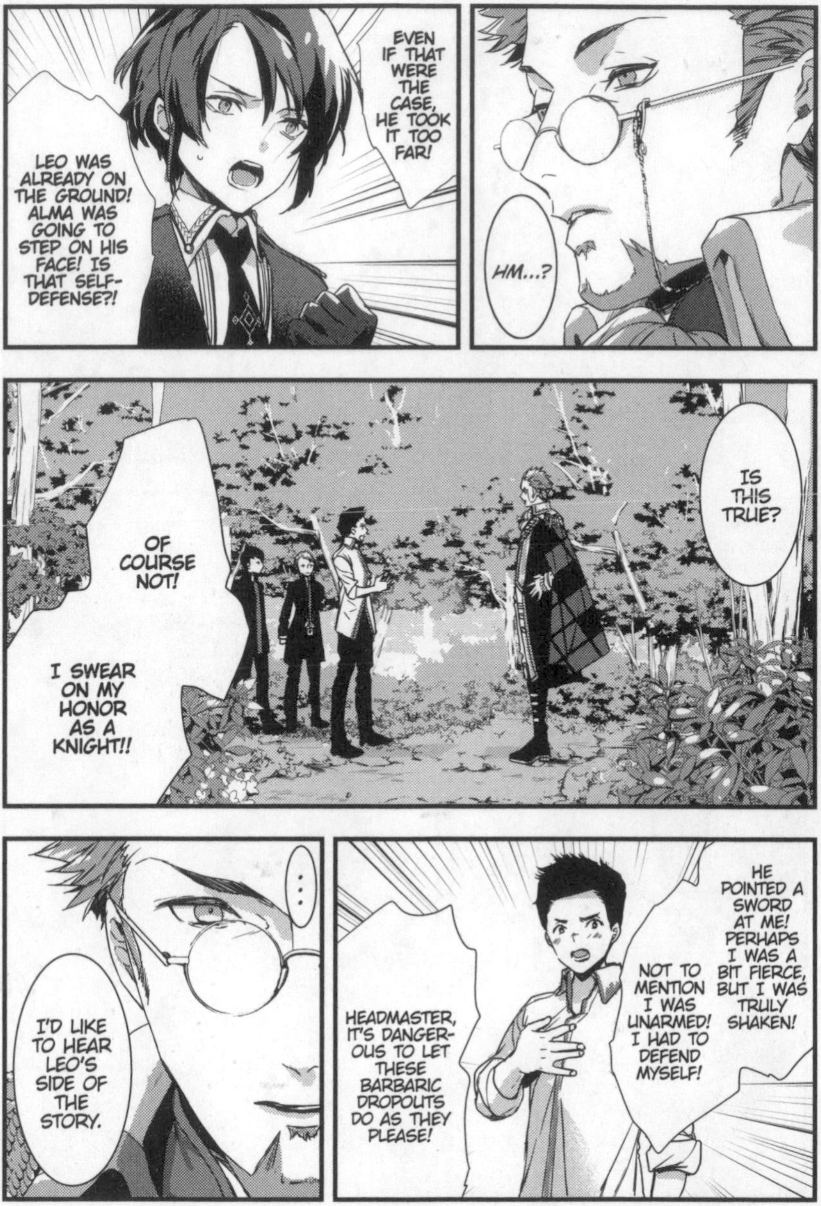
HM...?
EVEN IF THAT WERE THE CASE, HE TOOK IT TOO FAR!
LEO WAS ALREADY ON THE GROUND! ALMA WAS GOING TO STEP ON HIS FACE! IS THAT SELF-DEFENSE?!
IS THIS TRUE?
OF COURSE NOT!
I SWEAR ON MY HONOR AS A KNIGHT!!
HE POINTED A SWORD AT ME! PERHAPS I WAS A BIT FIERCE, BUT I WAS TRULY SHAKEN!
NOT TO MENTION I WAS UNARMED! I HAD TO DEFEND MYSELF!
HEADMASTER, IT'S DANGEROUS TO LET THESE BARBARIC DROPOUTS DO AS THEY PLEASE!
...
I'D LIKE TO HEAR LEO'S SIDE OF THE STORY.

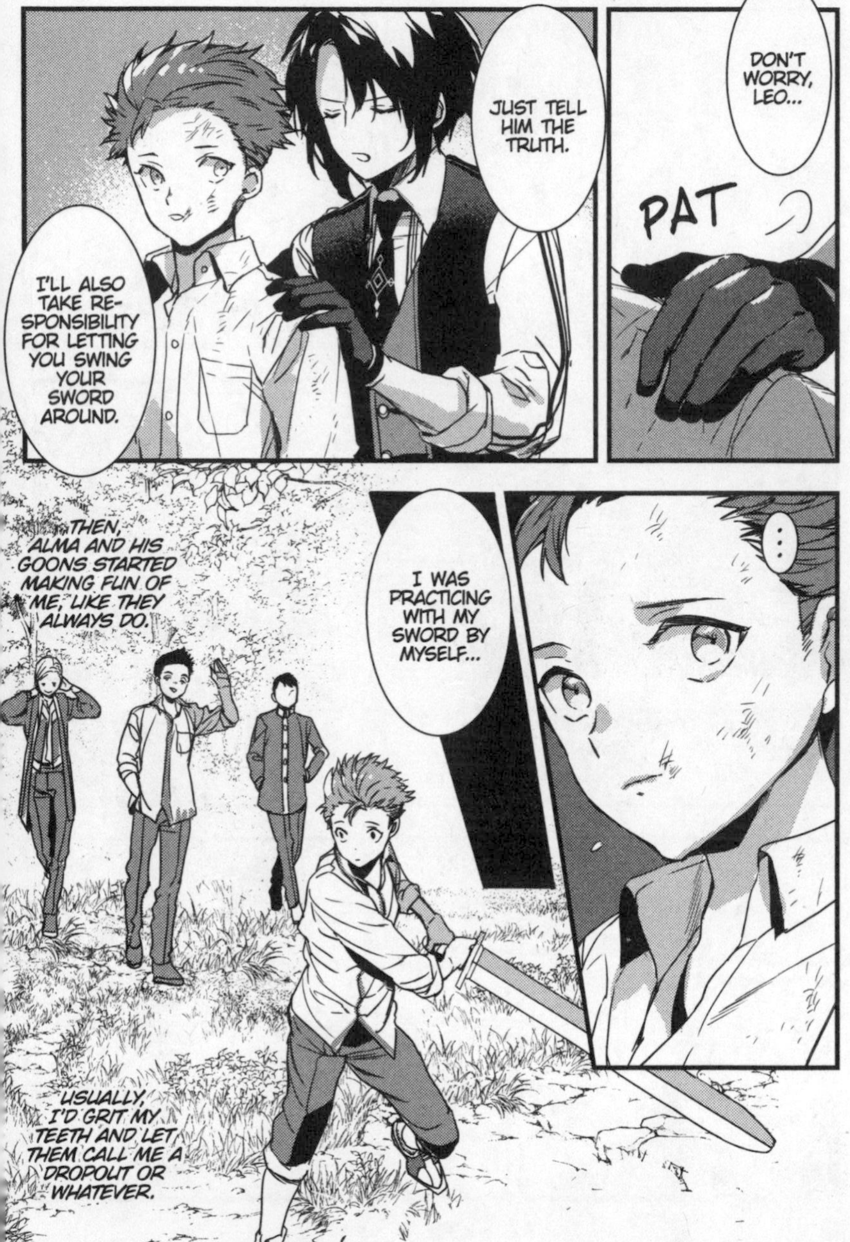
DON'T WORRY, LEO...
PAT
JUST TELL HIM THE TRUTH.
I'LL ALSO TAKE RE-SPONSIBILITY FOR LETTING YOU SWING YOUR SWORD AROUND.
...
I WAS PRACTICING WITH MY SWORD BY MYSELF...
THEN, ALMA AND HIS GOONS STARTED MAKING FUN OF ME, LIKE THEY ALWAYS DO.
USUALLY, I'D GRIT MY TEETH AND LET THEM CALL ME A DROPOUT OR WHATEVER.

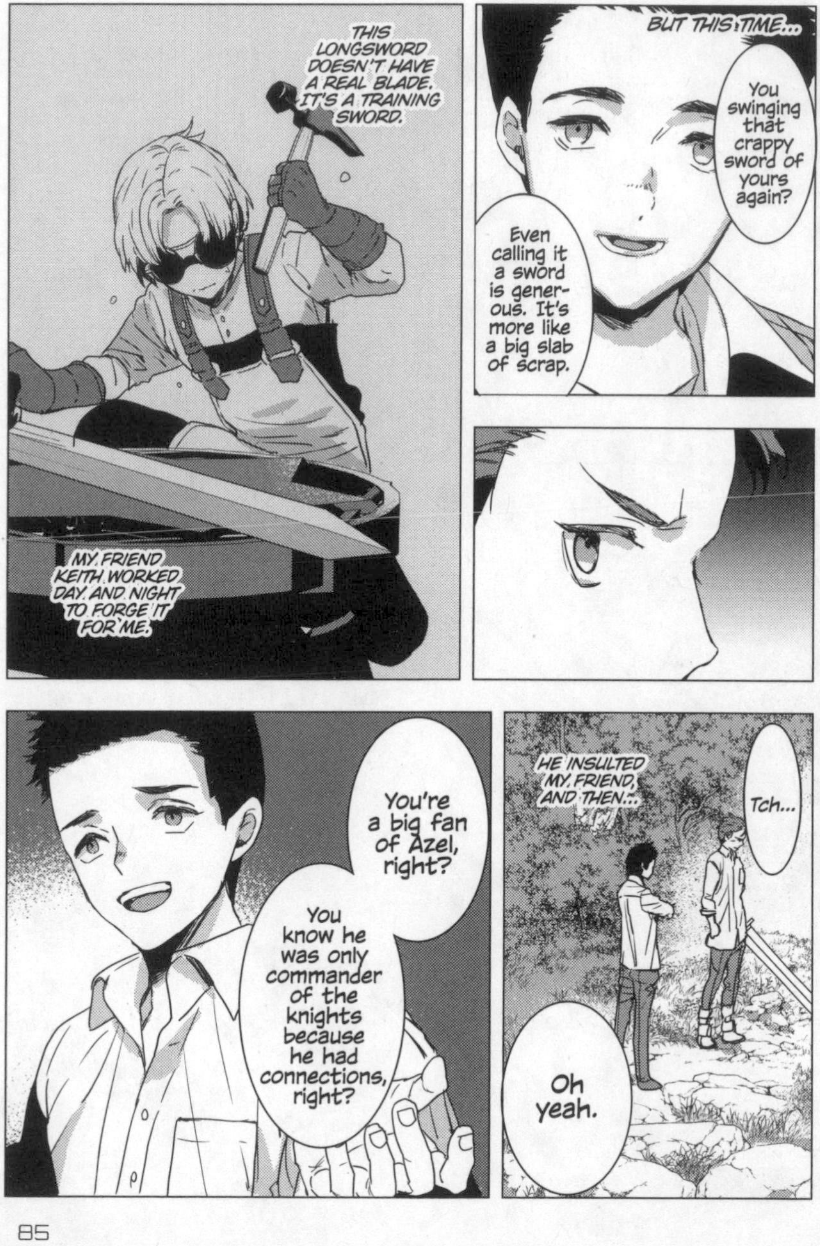
BUT THIS TIME...
You swinging that crappy sword of yours again?
Even calling it a sword is generous. It's more like a big slab of scrap.
THIS LONGSWORD DOESN'T HAVE A REAL BLADE. IT'S A TRAINING SWORD.
MY FRIEND KEITH WORKED DAY AND NIGHT TO FORGE IT FOR ME.
HE INSULTED MY FRIEND, AND THEN...
Tch...
Oh yeah.
You're a big fan of Azel, right?
You know he was only commander of the knights because he had connections, right?

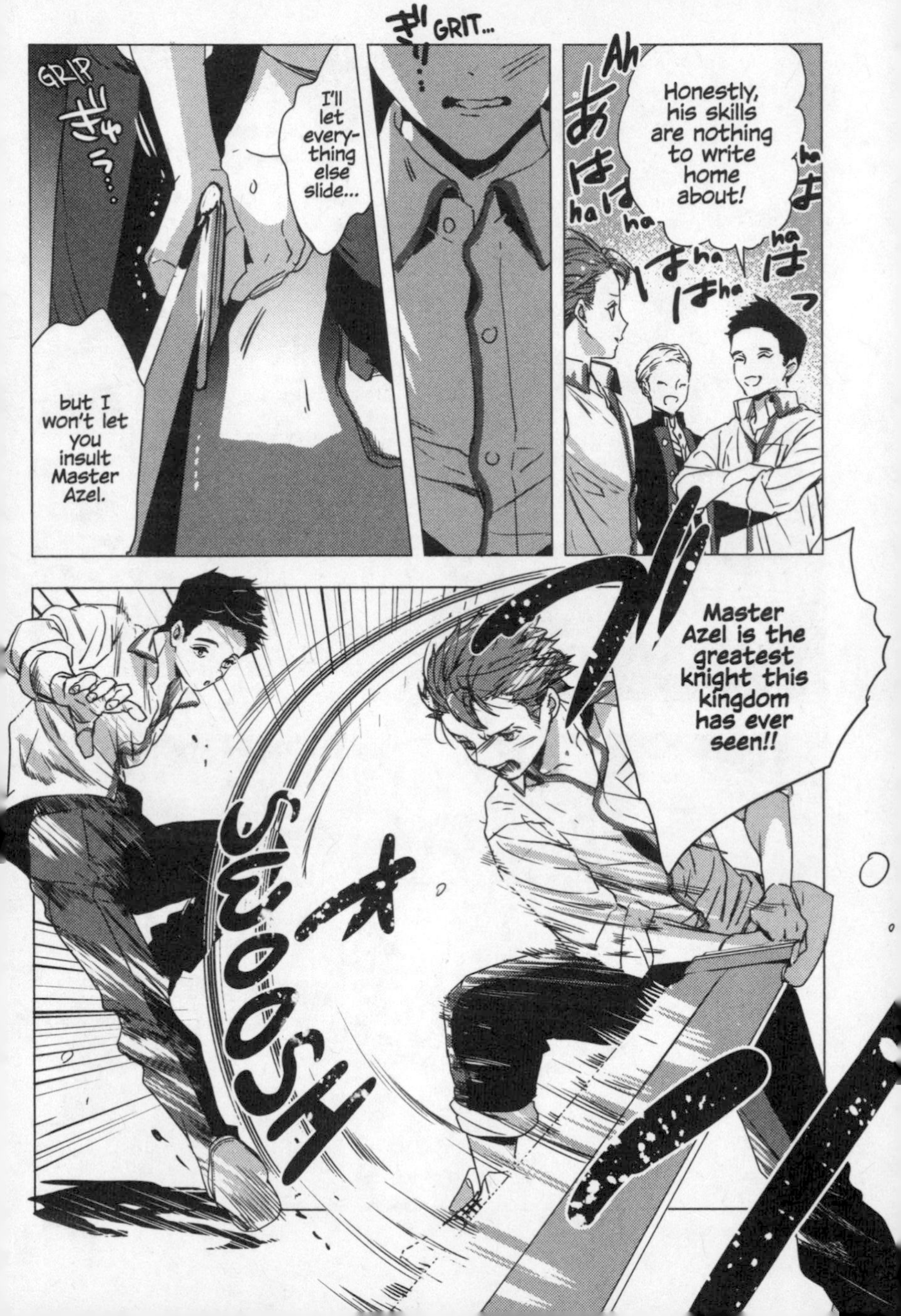
Ah
Honestly, his skills are nothing to write home about!
ha ha ha ha ha ha ha
GRIT...
GRIP
I'll let every-thing else slide...
but I won't let you insult Master Azel.
Master Azel is the greatest knight this kingdom has ever seen!!
SWOOSH

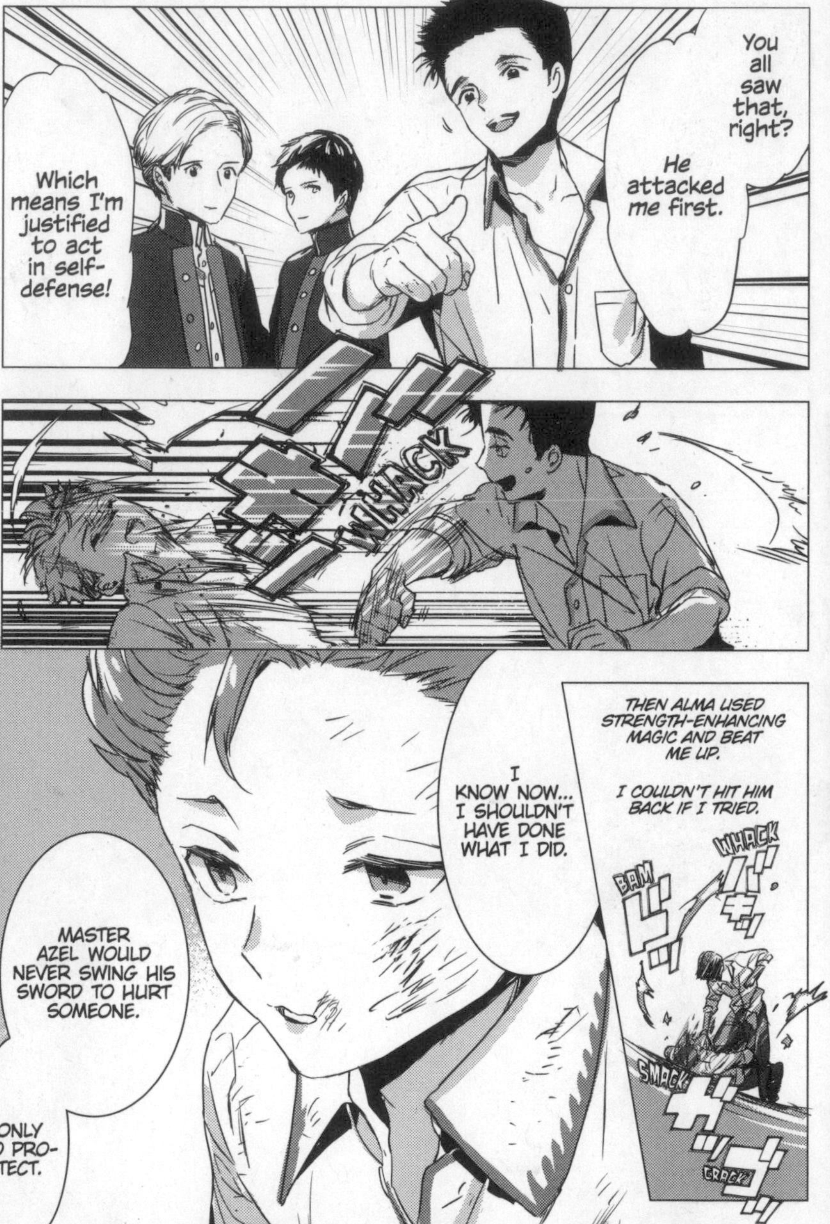
You all saw that, right?
He attacked me first.
Which means I'm justified to act in self-defense!
WHACK
THEN ALMA USED STRENGTH-ENHANCING MAGIC AND BEAT ME UP.
I COULDN'T HIT HIM BACK IF I TRIED.
WHACK
BAM
SMACK
CRACK
I KNOW NOW... I SHOULDN'T HAVE DONE WHAT I DID.
MASTER AZEL WOULD NEVER SWING HIS SWORD TO HURT SOMEONE.
ONLY TO PRO-TECT.

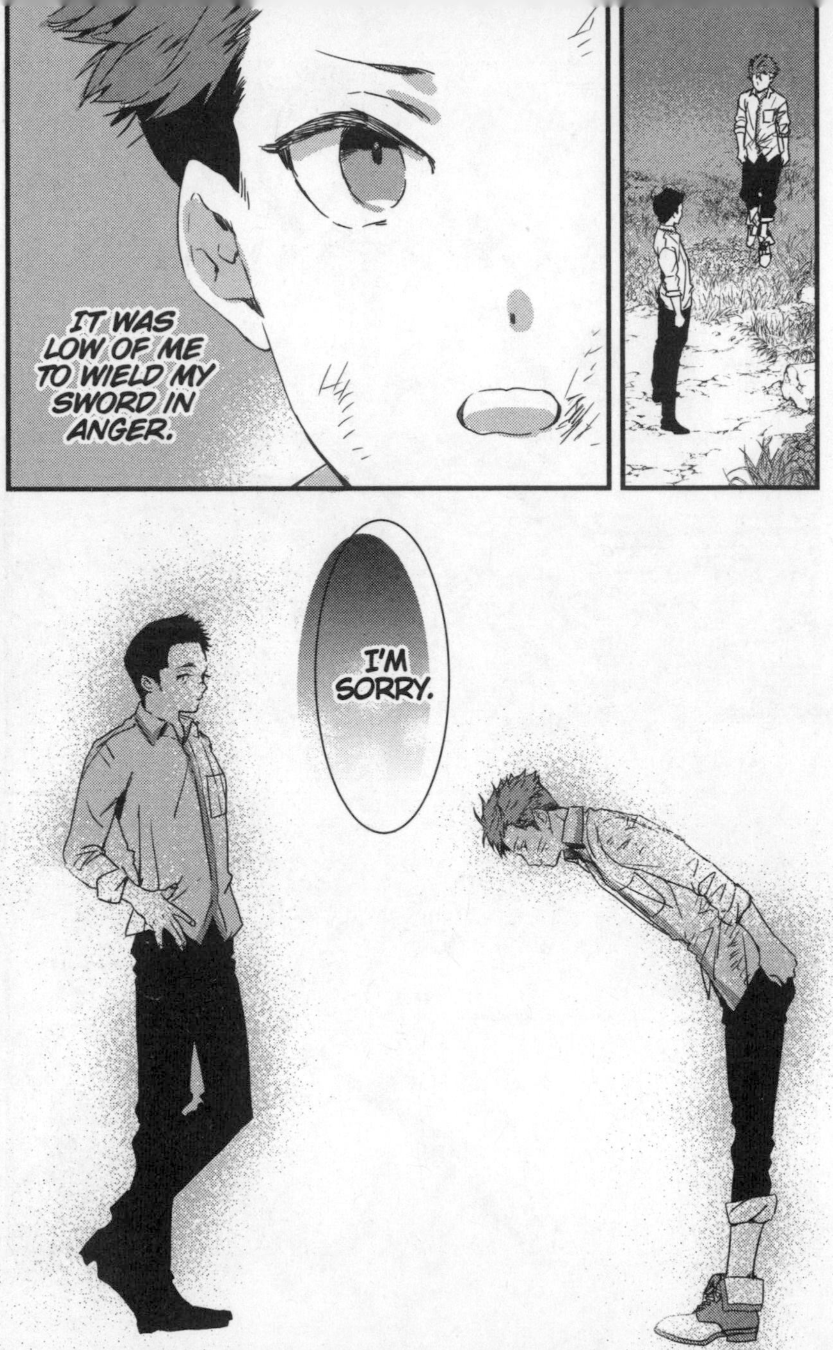
IT WAS LOW OF ME TO WIELD MY SWORD IN ANGER.
I'M SORRY.

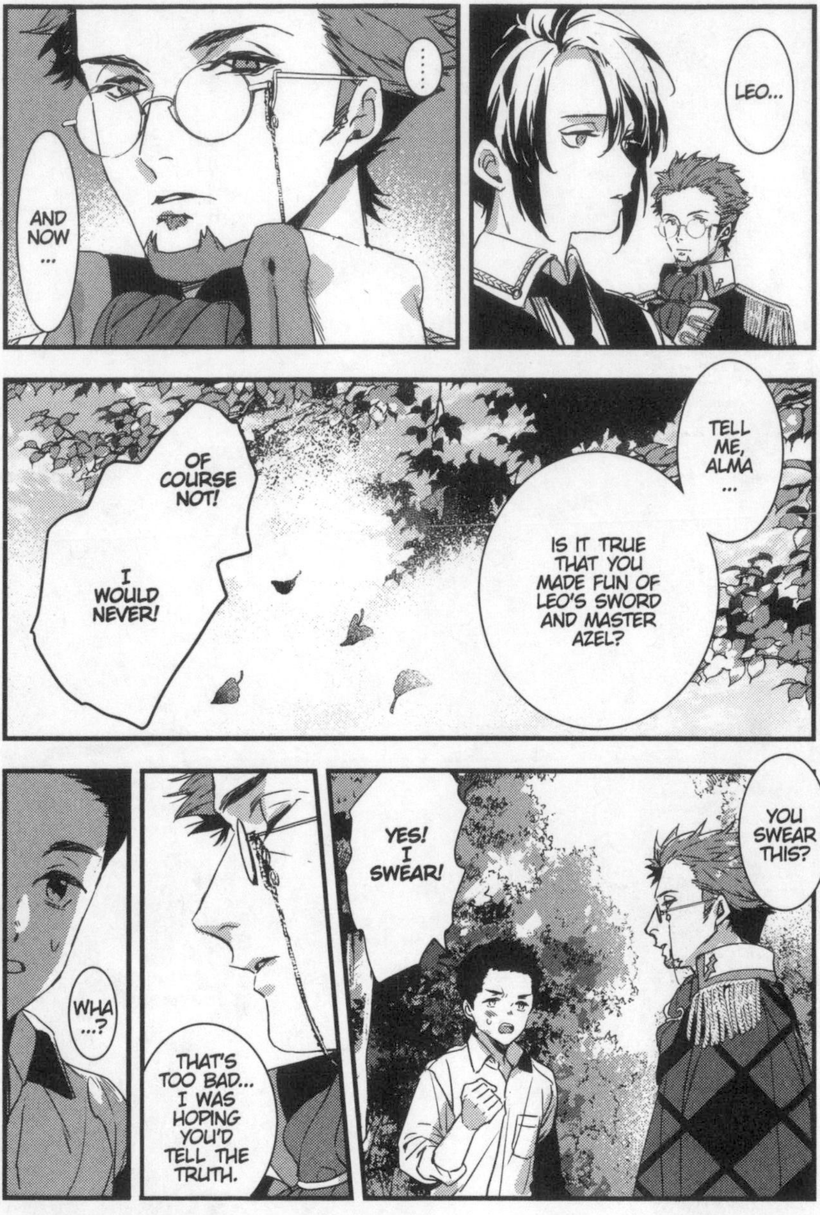
LEO...
......
AND NOW ...
TELL ME, ALMA ...
IS IT TRUE THAT YOU MADE FUN OF LEO'S SWORD AND MASTER AZEL?
OF COURSE NOT!
I WOULD NEVER!
YOU SWEAR THIS?
YES! I SWEAR!
THAT'S TOO BAD... I WAS HOPING YOU'D TELL THE TRUTH.
WHA ...?

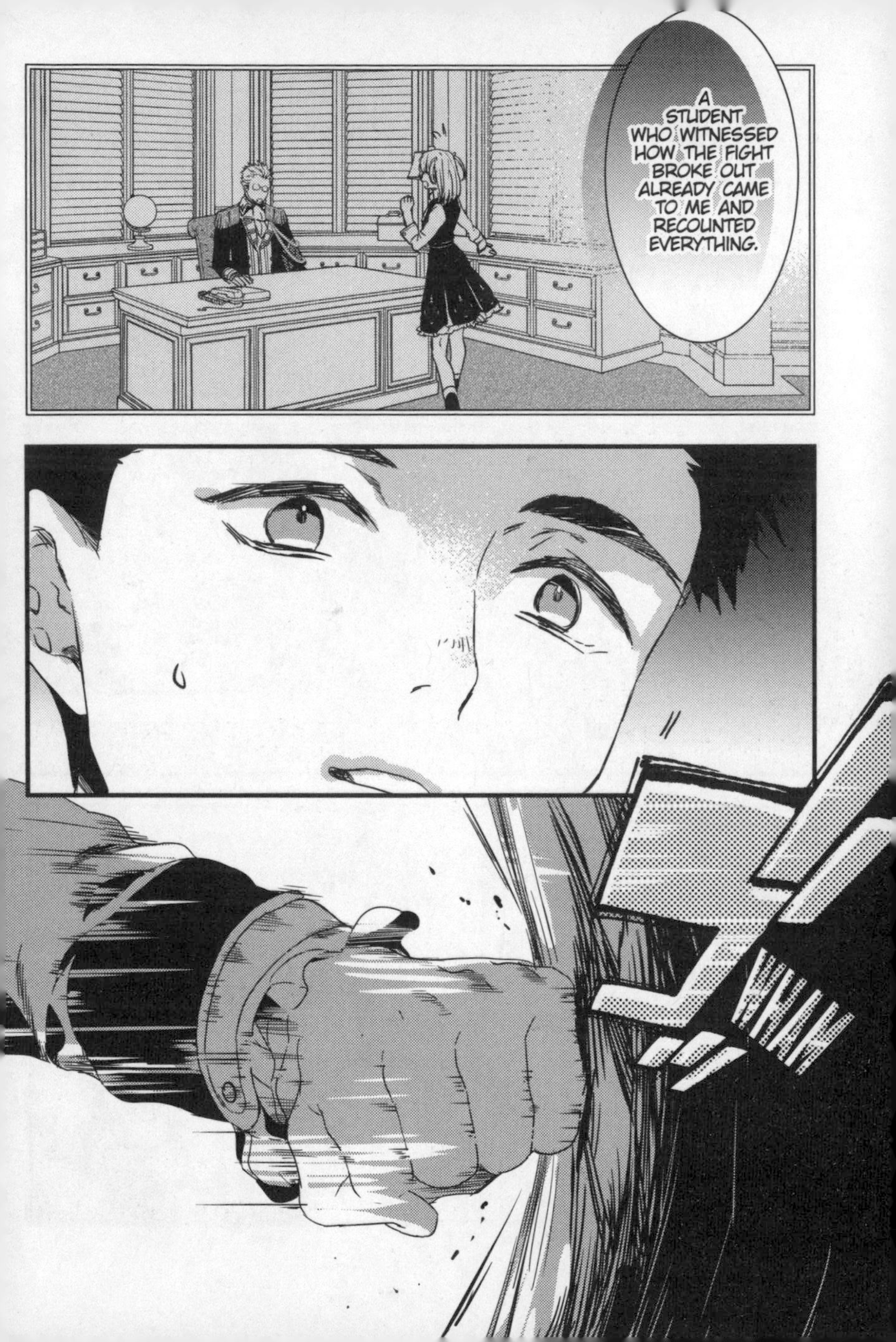
A STUDENT WHO WITNESSED HOW THE FIGHT BROKE OUT ALREADY CAME TO ME AND RECOUNTED EVERYTHING.
WHAM

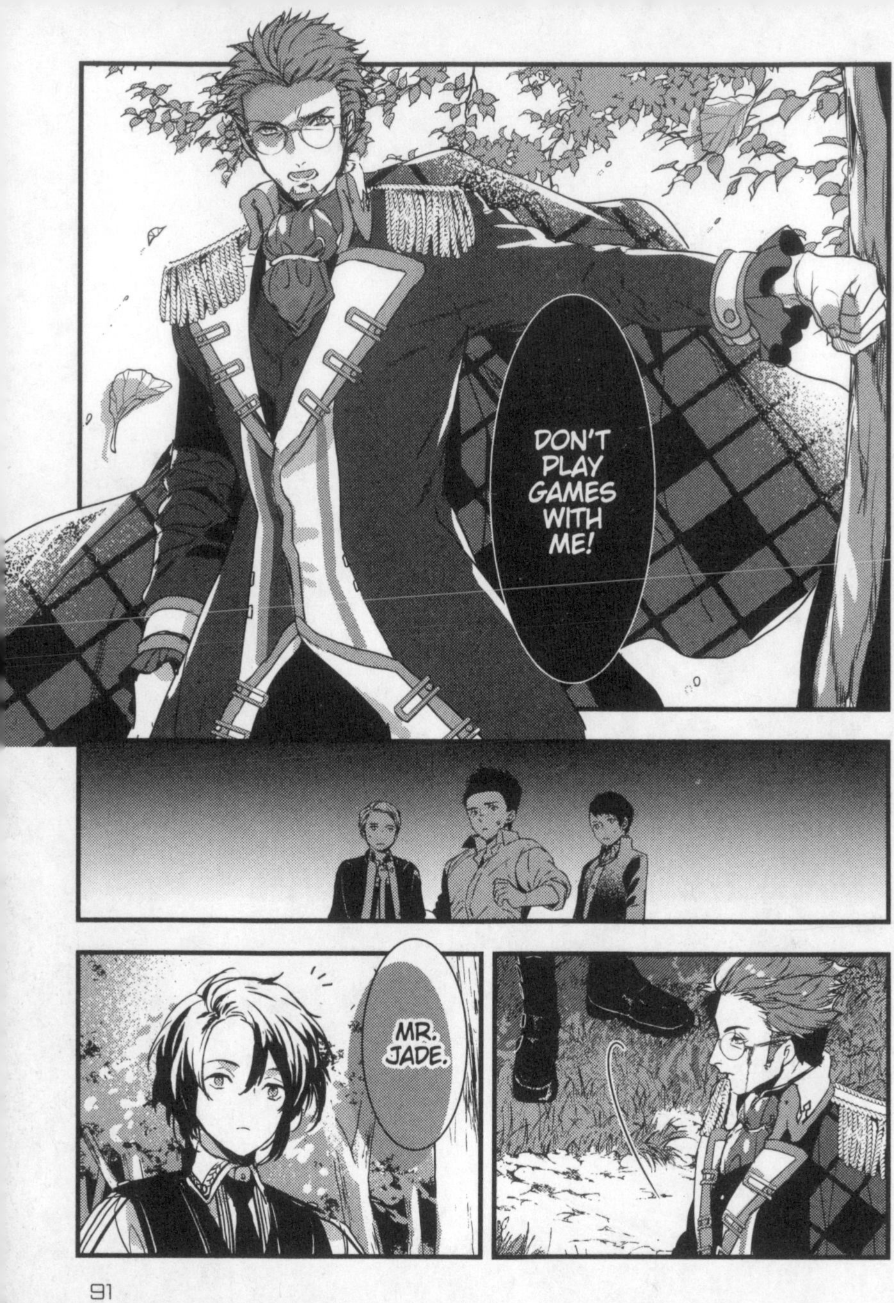
DON'T PLAY GAMES WITH ME!
MR. JADE.

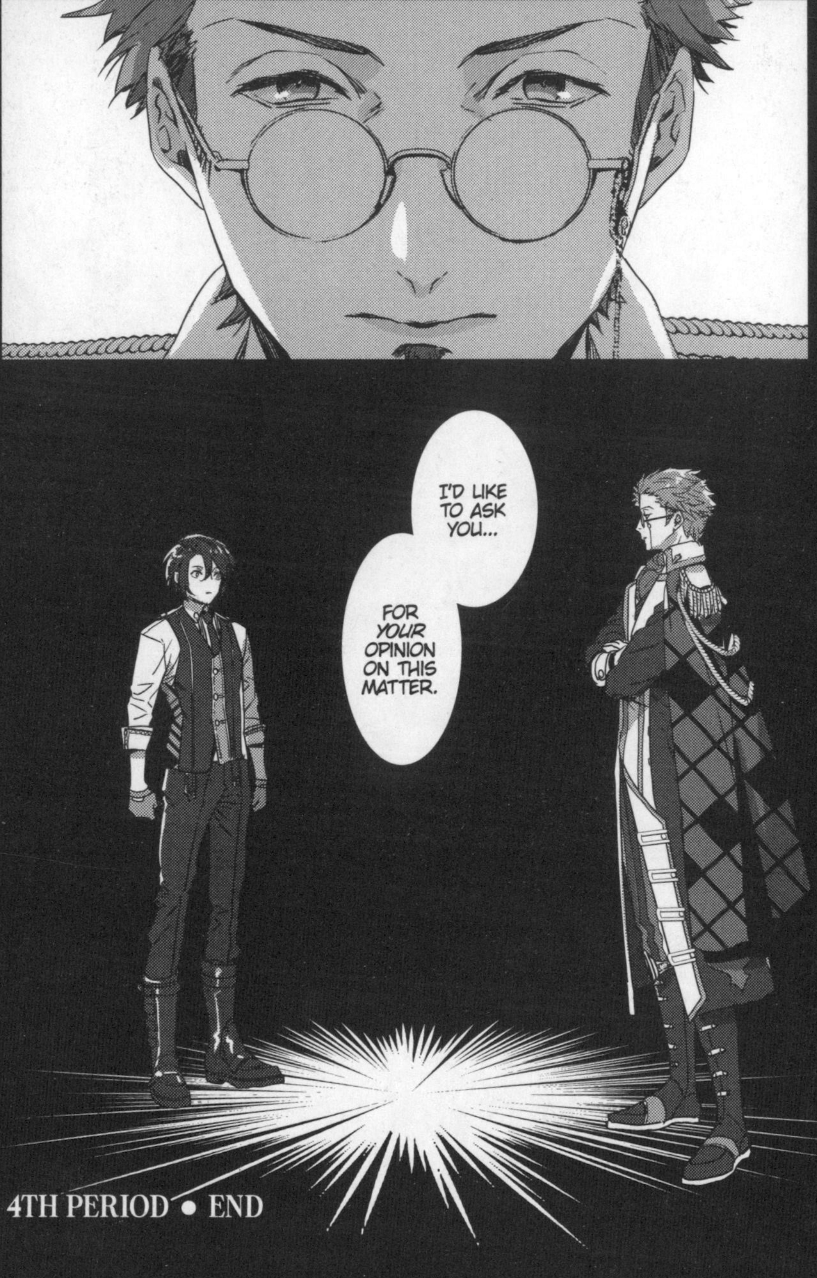
I'D LIKE TO ASK YOU...
FOR *YOUR* OPINION ON THIS MATTER.
4TH PERIOD • END

I Got
FIRED
as a
Court Wizard
so Now I'm Moving
to the Country
to Become a
Magic Teacher

I Got Fired as a COURT WIZARD so Now I'm Moving to the Country to Become a MAGIC TEACHER

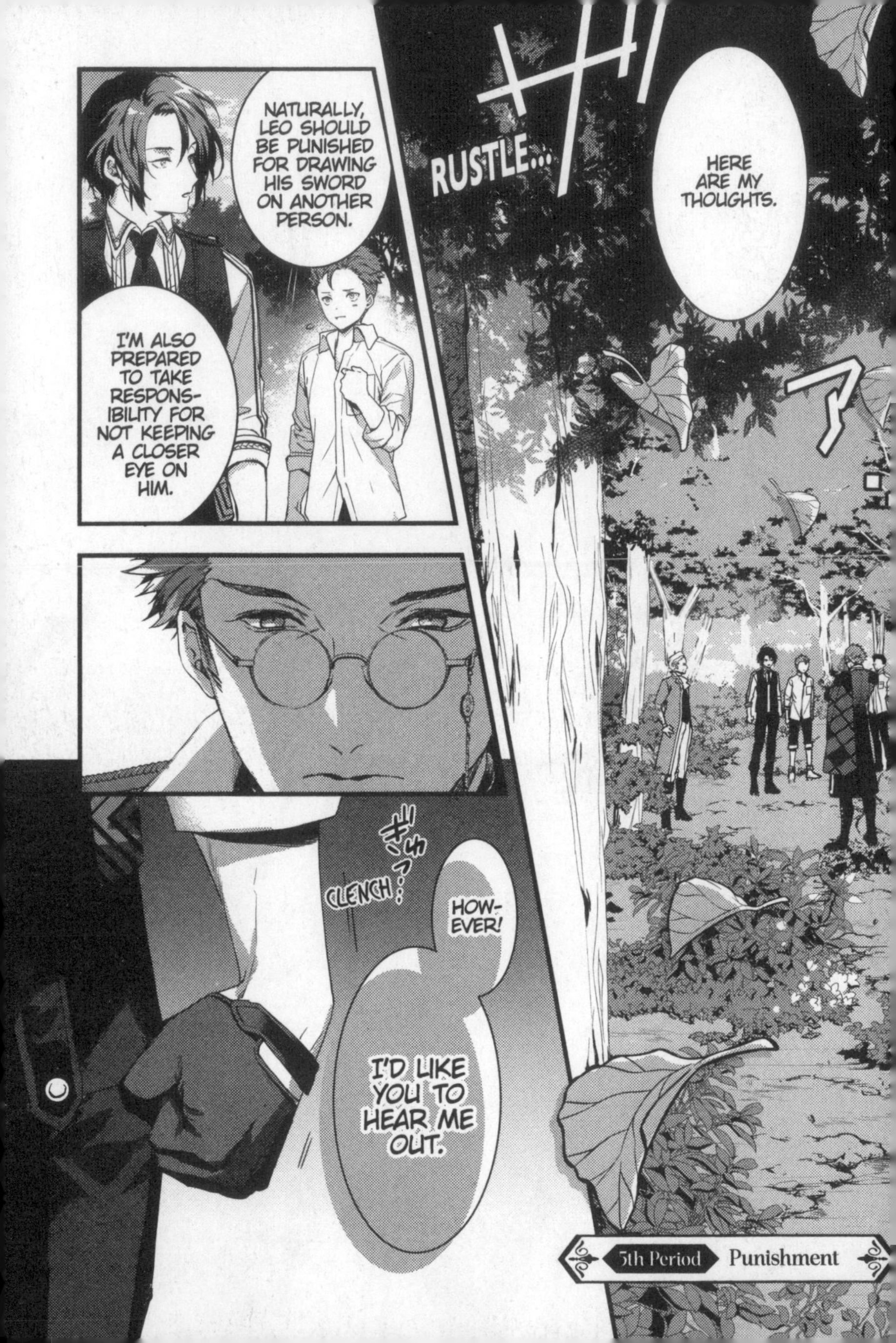
RUSTLE...
HERE ARE MY THOUGHTS.
5th Period Punishment
NATURALLY, LEO SHOULD BE PUNISHED FOR DRAWING HIS SWORD ON ANOTHER PERSON.
I'M ALSO PREPARED TO TAKE RESPONS-IBILITY FOR NOT KEEPING A CLOSER EYE ON HIM.
CLENCH...
HOW-EVER!
I'D LIKE YOU TO HEAR ME OUT.

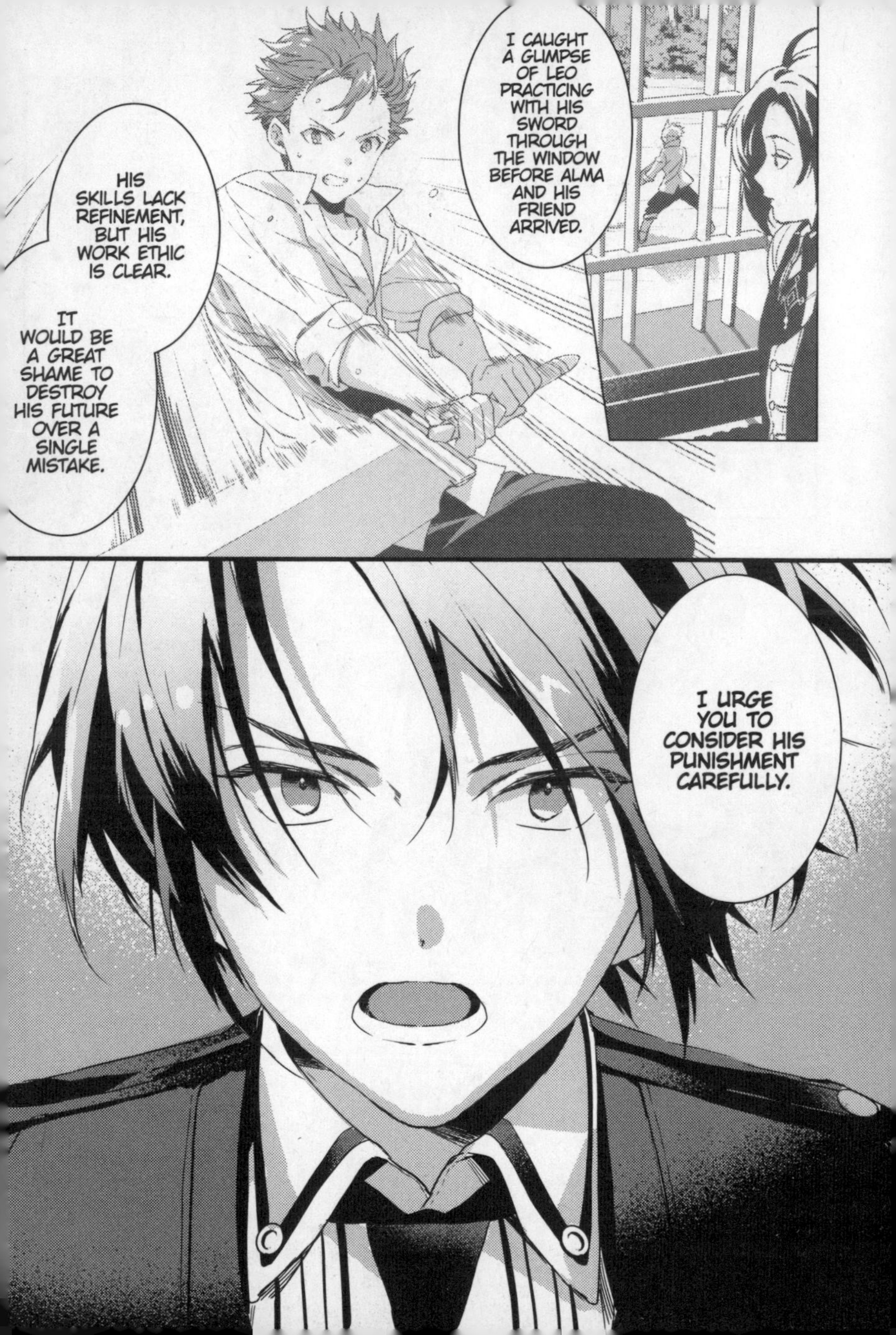
I CAUGHT A GLIMPSE OF LEO PRACTICING WITH HIS SWORD THROUGH THE WINDOW BEFORE ALMA AND HIS FRIEND ARRIVED.
HIS SKILLS LACK REFINEMENT, BUT HIS WORK ETHIC IS CLEAR.
IT WOULD BE A GREAT SHAME TO DESTROY HIS FUTURE OVER A SINGLE MISTAKE.
I URGE YOU TO CONSIDER HIS PUNISHMENT CAREFULLY.

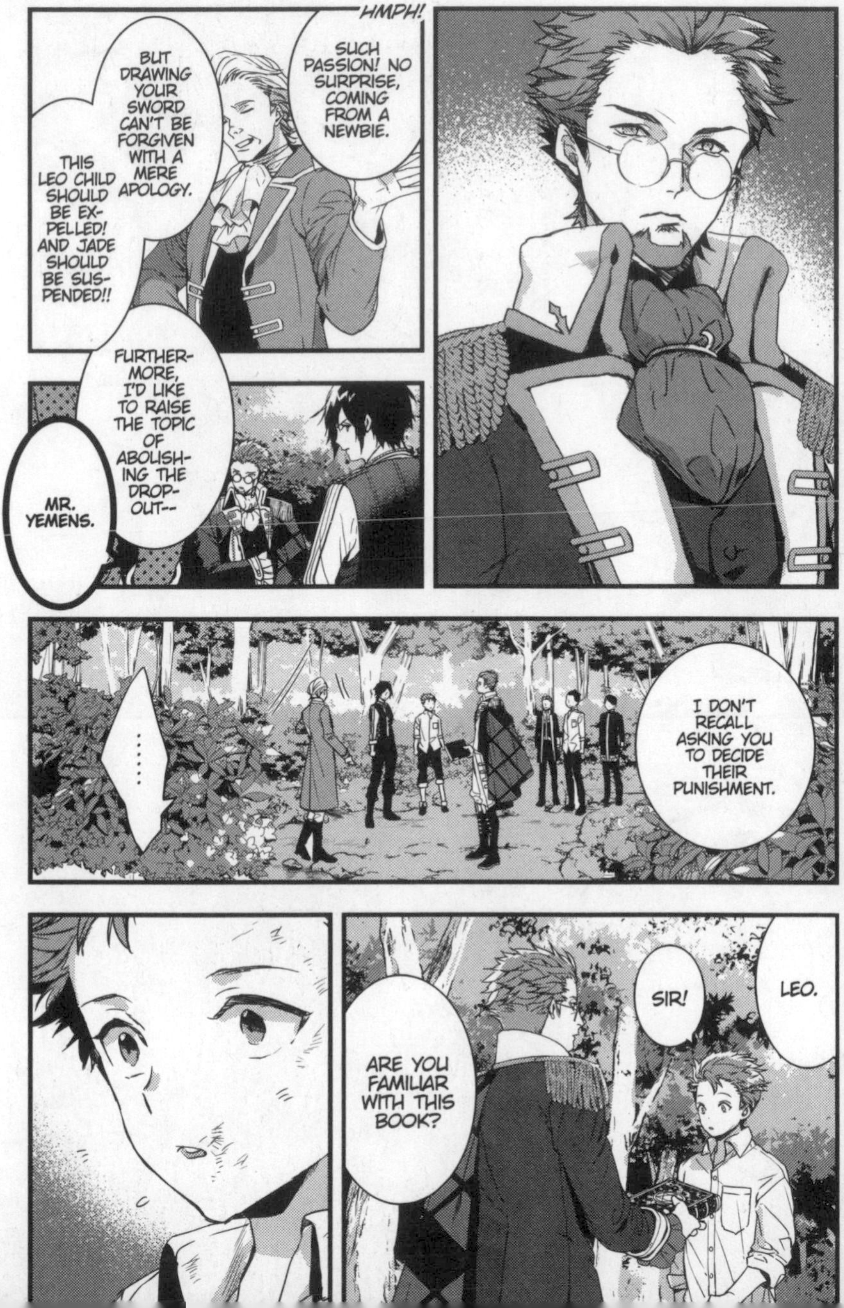
HMPH!
SUCH PASSION! NO SURPRISE, COMING FROM A NEWBIE.
BUT DRAWING YOUR SWORD CAN'T BE FORGIVEN WITH A MERE APOLOGY.
THIS LEO CHILD SHOULD BE EX-PELLED! AND JADE SHOULD BE SUS-PENDED!!
FURTHER-MORE, I'D LIKE TO RAISE THE TOPIC OF ABOLISH-ING THE DROP-OUT--
MR. YEMENS.
I DON'T RECALL ASKING YOU TO DECIDE THEIR PUNISHMENT.
......
LEO.
SIR!
ARE YOU FAMILIAR WITH THIS BOOK?

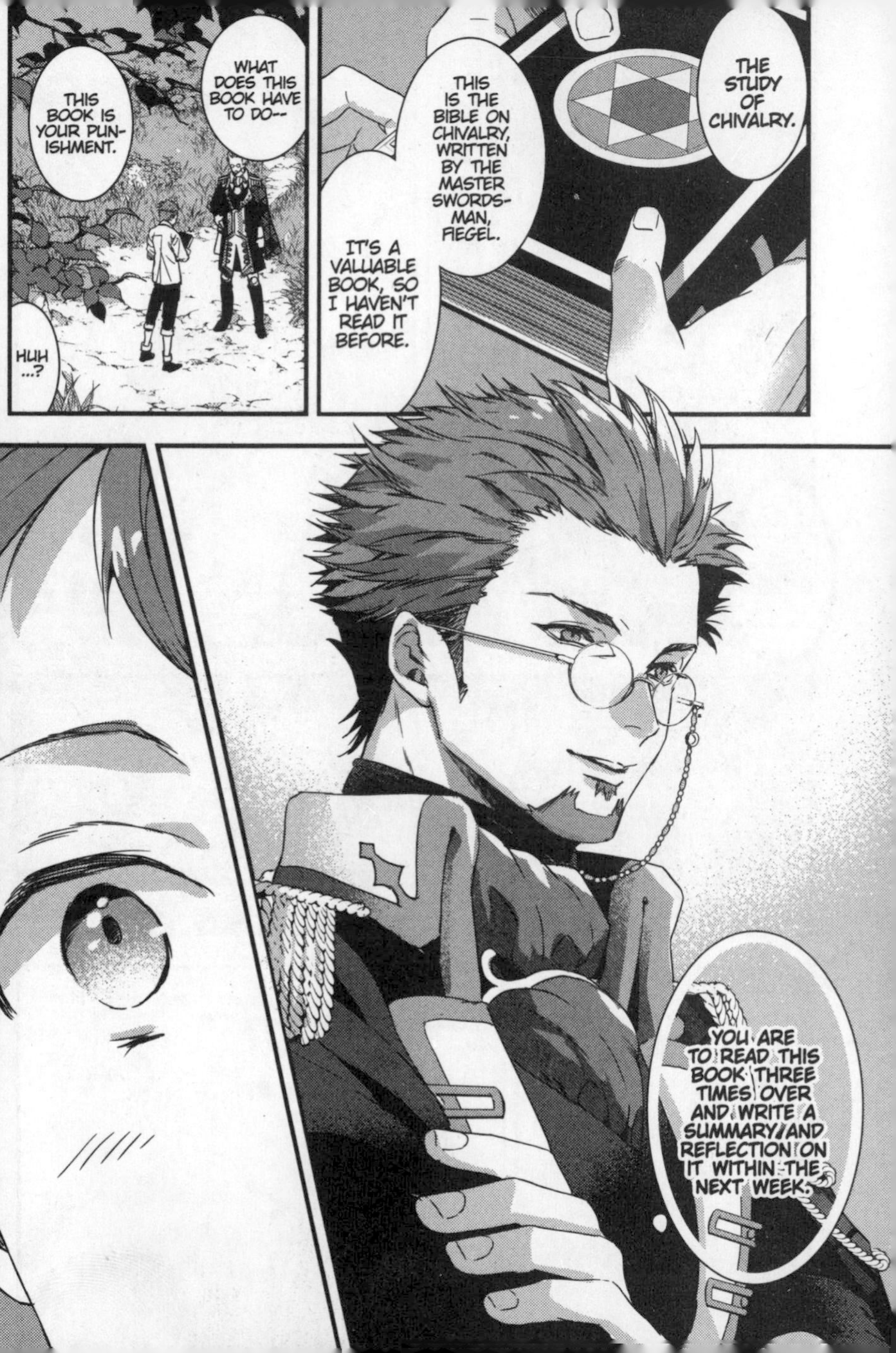
THE STUDY OF CHIVALRY.
THIS IS THE BIBLE ON CHIVALRY, WRITTEN BY THE MASTER SWORDSMAN, FIEGEL.
IT'S A VALUABLE BOOK, SO I HAVEN'T READ IT BEFORE.
WHAT DOES THIS BOOK HAVE TO DO--
THIS BOOK IS YOUR PUNISHMENT.
HUH ...?
YOU ARE TO READ THIS BOOK THREE TIMES OVER AND WRITE A SUMMARY AND REFLECTION ON IT WITHIN THE NEXT WEEK.

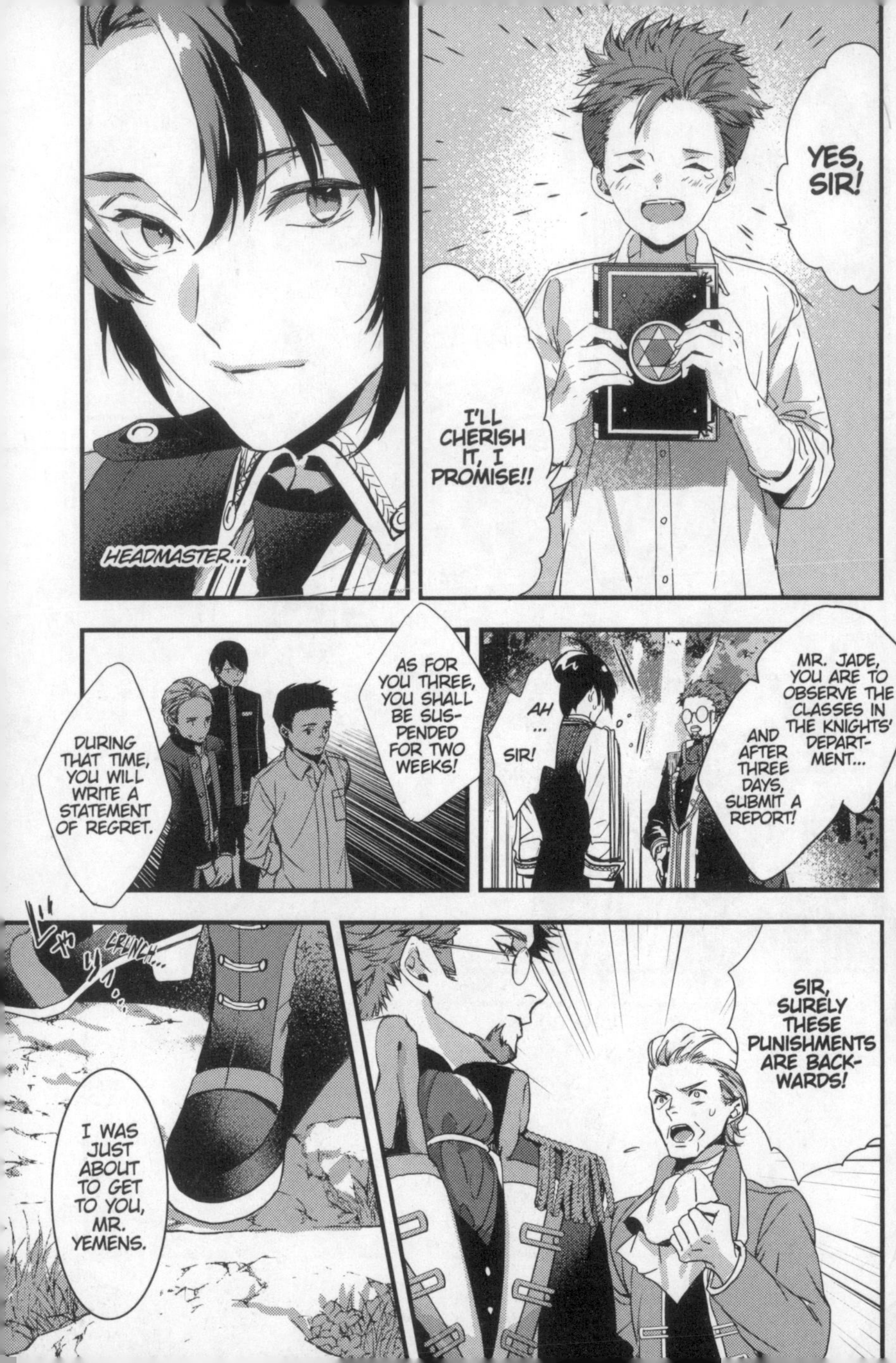
YES, SIR!
I'LL CHERISH IT, I PROMISE!!
HEADMASTER...
MR. JADE, YOU ARE TO OBSERVE THE CLASSES IN THE KNIGHTS' DEPARTMENT...
AND AFTER THREE DAYS, SUBMIT A REPORT!
AH ... SIR!
AS FOR YOU THREE, YOU SHALL BE SUSPENDED FOR TWO WEEKS!
DURING THAT TIME, YOU WILL WRITE A STATEMENT OF REGRET.
SIR, SURELY THESE PUNISHMENTS ARE BACKWARDS!
CRUNCH...
I WAS JUST ABOUT TO GET TO YOU, MR. YEMENS.

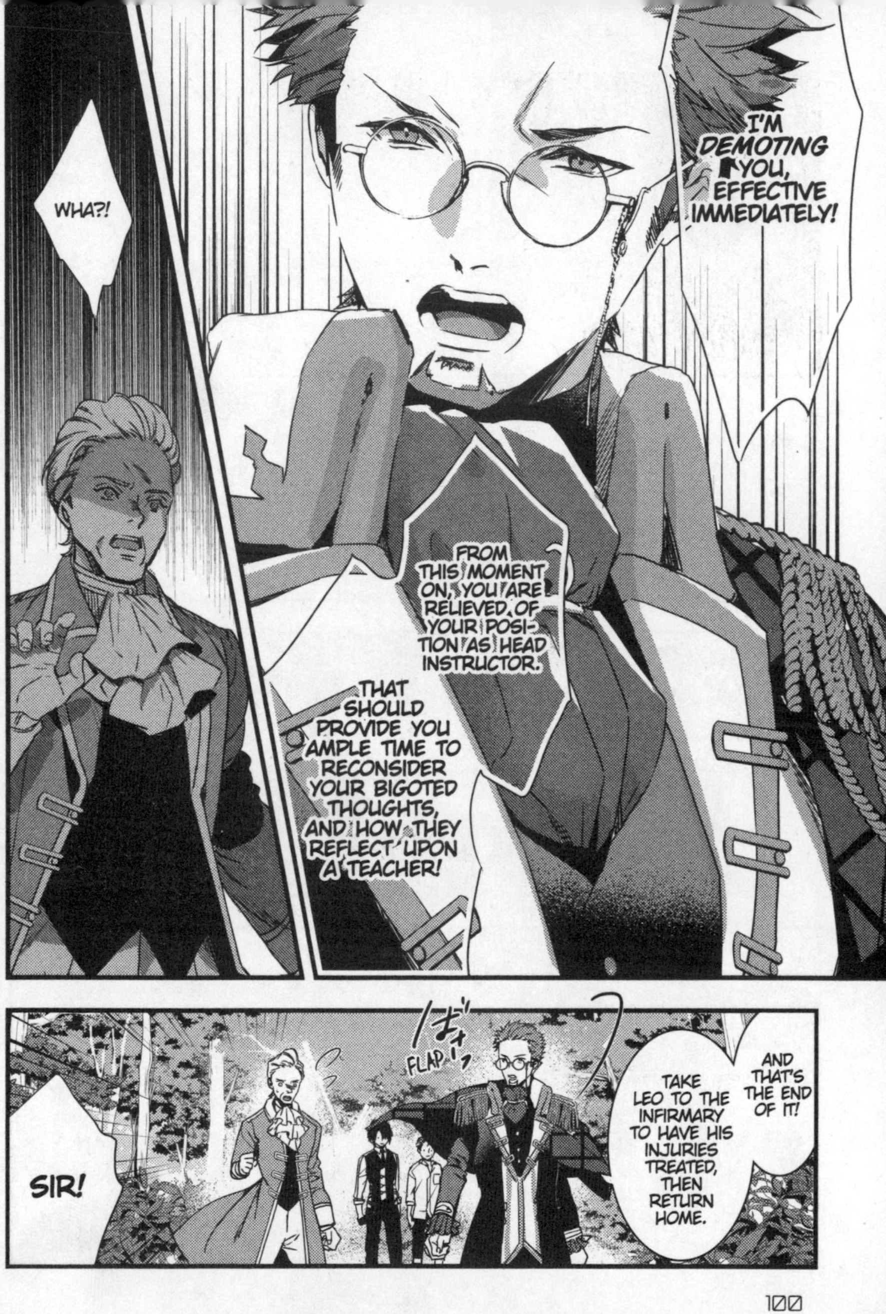
I'M DEMOTING YOU, EFFECTIVE IMMEDIATELY!
FROM THIS MOMENT ON, YOU ARE RELIEVED OF YOUR POSITION AS HEAD INSTRUCTOR.
THAT SHOULD PROVIDE YOU AMPLE TIME TO RECONSIDER YOUR BIGOTED THOUGHTS, AND HOW THEY REFLECT UPON A TEACHER!
WHA?!
AND THAT'S THE END OF IT!
TAKE LEO TO THE INFIRMARY TO HAVE HIS INJURIES TREATED, THEN RETURN HOME.
FLAP
SIR!

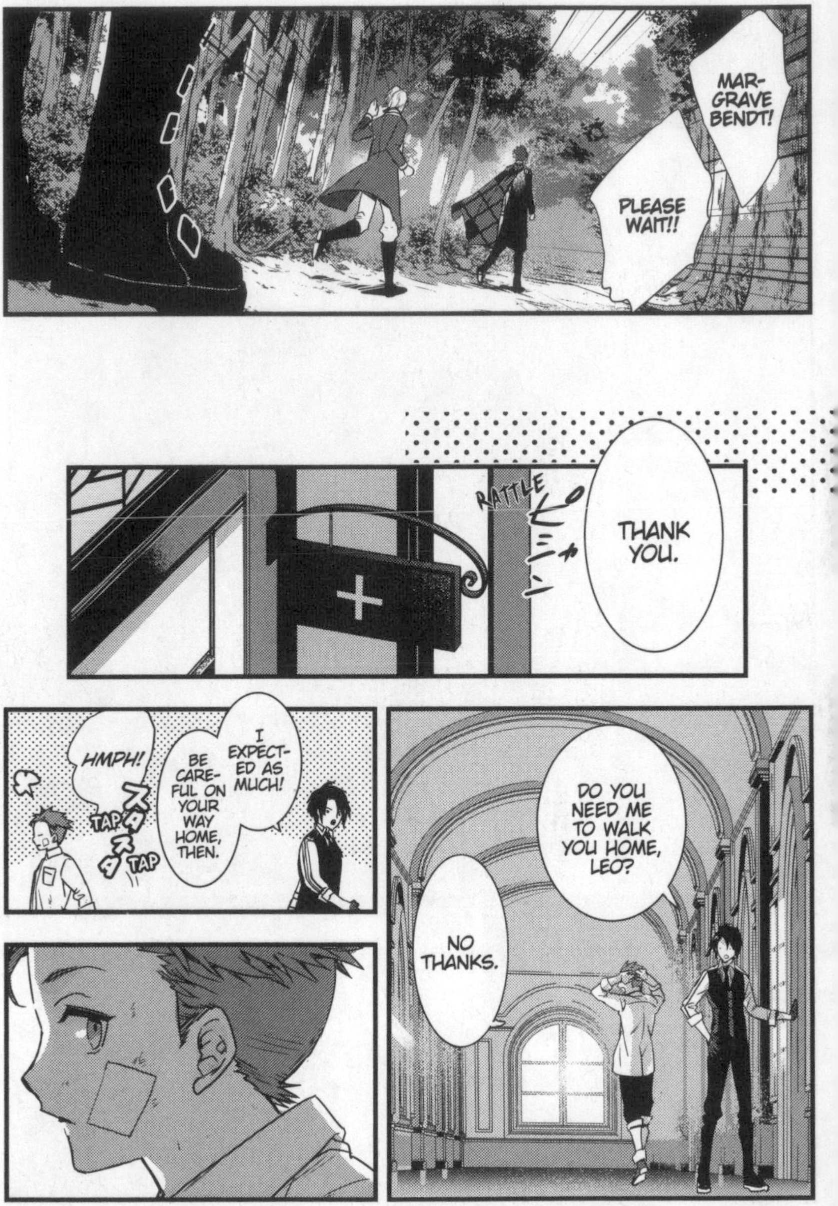

MAR-GRAVE BENDT!
PLEASE WAIT!!
THANK YOU.
RATTLE
ピシャン
DO YOU NEED ME TO WALK YOU HOME, LEO?
NO THANKS.
I EXPECT-ED AS MUCH!
BE CARE-FUL ON YOUR WAY HOME, THEN.
HMPH!
スタスタ
TAP TAP

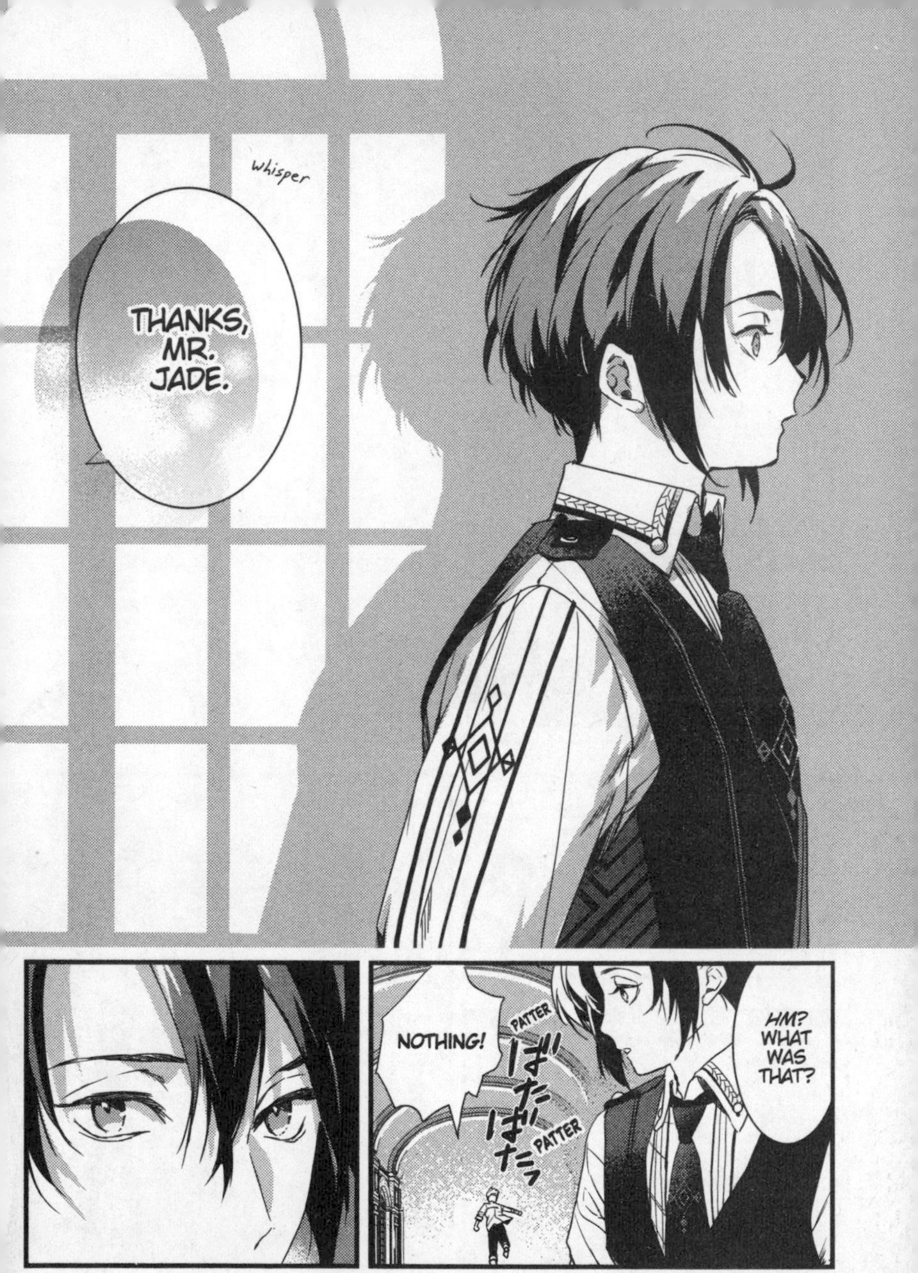
whisper
THANKS, MR. JADE.
HM? WHAT WAS THAT?
PATTER
ばたばたっ
PATTER
NOTHING!

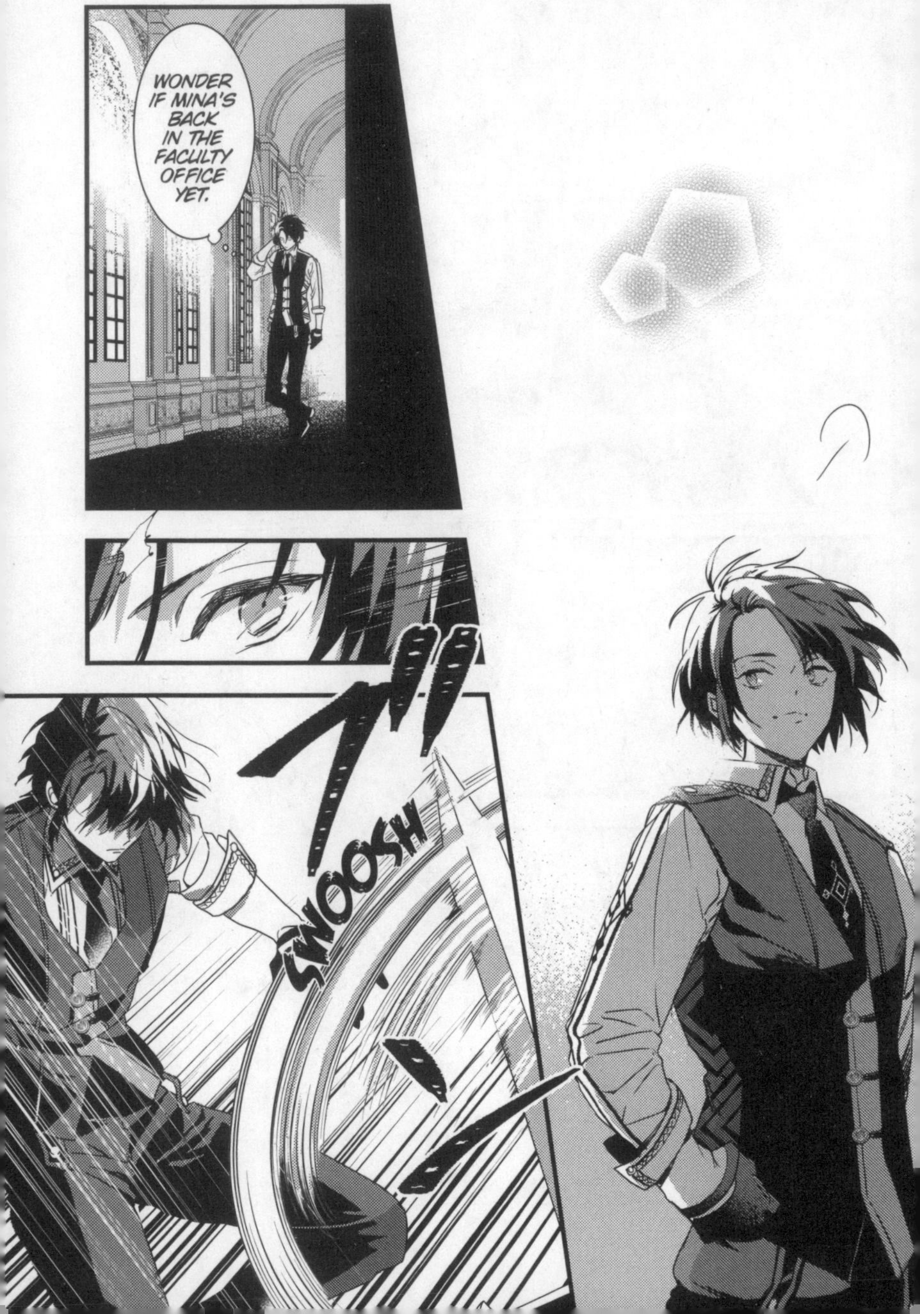
WONDER IF MINA'S BACK IN THE FACULTY OFFICE YET.
SWOOSH

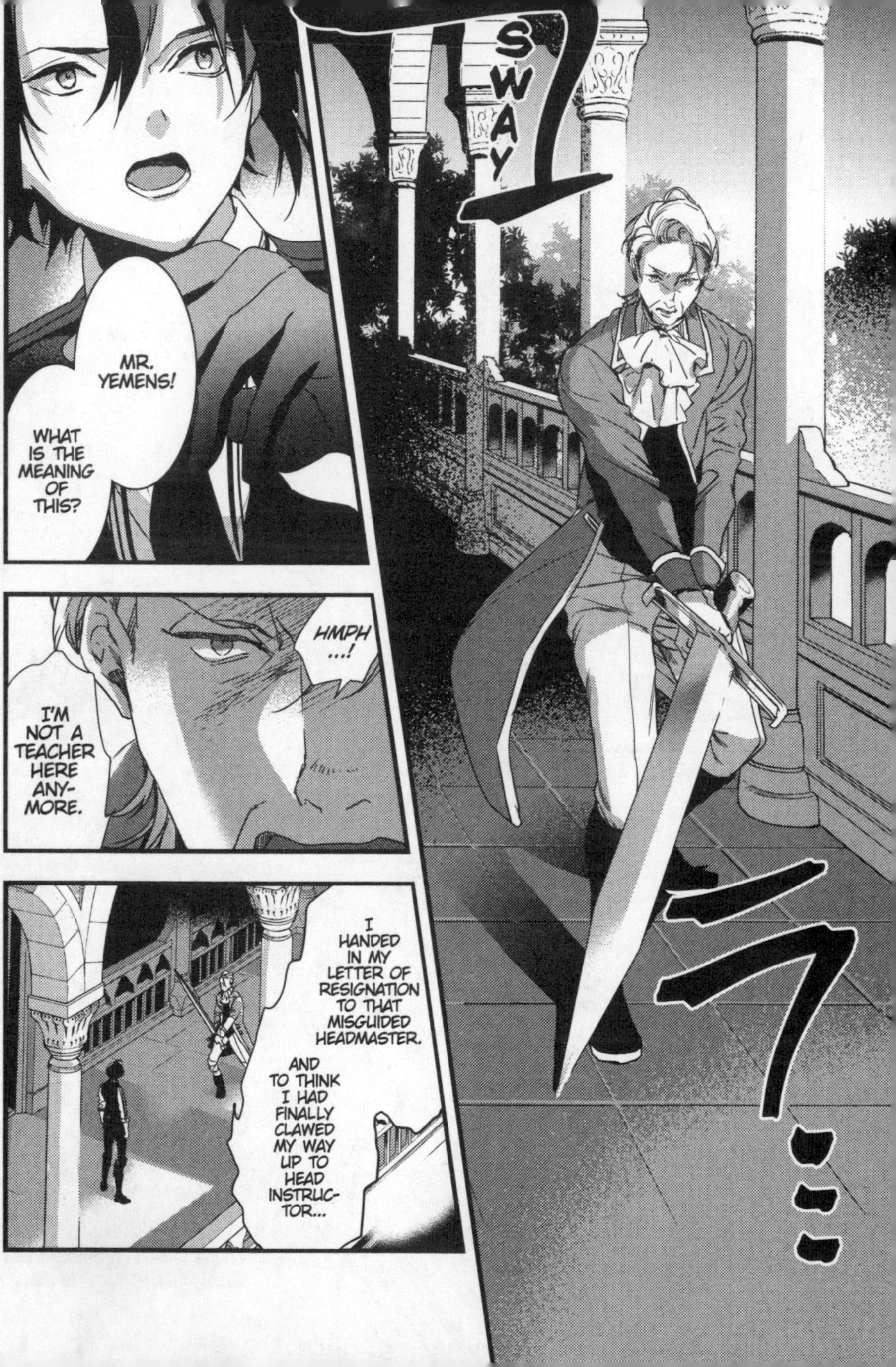
SWAY
MR. YEMENS!
WHAT IS THE MEANING OF THIS?
HMPH ...!
I'M NOT A TEACHER HERE ANY-MORE.
I HANDED IN MY LETTER OF RESIGNATION TO THAT MISGUIDED HEADMASTER.
AND TO THINK I HAD FINALLY CLAWED MY WAY UP TO HEAD INSTRUC-TOR...

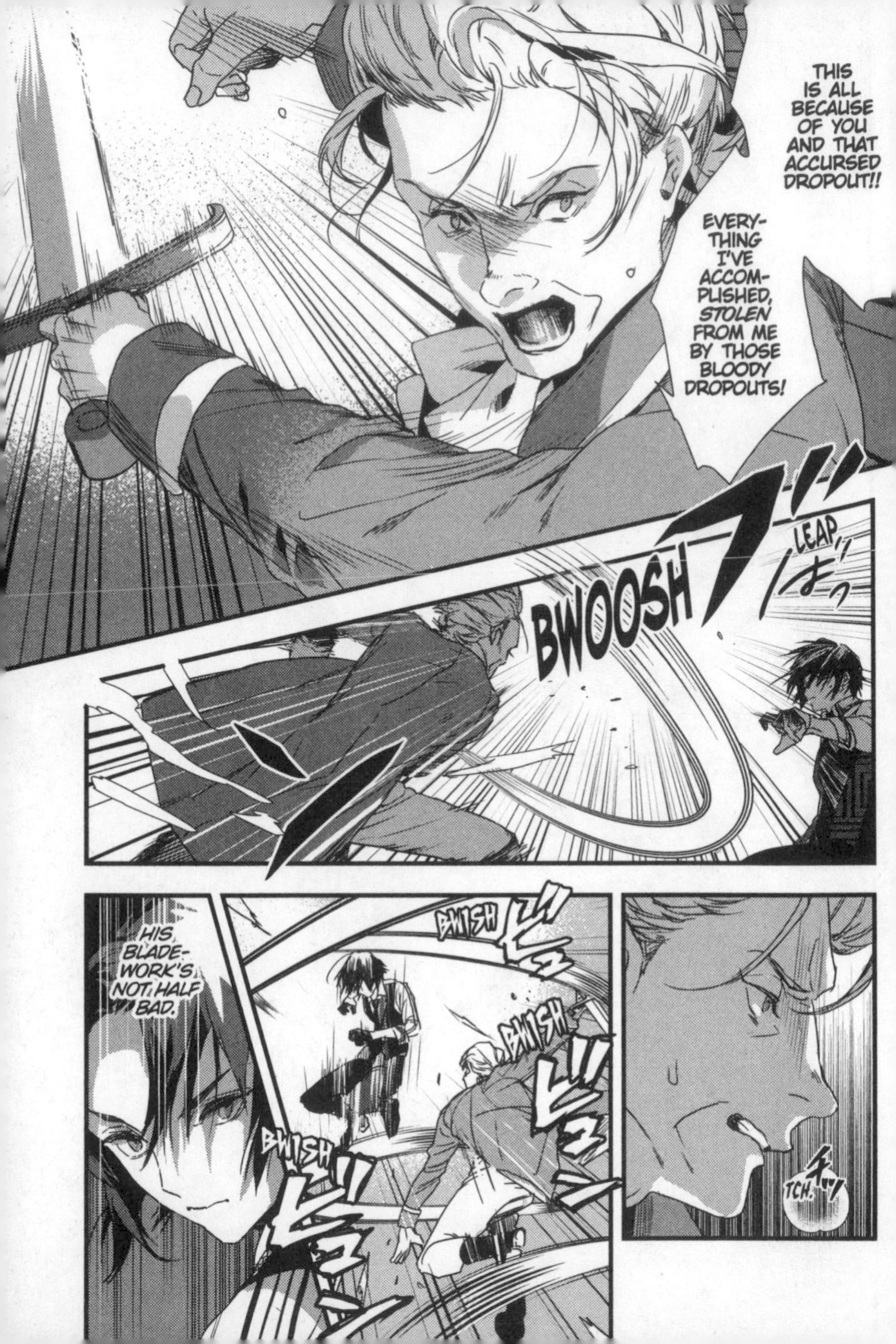
THIS IS ALL BECAUSE OF YOU AND THAT ACCURSED DROPOUT!!
EVERY-THING I'VE ACCOM-PLISHED, STOLEN FROM ME BY THOSE BLOODY DROPOUTS!
LEAP
ぱっ
BWOOSH
TCH.
チッ
BWISH
BWISH
BWISH
HIS BLADE-WORK'S NOT HALF BAD.

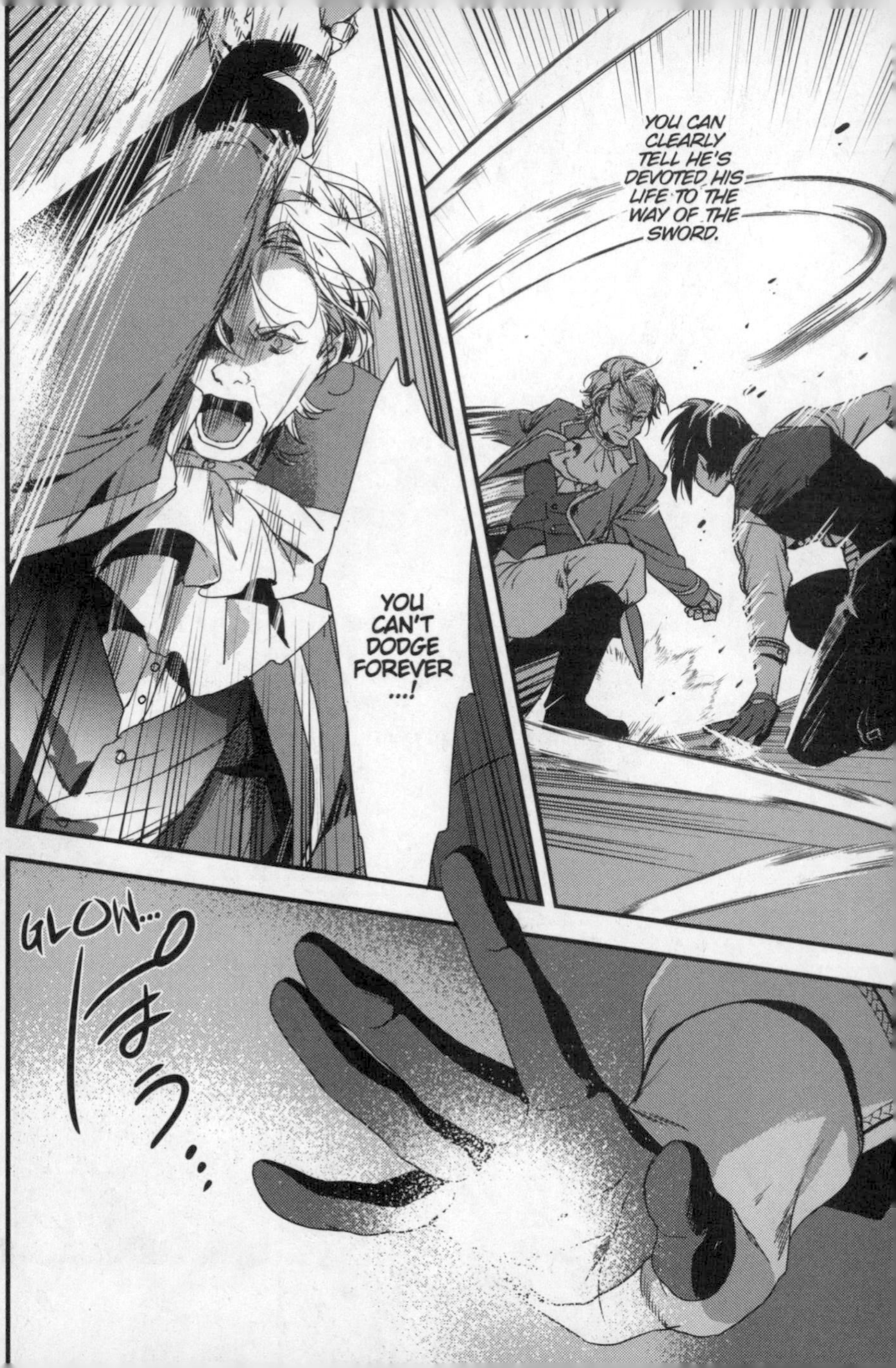
YOU CAN CLEARLY TELL HE'S DEVOTED HIS LIFE TO THE WAY OF THE SWORD.
YOU CAN'T DODGE FOREVER ...!
GLOW...
ぽう...

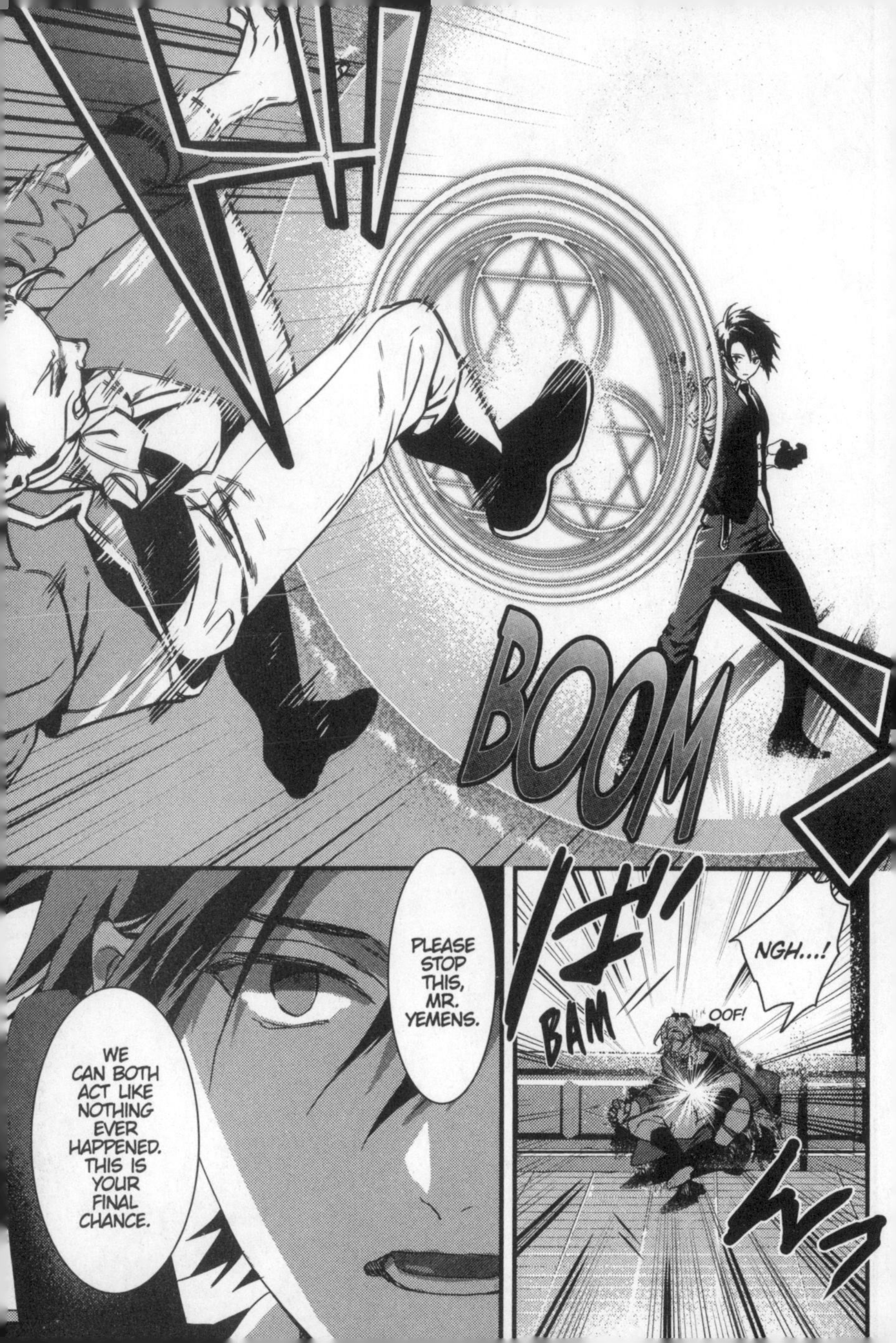
BOOM
NGH...!
BAM
OOF!
PLEASE STOP THIS, MR. YEMENS.
WE CAN BOTH ACT LIKE NOTHING EVER HAPPENED. THIS IS YOUR FINAL CHANCE.

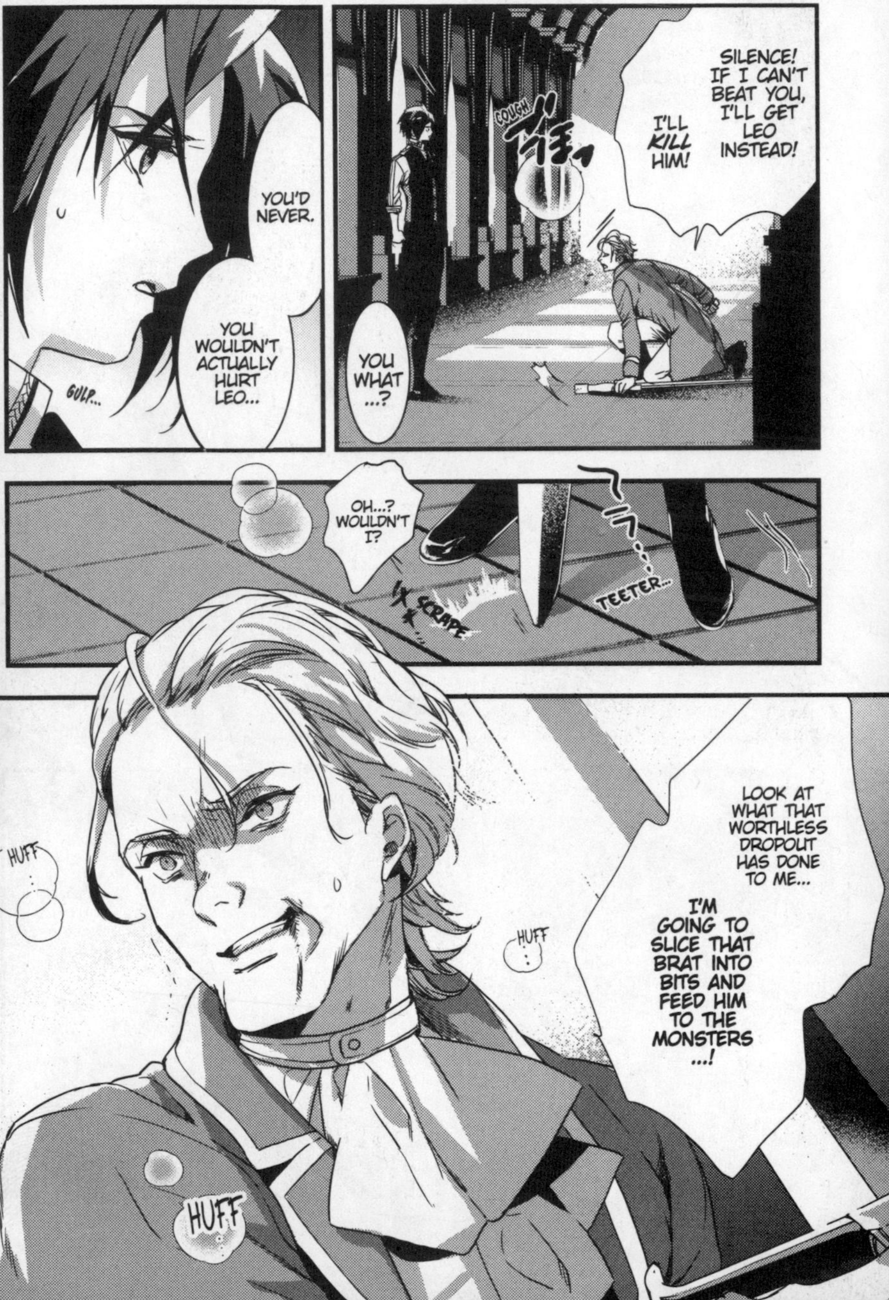
SILENCE! IF I CAN'T BEAT YOU, I'LL GET LEO INSTEAD!
I'LL KILL HIM!
COUGH
YOU WHAT ...?
YOU'D NEVER.
YOU WOULDN'T ACTUALLY HURT LEO...
GULP...
TEETER...
SCRAPE
OH...? WOULDN'T I?
LOOK AT WHAT THAT WORTHLESS DROPOUT HAS DONE TO ME...
I'M GOING TO SLICE THAT BRAT INTO BITS AND FEED HIM TO THE MONSTERS ...!
HUFF...
HUFF...
HUFF...

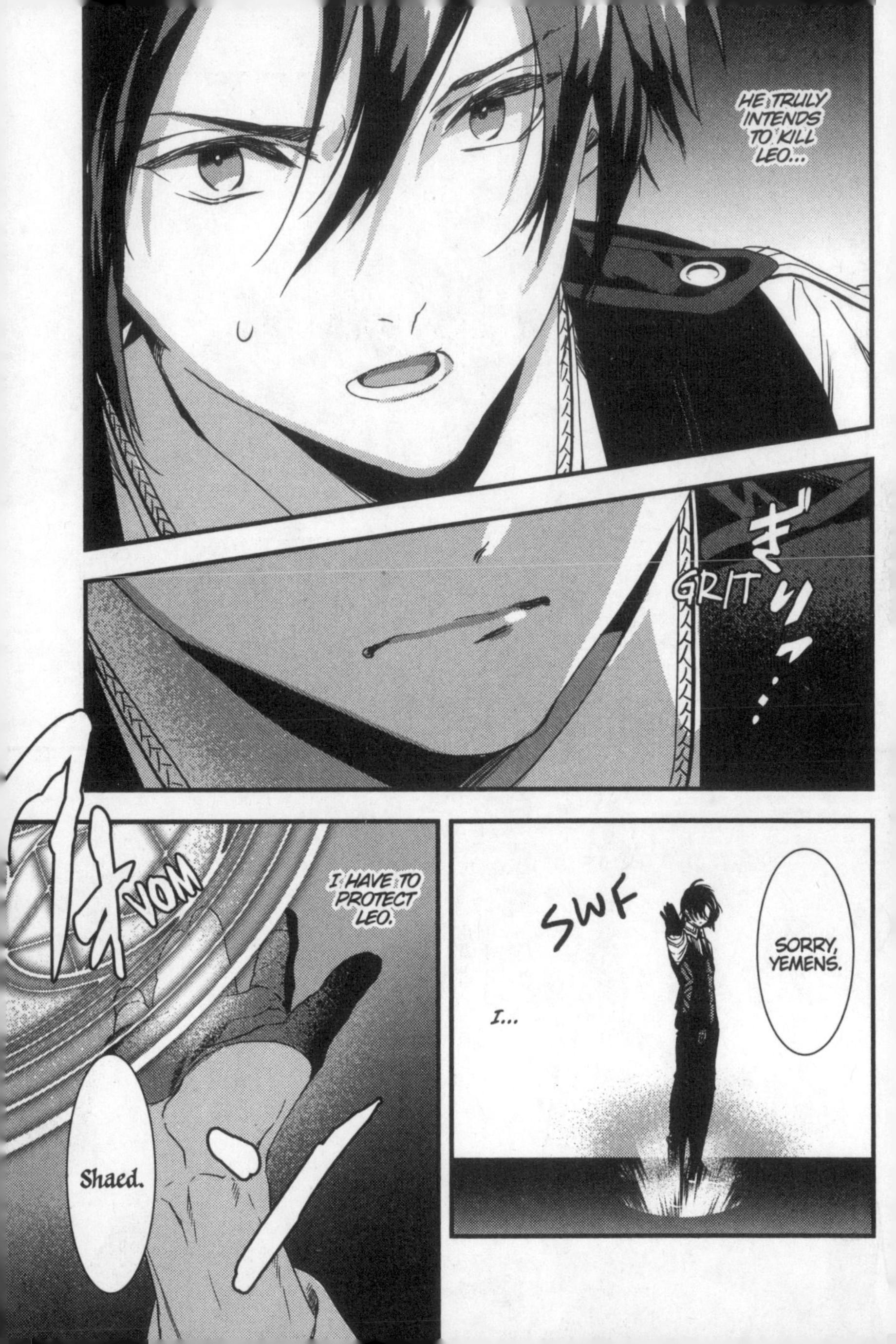
HE TRULY INTENDS TO KILL LEO...
ぎりっ
GRIT
SORRY, YEMENS.
SWF
I...
VOM
I HAVE TO PROTECT LEO.
Shaed.

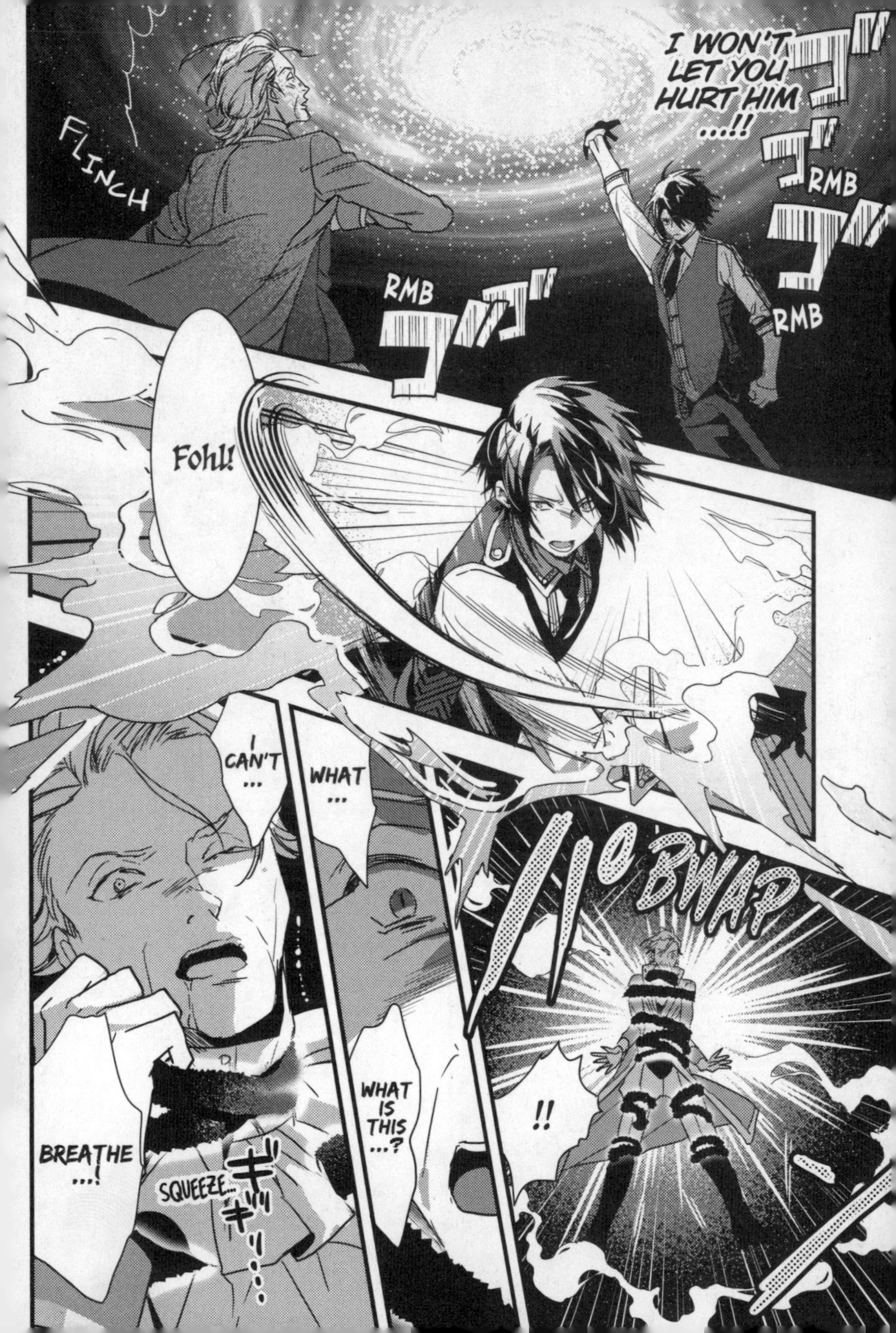
I WON'T LET YOU HURT HIM ...!!
RMB
RMB
RMB
FLINCH
Fohl!
BWAP
!!
WHAT ...
WHAT IS THIS ...?
I CAN'T ...
BREATHE ...!
SQUEEZE...

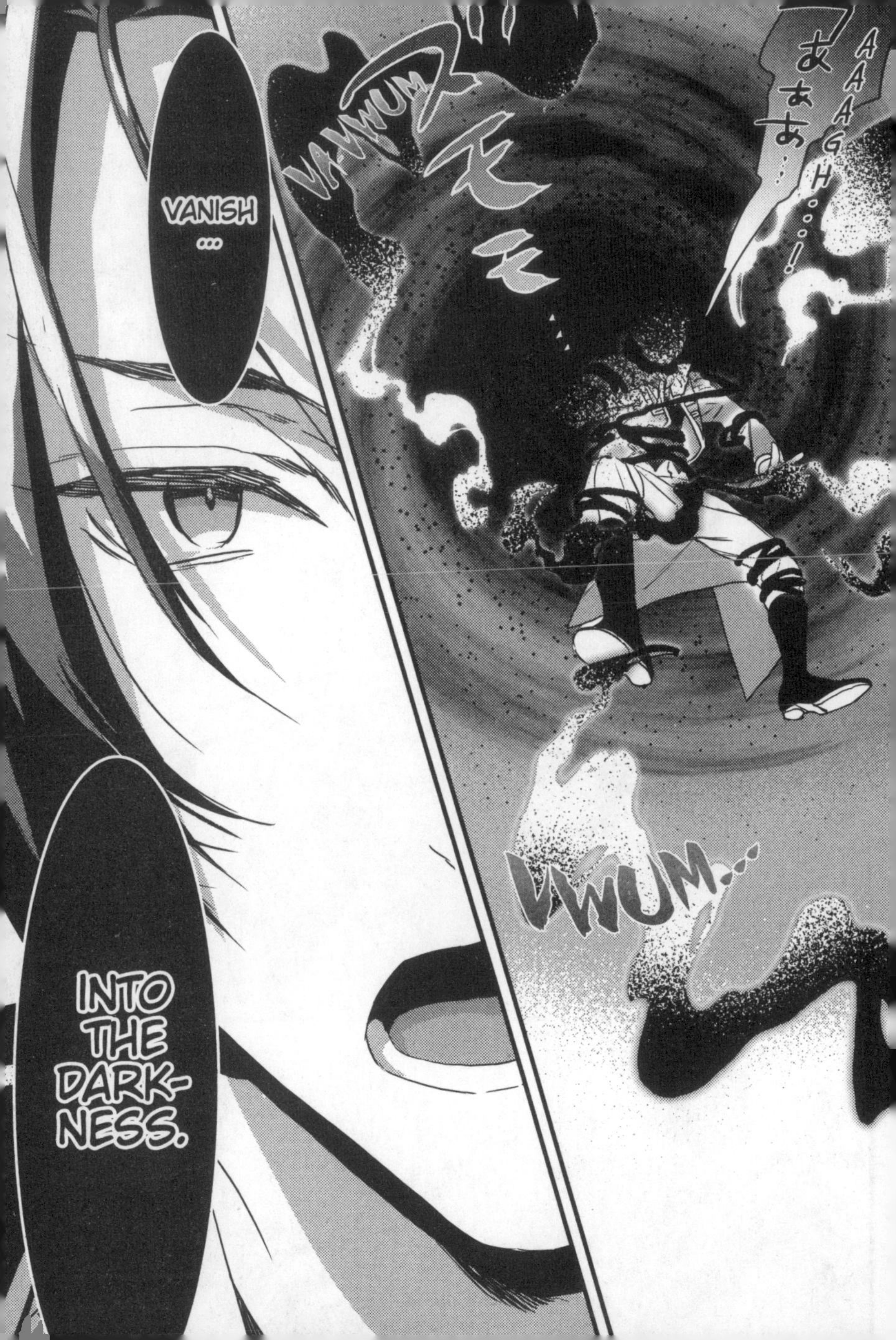
AAAAGH...!
VA-VWUM
VWUM...
VANISH ...
INTO THE DARKNESS.

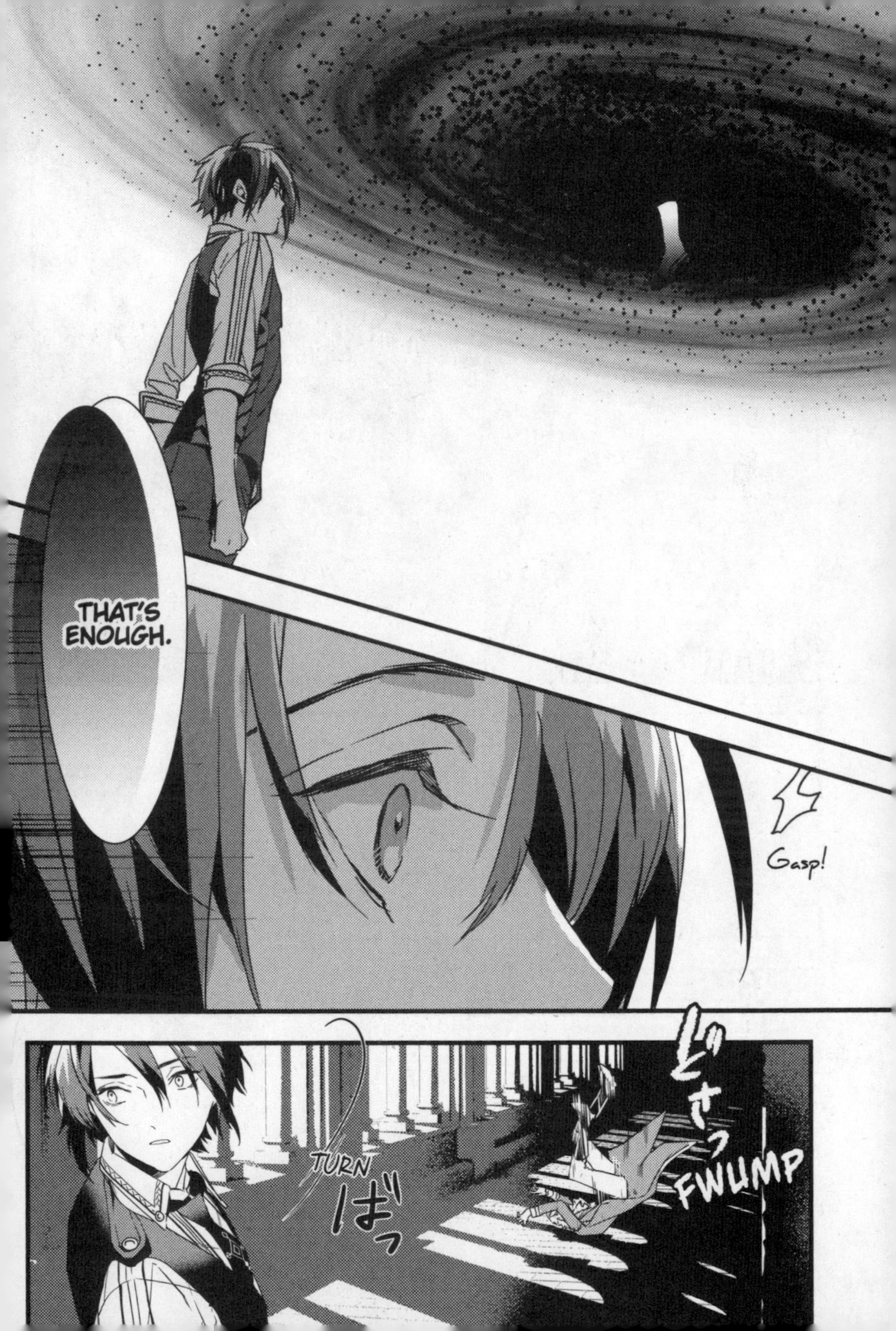
THAT'S ENOUGH.
Gasp!
どさっ
FWUMP
TURN
ばっ

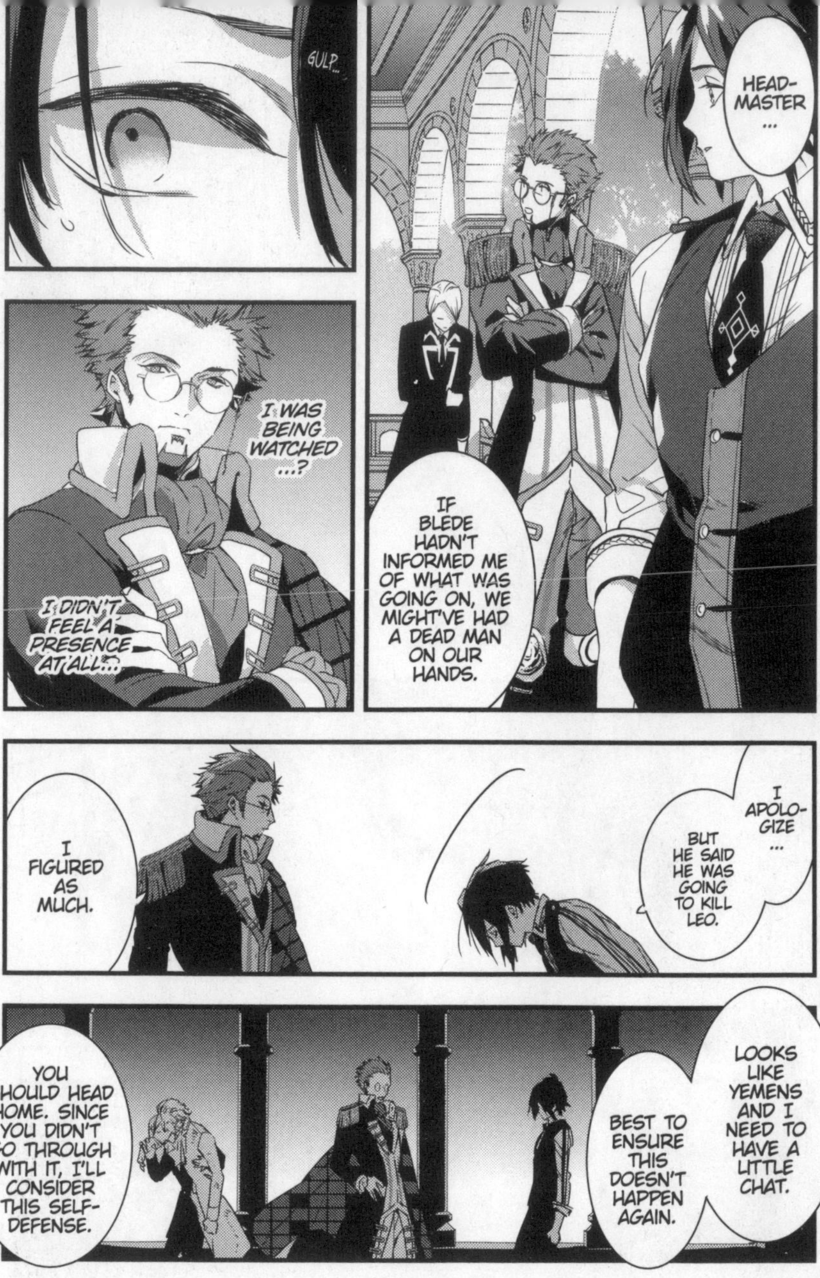
HEAD-MASTER ...
IF BLEDE HADN'T INFORMED ME OF WHAT WAS GOING ON, WE MIGHT'VE HAD A DEAD MAN ON OUR HANDS.
GULP...
I WAS BEING WATCHED ...?
I DIDN'T FEEL A PRESENCE AT ALL...
I APOLO-GIZE ...
BUT HE SAID HE WAS GOING TO KILL LEO.
I FIGURED AS MUCH.
LOOKS LIKE YEMENS AND I NEED TO HAVE A LITTLE CHAT.
BEST TO ENSURE THIS DOESN'T HAPPEN AGAIN.
YOU SHOULD HEAD HOME. SINCE YOU DIDN'T GO THROUGH WITH IT, I'LL CONSIDER THIS SELF-DEFENSE.

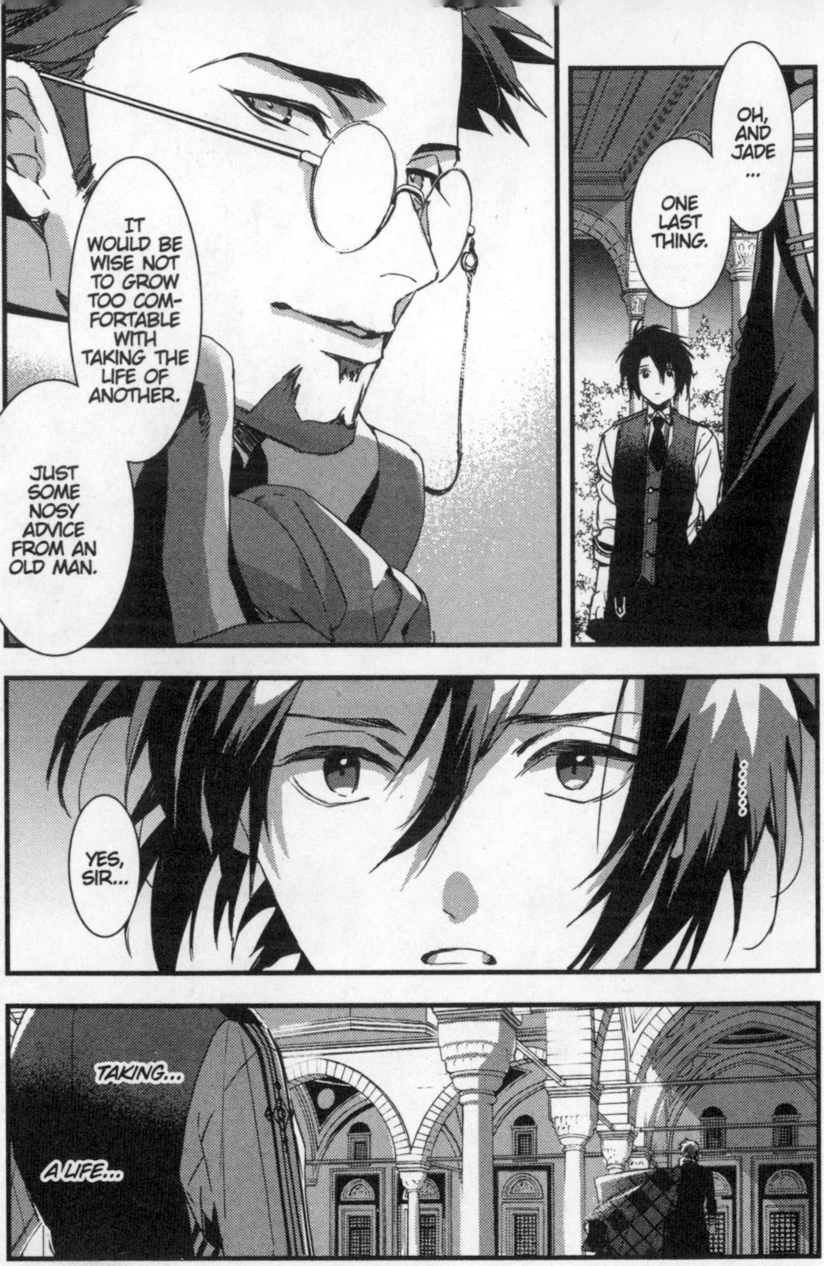

OH, AND JADE ...
ONE LAST THING.
IT WOULD BE WISE NOT TO GROW TOO COM-FORTABLE WITH TAKING THE LIFE OF ANOTHER.
JUST SOME NOSY ADVICE FROM AN OLD MAN.
YES, SIR...
TAKING...
A LIFE...

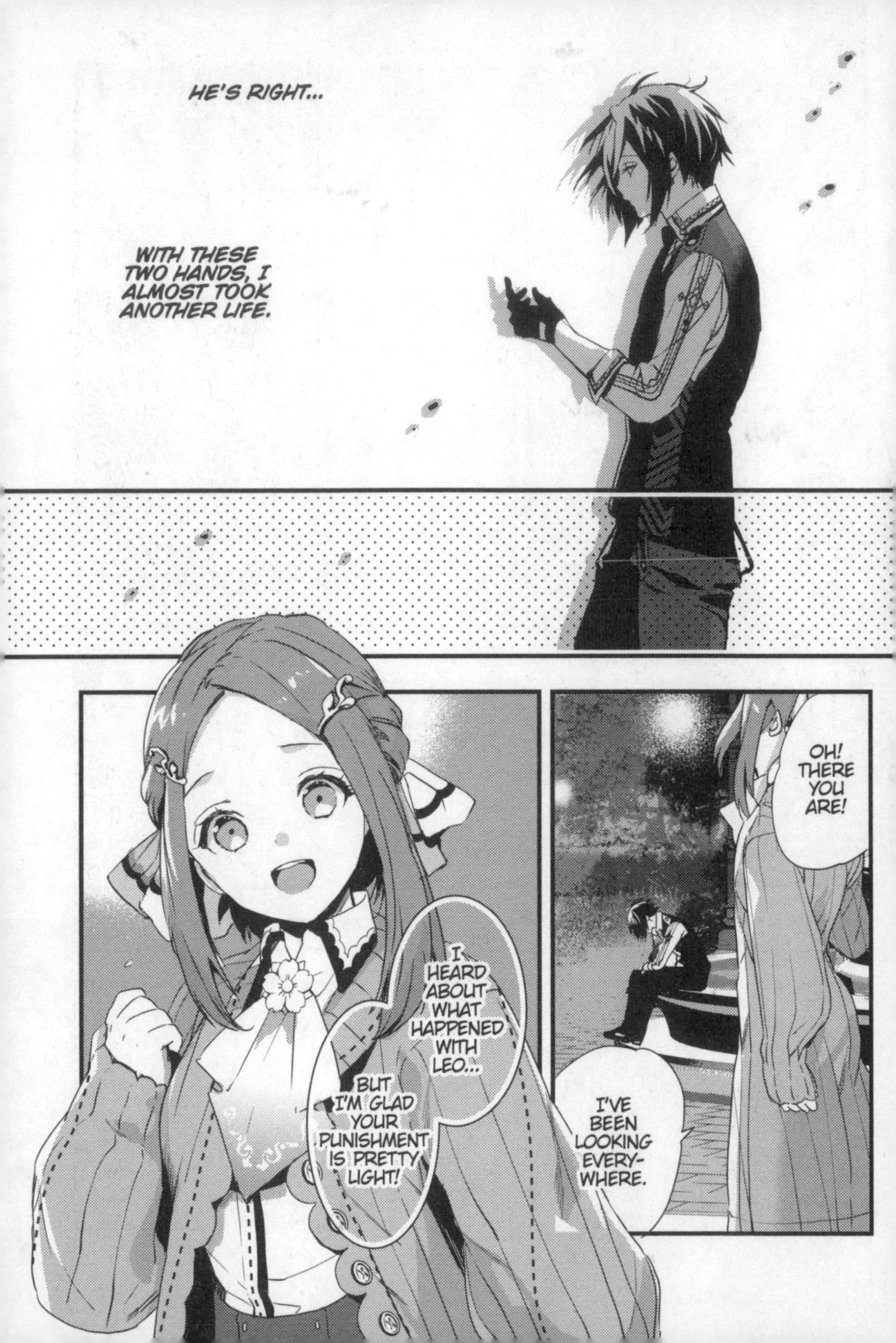
HE'S RIGHT...
WITH THESE TWO HANDS, I ALMOST TOOK ANOTHER LIFE.
OH! THERE YOU ARE!
I'VE BEEN LOOKING EVERY-WHERE.
I HEARD ABOUT WHAT HAPPENED WITH LEO...
BUT I'M GLAD YOUR PUNISHMENT IS PRETTY LIGHT!

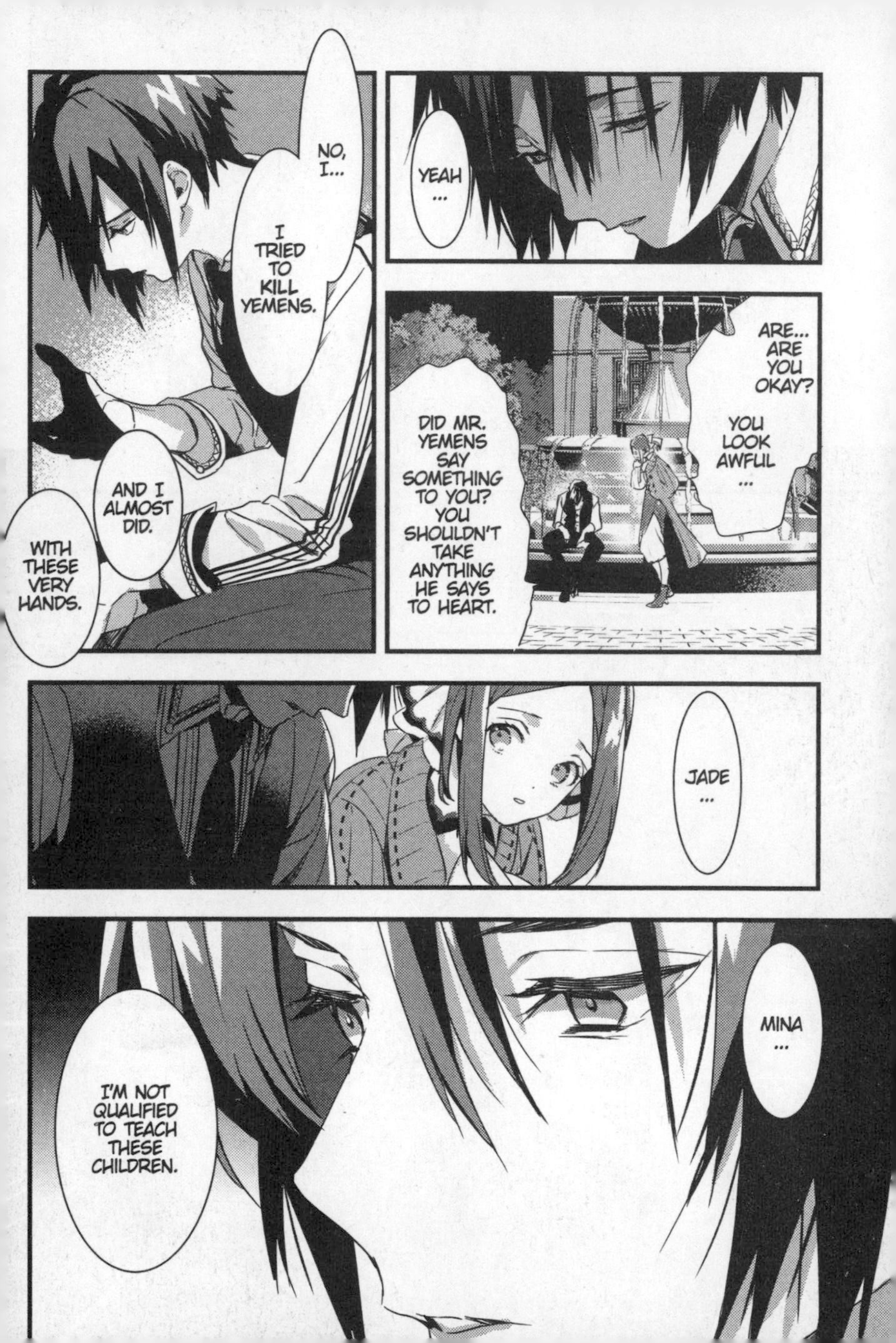
YEAH ...
ARE... ARE YOU OKAY?
YOU LOOK AWFUL ...
DID MR. YEMENS SAY SOMETHING TO YOU? YOU SHOULDN'T TAKE ANYTHING HE SAYS TO HEART.
NO, I...
I TRIED TO KILL YEMENS.
AND I ALMOST DID.
WITH THESE VERY HANDS.
JADE ...
MINA ...
I'M NOT QUALIFIED TO TEACH THESE CHILDREN.

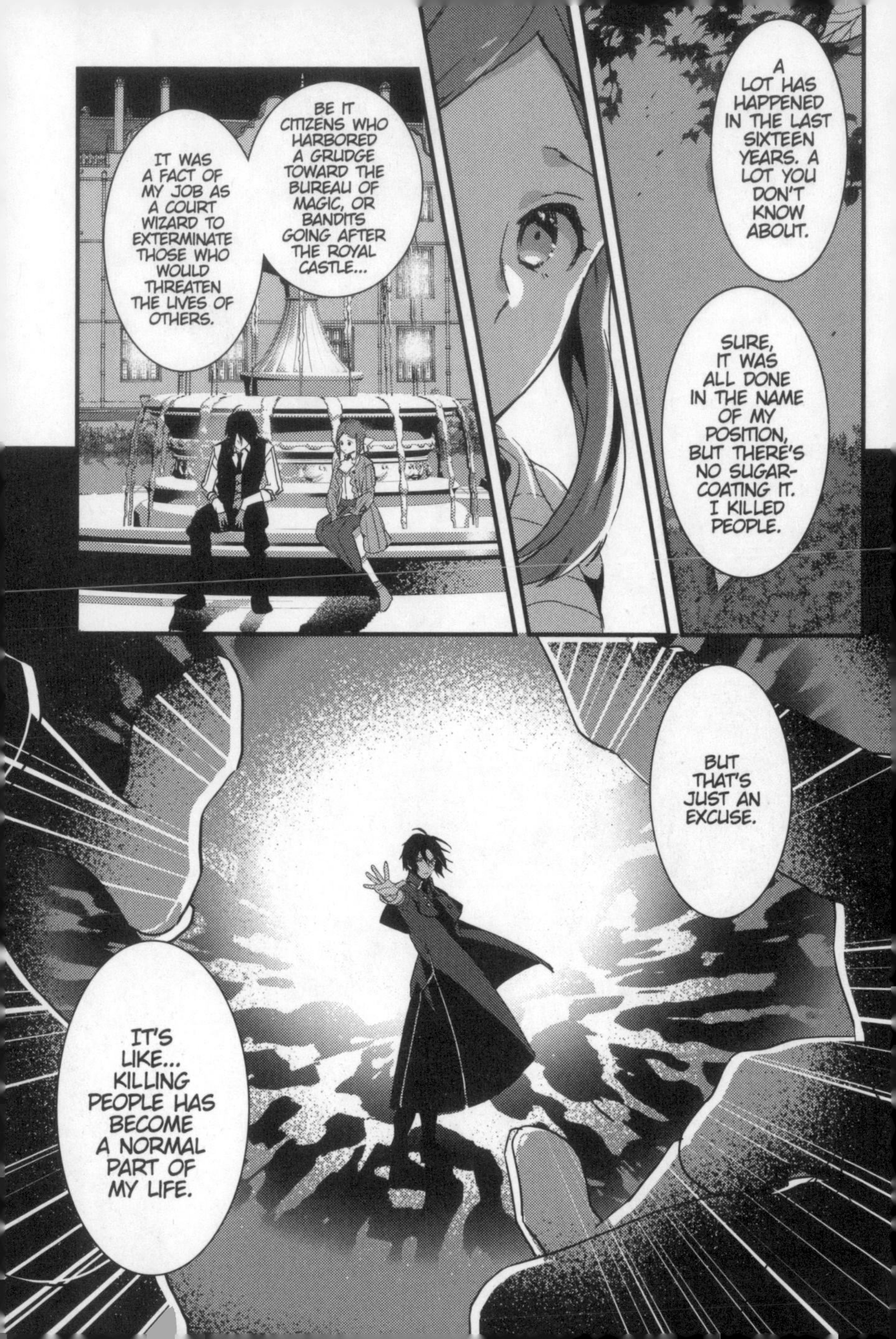
A LOT HAS HAPPENED IN THE LAST SIXTEEN YEARS. A LOT YOU DON'T KNOW ABOUT.
SURE, IT WAS ALL DONE IN THE NAME OF MY POSITION, BUT THERE'S NO SUGAR-COATING IT. I KILLED PEOPLE.
BE IT CITIZENS WHO HARBORED A GRUDGE TOWARD THE BUREAU OF MAGIC, OR BANDITS GOING AFTER THE ROYAL CASTLE...
IT WAS A FACT OF MY JOB AS A COURT WIZARD TO EXTERMINATE THOSE WHO WOULD THREATEN THE LIVES OF OTHERS.
BUT THAT'S JUST AN EXCUSE.
IT'S LIKE... KILLING PEOPLE HAS BECOME A NORMAL PART OF MY LIFE.

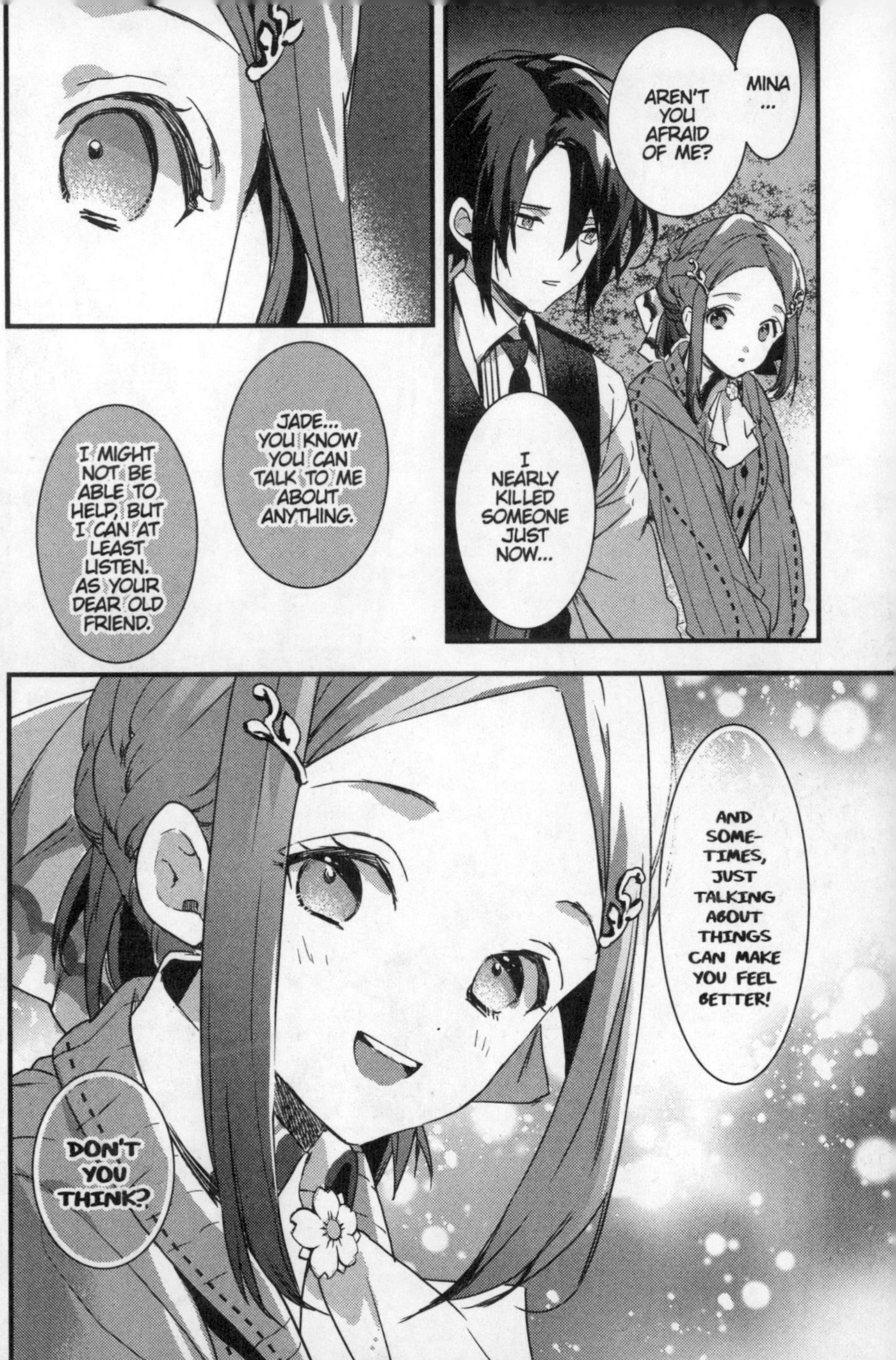
MINA...
AREN'T YOU AFRAID OF ME?
I NEARLY KILLED SOMEONE JUST NOW...
JADE... YOU KNOW YOU CAN TALK TO ME ABOUT ANYTHING.
I MIGHT NOT BE ABLE TO HELP, BUT I CAN AT LEAST LISTEN. AS YOUR DEAR OLD FRIEND.
AND SOME-TIMES, JUST TALKING ABOUT THINGS CAN MAKE YOU FEEL BETTER!
DON'T YOU THINK?

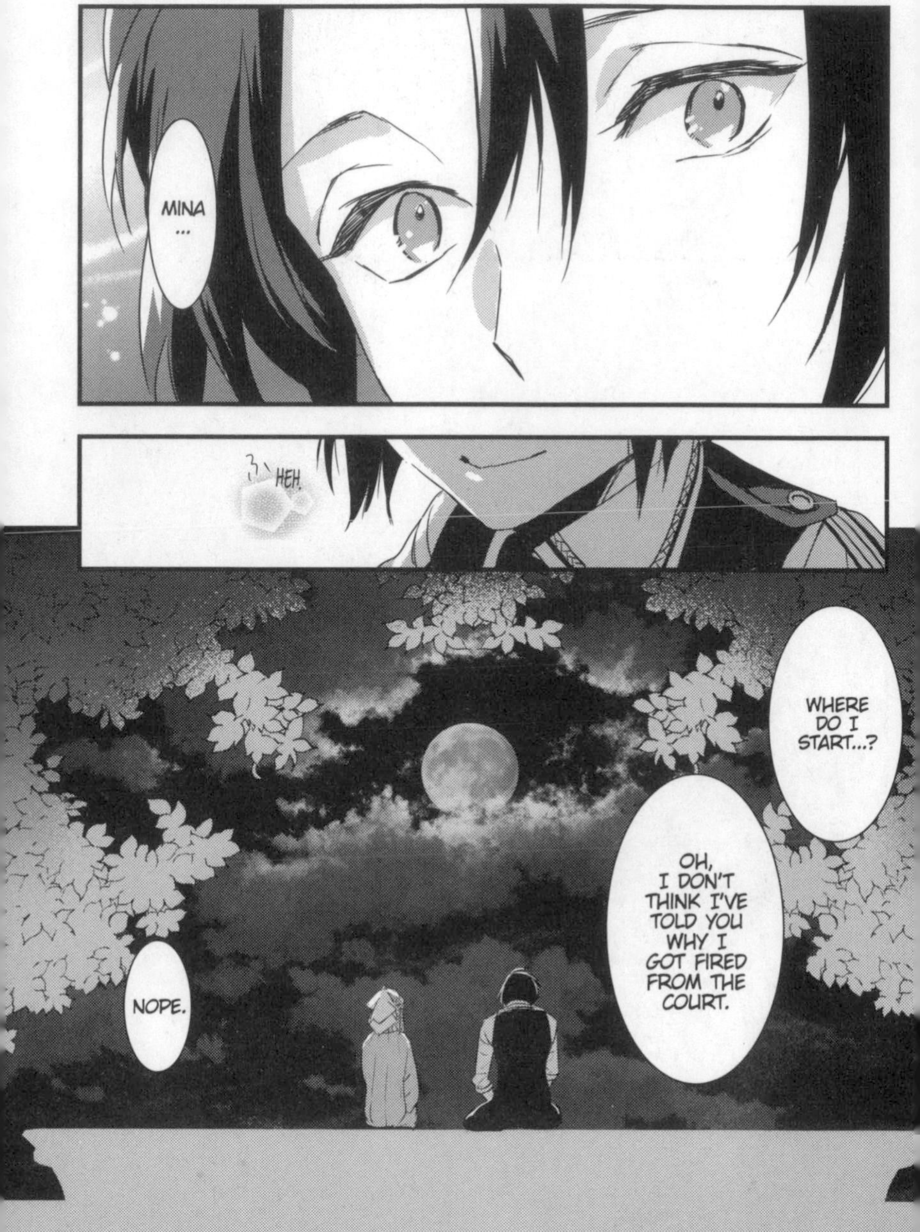
MINA...
HEH.
WHERE DO I START...?
OH, I DON'T THINK I'VE TOLD YOU WHY I GOT FIRED FROM THE COURT.
NOPE.

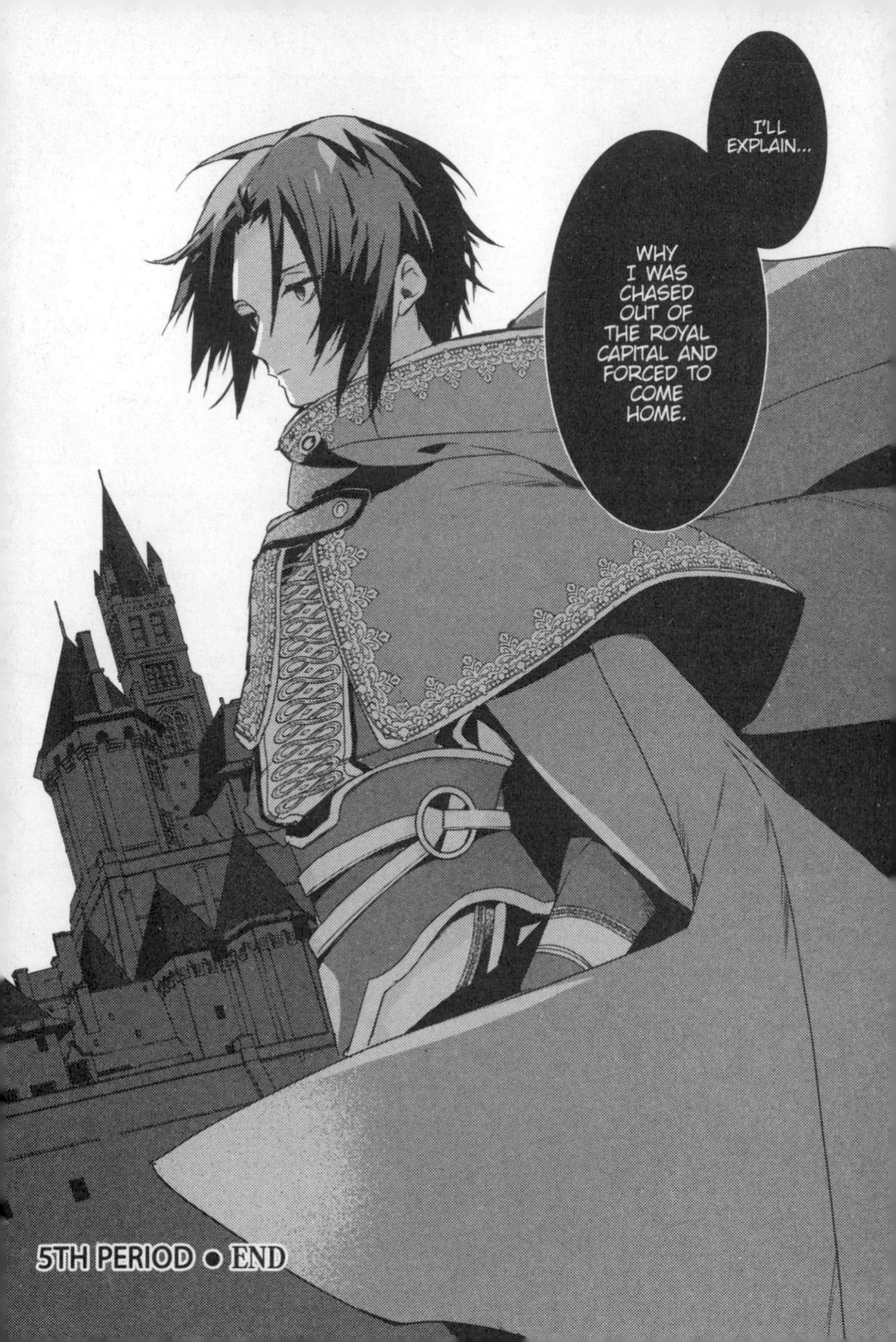
I'LL EXPLAIN...
WHY I WAS CHASED OUT OF THE ROYAL CAPITAL AND FORCED TO COME HOME.
5TH PERIOD • END

I Got

FIRED

as a
Court Wizard
so Now I'm Moving
to the Country
to Become a
Magic Teacher

I Got Fired as a
COURT WIZARD
so Now I'm Moving to the Country to Become a
MAGIC TEACHER

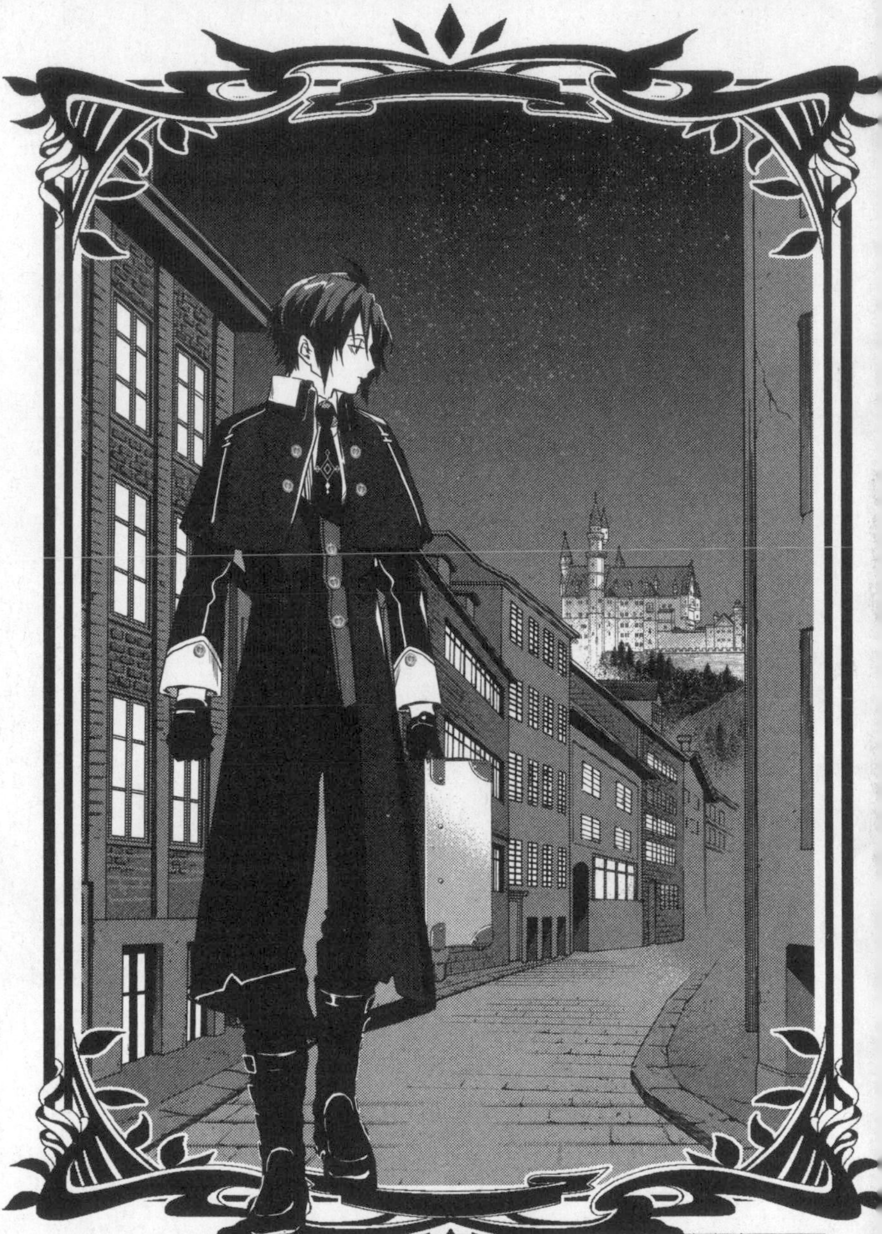

6th Period The Bureau's Negligence

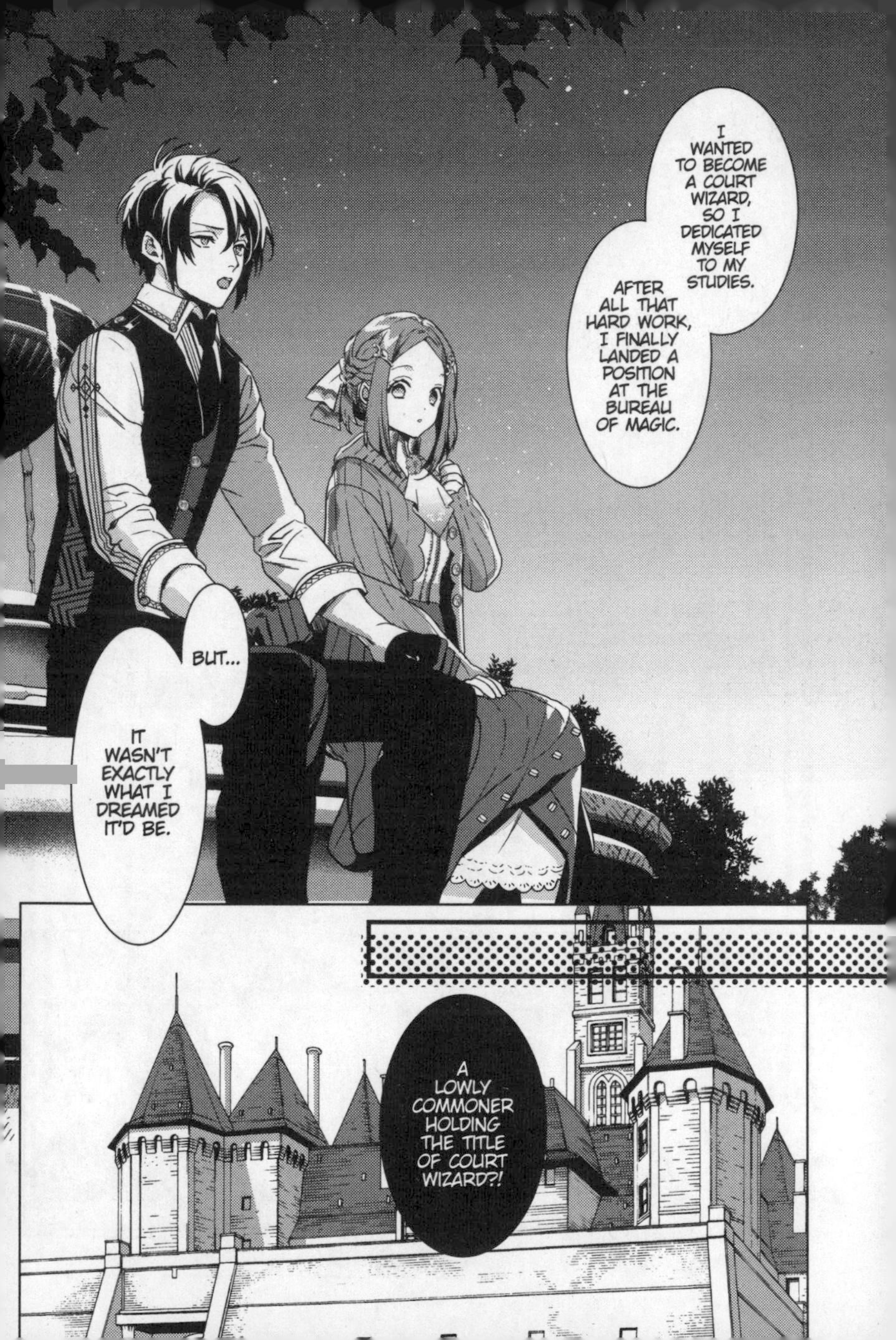
I WANTED TO BECOME A COURT WIZARD, SO I DEDICATED MYSELF TO MY STUDIES.
AFTER ALL THAT HARD WORK, I FINALLY LANDED A POSITION AT THE BUREAU OF MAGIC.
BUT...
IT WASN'T EXACTLY WHAT I DREAMED IT'D BE.
A LOWLY COMMONER HOLDING THE TITLE OF COURT WIZARD?!

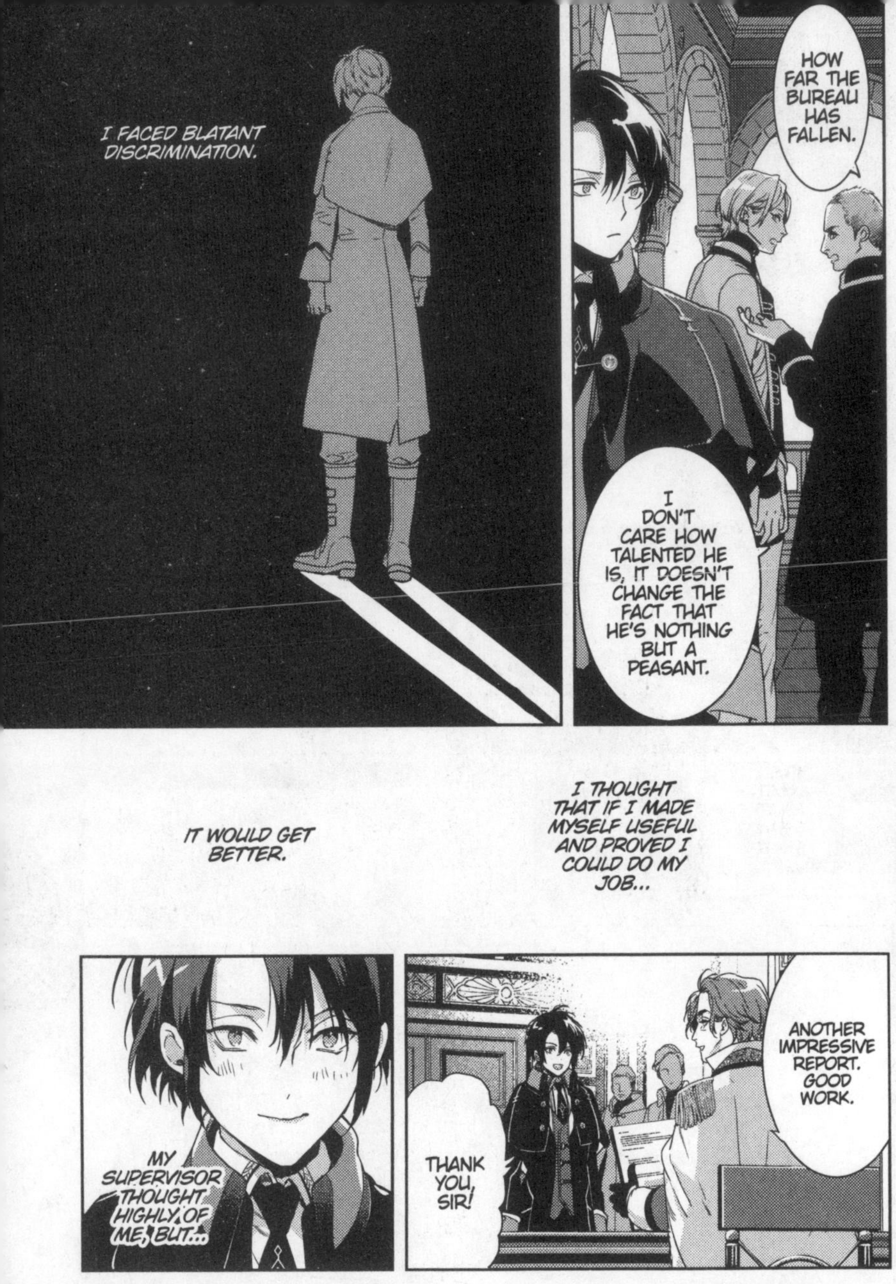
HOW FAR THE BUREAU HAS FALLEN.
I DON'T CARE HOW TALENTED HE IS, IT DOESN'T CHANGE THE FACT THAT HE'S NOTHING BUT A PEASANT.
I FACED BLATANT DISCRIMINATION.
I THOUGHT THAT IF I MADE MYSELF USEFUL AND PROVED I COULD DO MY JOB...
IT WOULD GET BETTER.
ANOTHER IMPRESSIVE REPORT. GOOD WORK.
THANK YOU, SIR!
MY SUPERVISOR THOUGHT HIGHLY OF ME, BUT...

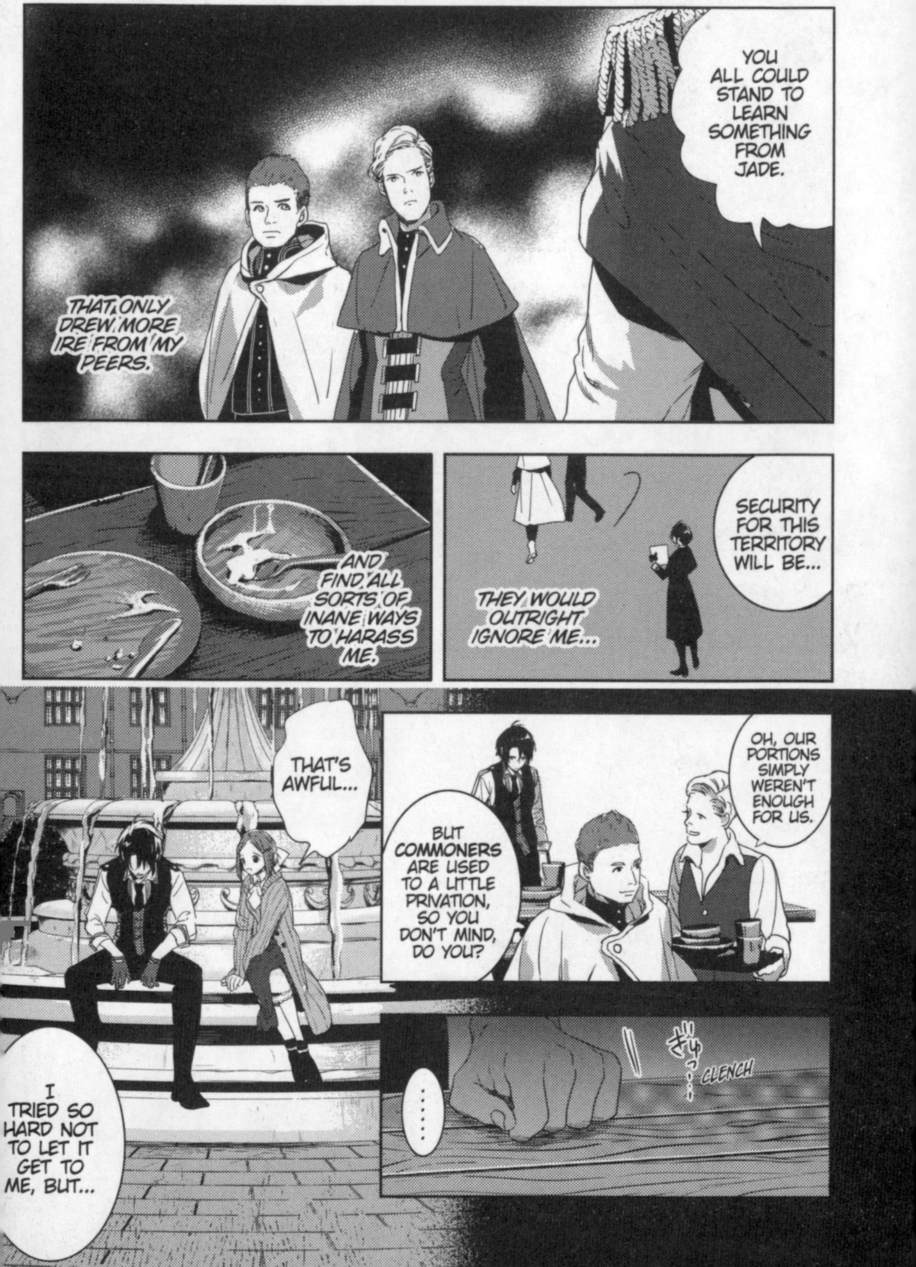
YOU ALL COULD STAND TO LEARN SOMETHING FROM JADE.
THAT ONLY DREW MORE IRE FROM MY PEERS.
SECURITY FOR THIS TERRITORY WILL BE...
THEY WOULD OUTRIGHT IGNORE ME...
AND FIND ALL SORTS OF INANE WAYS TO HARASS ME.
OH, OUR PORTIONS SIMPLY WEREN'T ENOUGH FOR US.
BUT COMMONERS ARE USED TO A LITTLE PRIVATION, SO YOU DON'T MIND, DO YOU?
ぎゅっ…
CLENCH
......
THAT'S AWFUL...
I TRIED SO HARD NOT TO LET IT GET TO ME, BUT...

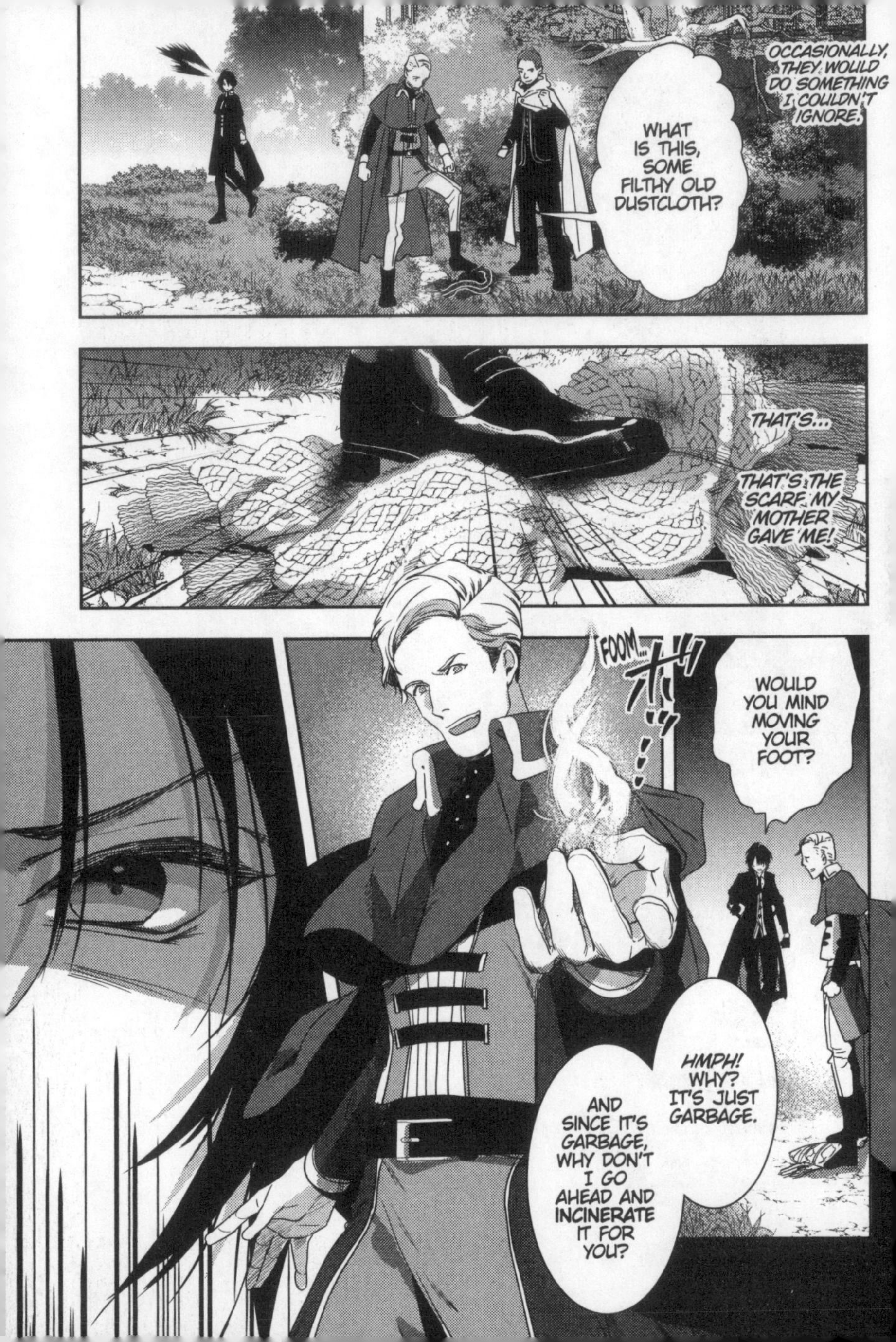
OCCASIONALLY, THEY WOULD DO SOMETHING I COULDN'T IGNORE.
WHAT IS THIS, SOME FILTHY OLD DUSTCLOTH?
THAT'S...
THAT'S THE SCARF MY MOTHER GAVE ME!
WOULD YOU MIND MOVING YOUR FOOT?
HMPH! WHY? IT'S JUST GARBAGE.
FOOM...
AND SINCE IT'S GARBAGE, WHY DON'T I GO AHEAD AND INCINERATE IT FOR YOU?

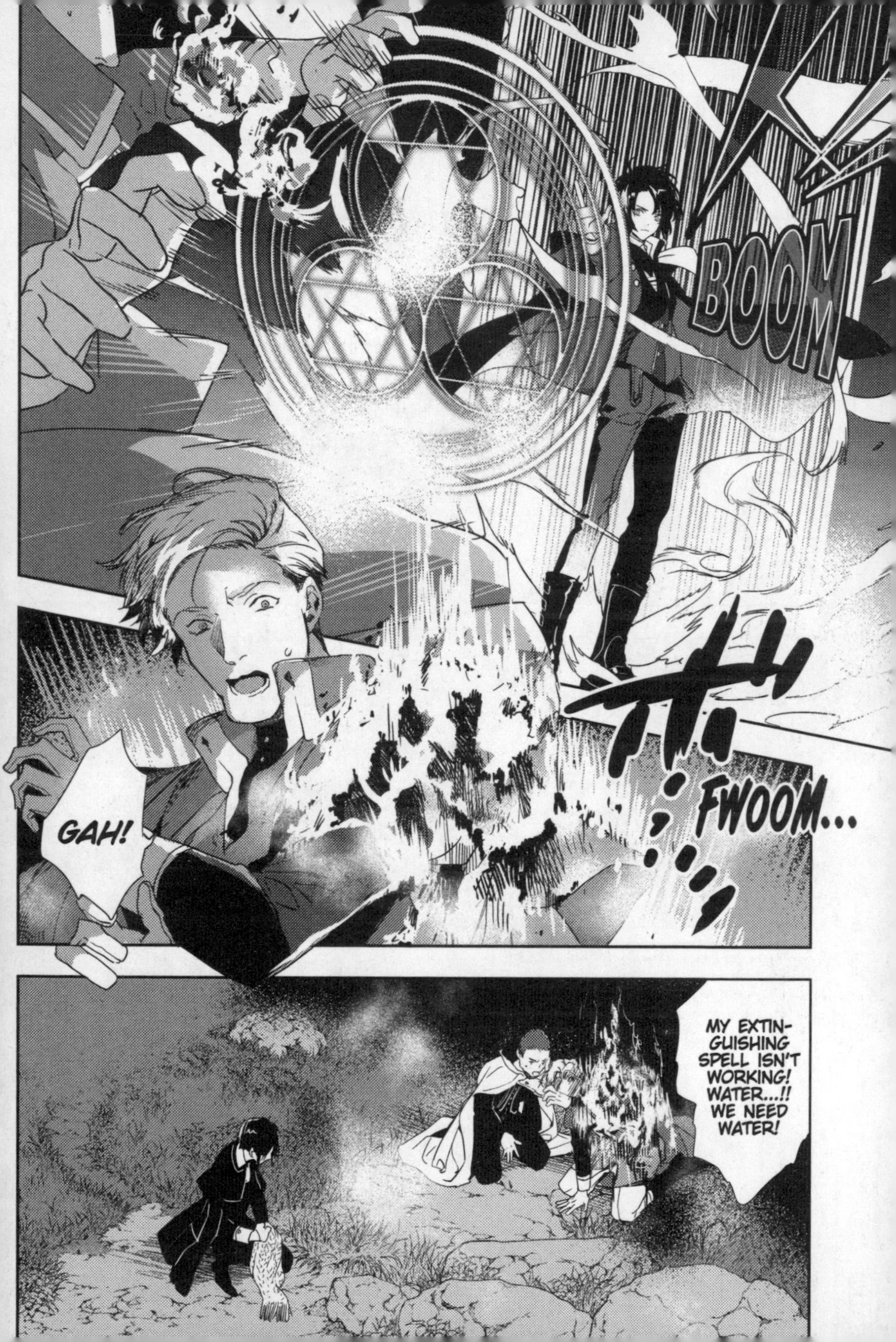
BOOM
FWOOM...
GAH!
MY EXTIN-
GUISHING
SPELL ISN'T
WORKING!
WATER...!!
WE NEED
WATER!

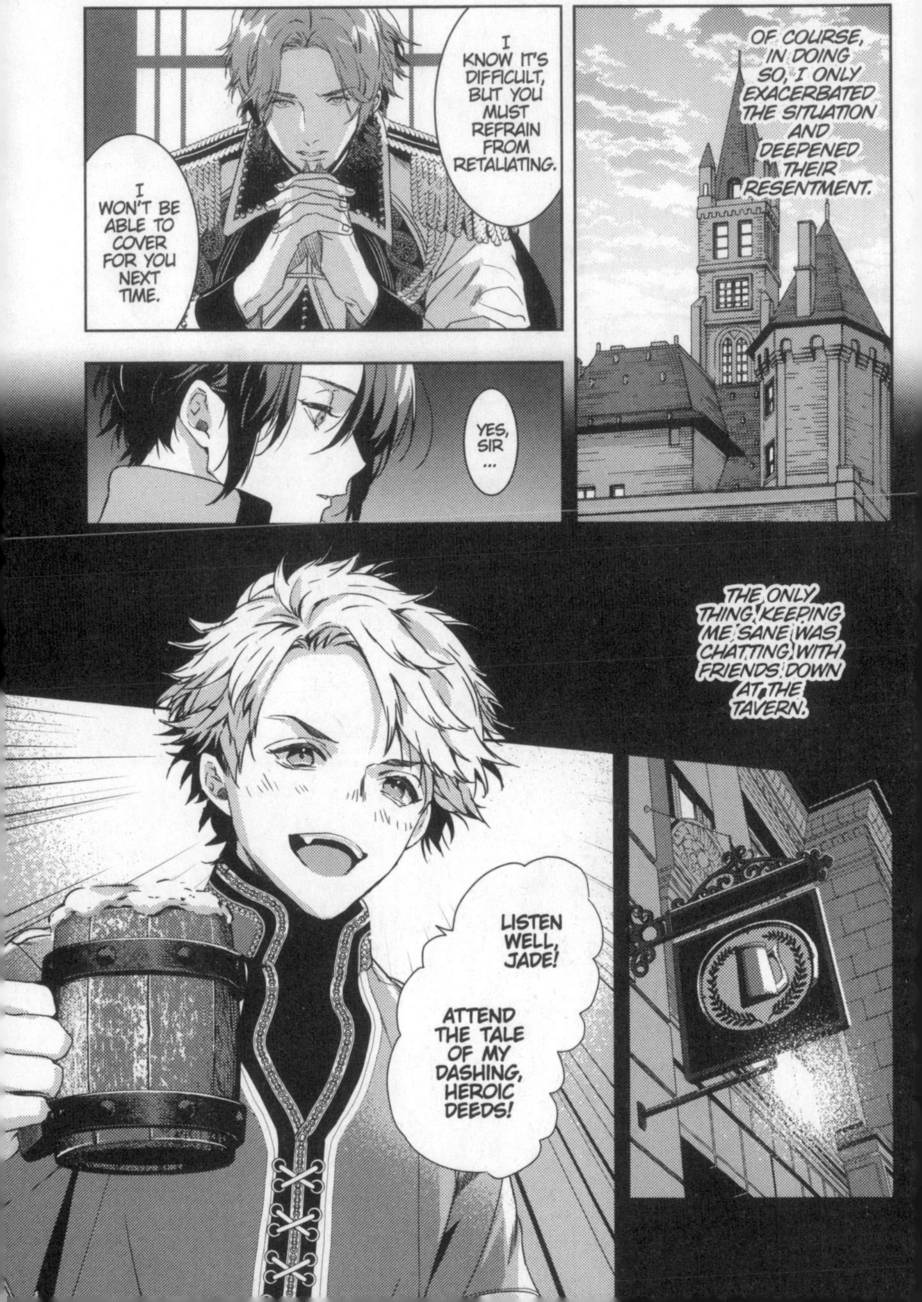
OF COURSE, IN DOING SO, I ONLY EXACERBATED THE SITUATION AND DEEPENED THEIR RESENTMENT.
I KNOW IT'S DIFFICULT, BUT YOU MUST REFRAIN FROM RETALIATING.
I WON'T BE ABLE TO COVER FOR YOU NEXT TIME.
YES, SIR...
THE ONLY THING KEEPING ME SANE WAS CHATTING WITH FRIENDS DOWN AT THE TAVERN.
LISTEN WELL, JADE!
ATTEND THE TALE OF MY DASHING, HEROIC DEEDS!

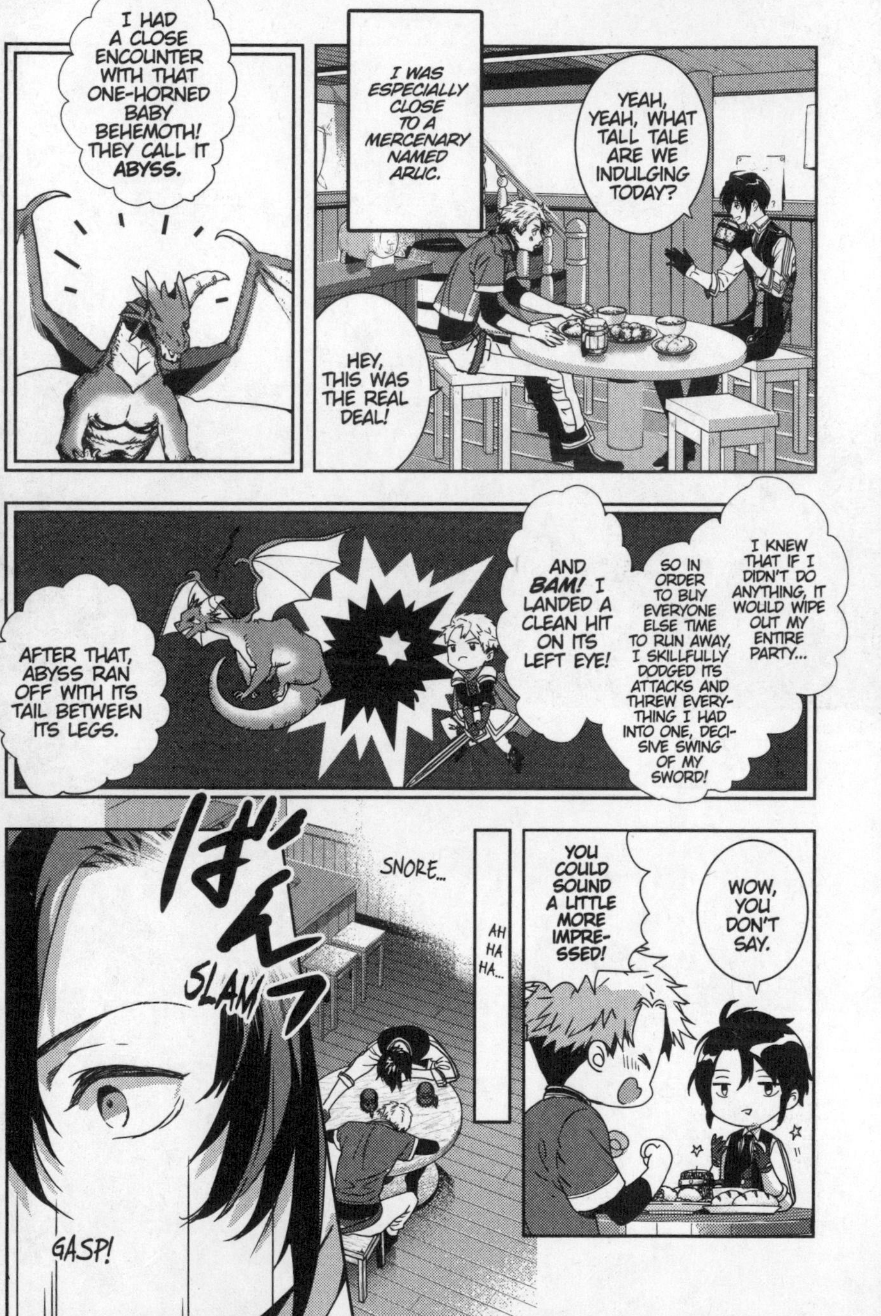
I WAS ESPECIALLY CLOSE TO A MERCENARY NAMED ARUC.
YEAH, YEAH, WHAT TALL TALE ARE WE INDULGING TODAY?
HEY, THIS WAS THE REAL DEAL!
I HAD A CLOSE ENCOUNTER WITH THAT ONE-HORNED BABY BEHEMOTH! THEY CALL IT **ABYSS.**
I KNEW THAT IF I DIDN'T DO ANYTHING, IT WOULD WIPE OUT MY ENTIRE PARTY...
SO IN ORDER TO BUY EVERYONE ELSE TIME TO RUN AWAY, I SKILLFULLY DODGED ITS ATTACKS AND THREW EVERY-THING I HAD INTO ONE, DECI-SIVE SWING OF MY SWORD!
AND ***BAM!*** I LANDED A CLEAN HIT ON ITS LEFT EYE!
AFTER THAT, ABYSS RAN OFF WITH ITS TAIL BETWEEN ITS LEGS.
WOW, YOU DON'T SAY.
YOU COULD SOUND A LITTLE MORE IMPRESSED!
AH HA HA...
SNORE...
ばんっ
SLAM
GASP!

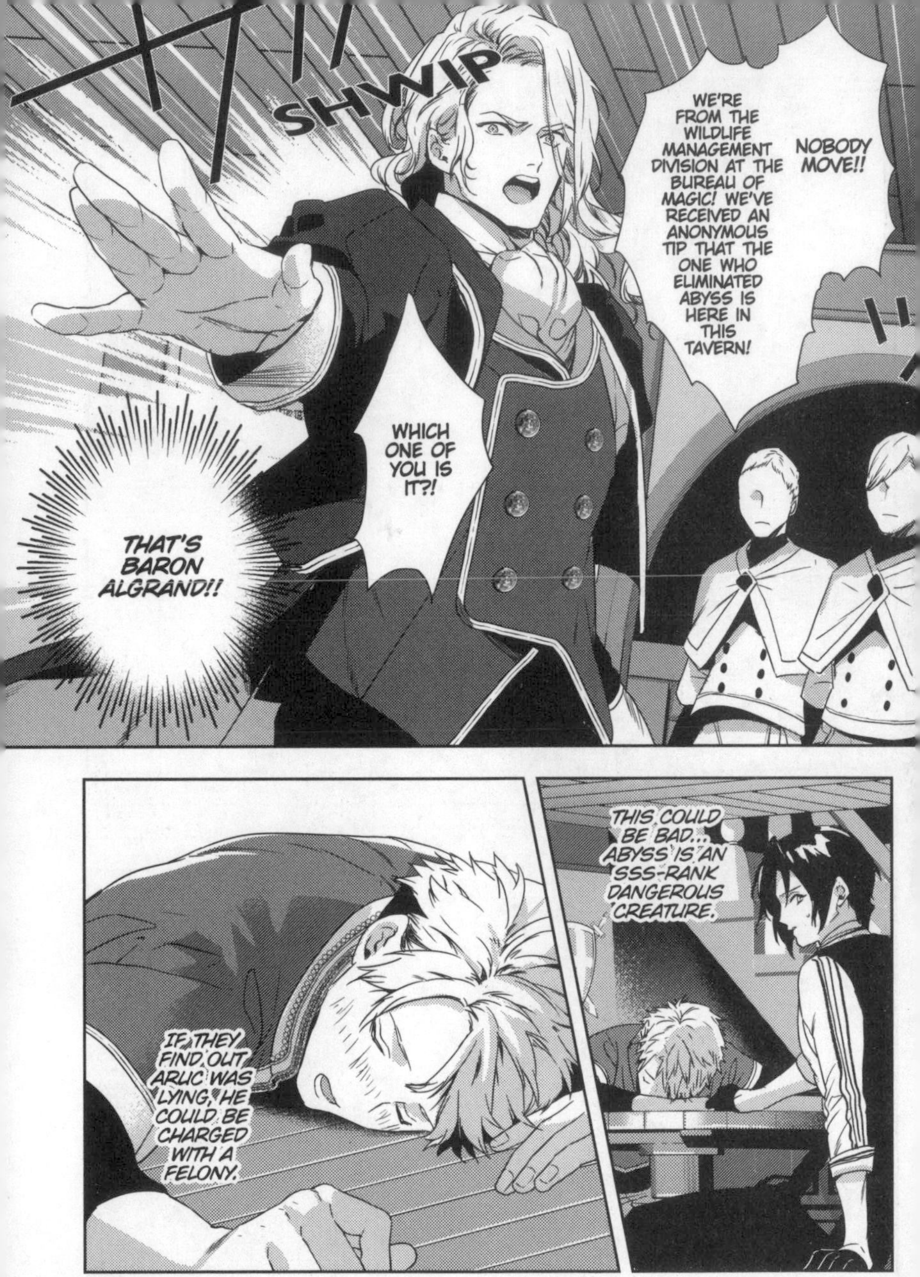
NOBODY MOVE!!
WE'RE FROM THE WILDLIFE MANAGEMENT DIVISION AT THE BUREAU OF MAGIC! WE'VE RECEIVED AN ANONYMOUS TIP THAT THE ONE WHO ELIMINATED ABYSS IS HERE IN THIS TAVERN!
SHWIP
WHICH ONE OF YOU IS IT?!
THAT'S BARON ALGRAND!!
THIS COULD BE BAD... ABYSS IS AN SSS-RANK DANGEROUS CREATURE.
IF THEY FIND OUT ARUC WAS LYING, HE COULD BE CHARGED WITH A FELONY.

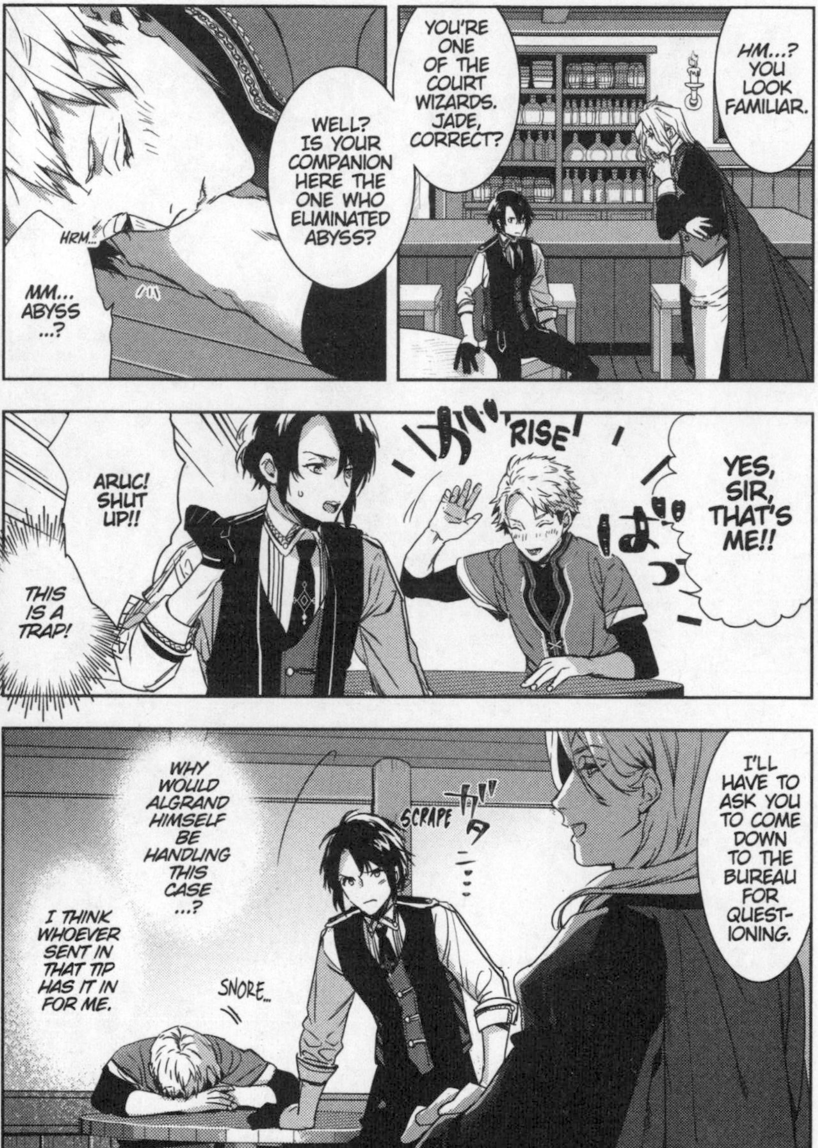
HM...? YOU LOOK FAMILIAR.
YOU'RE ONE OF THE COURT WIZARDS. JADE, CORRECT?
WELL? IS YOUR COMPANION HERE THE ONE WHO ELIMINATED ABYSS?
HRM...
MM... ABYSS ...?
YES, SIR, THAT'S ME!!
RISE
ARUC! SHUT UP!!
THIS IS A TRAP!
I'LL HAVE TO ASK YOU TO COME DOWN TO THE BUREAU FOR QUESTIONING.
SCRAPE
WHY WOULD ALGRAND HIMSELF BE HANDLING THIS CASE ...?
I THINK WHOEVER SENT IN THAT TIP HAS IT IN FOR ME.
SNORE...

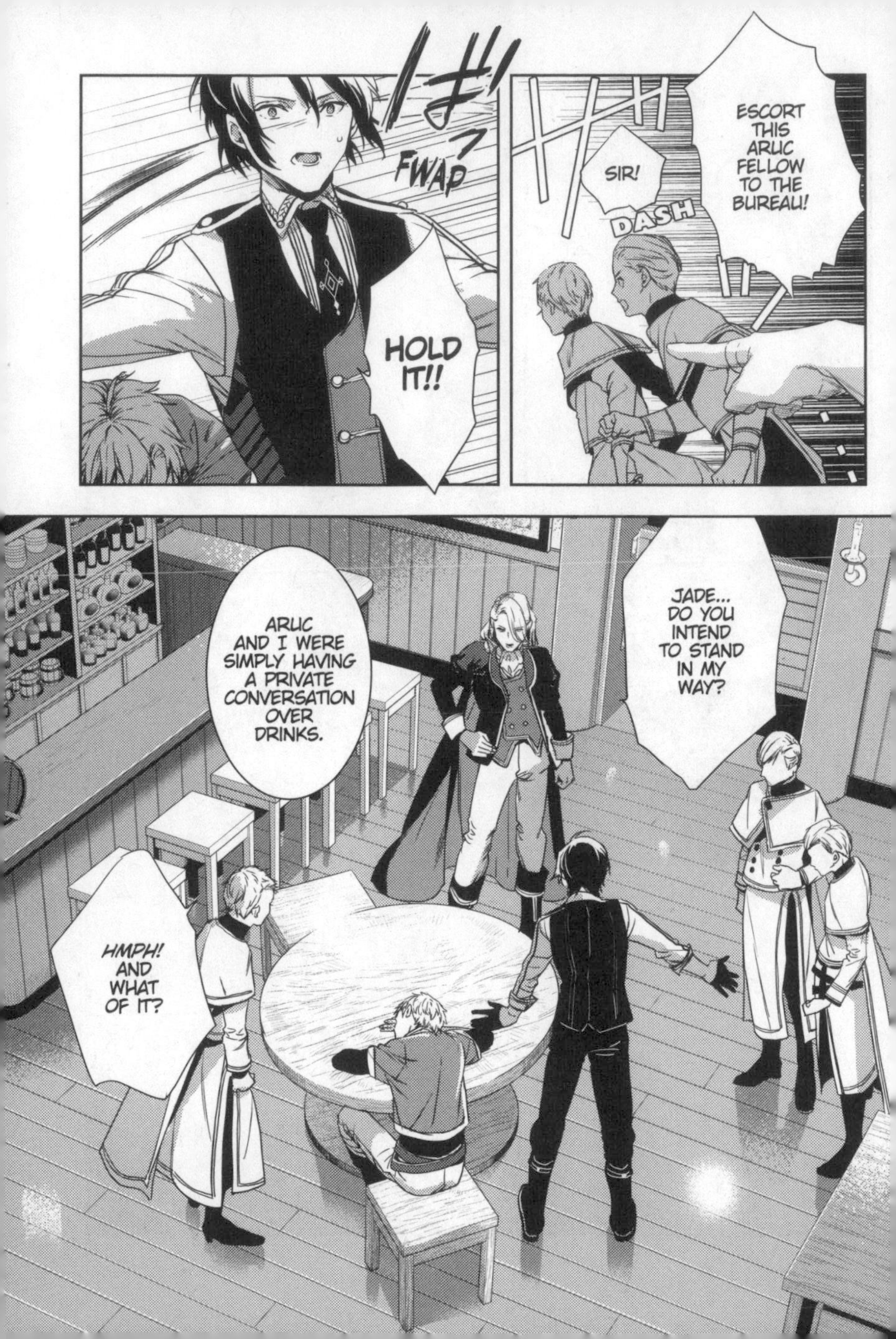
ESCORT THIS ARUC FELLOW TO THE BUREAU!
SIR!
DASH
FWAP
HOLD IT!!
JADE... DO YOU INTEND TO STAND IN MY WAY?
ARUC AND I WERE SIMPLY HAVING A PRIVATE CONVERSATION OVER DRINKS.
HMPH! AND WHAT OF IT?

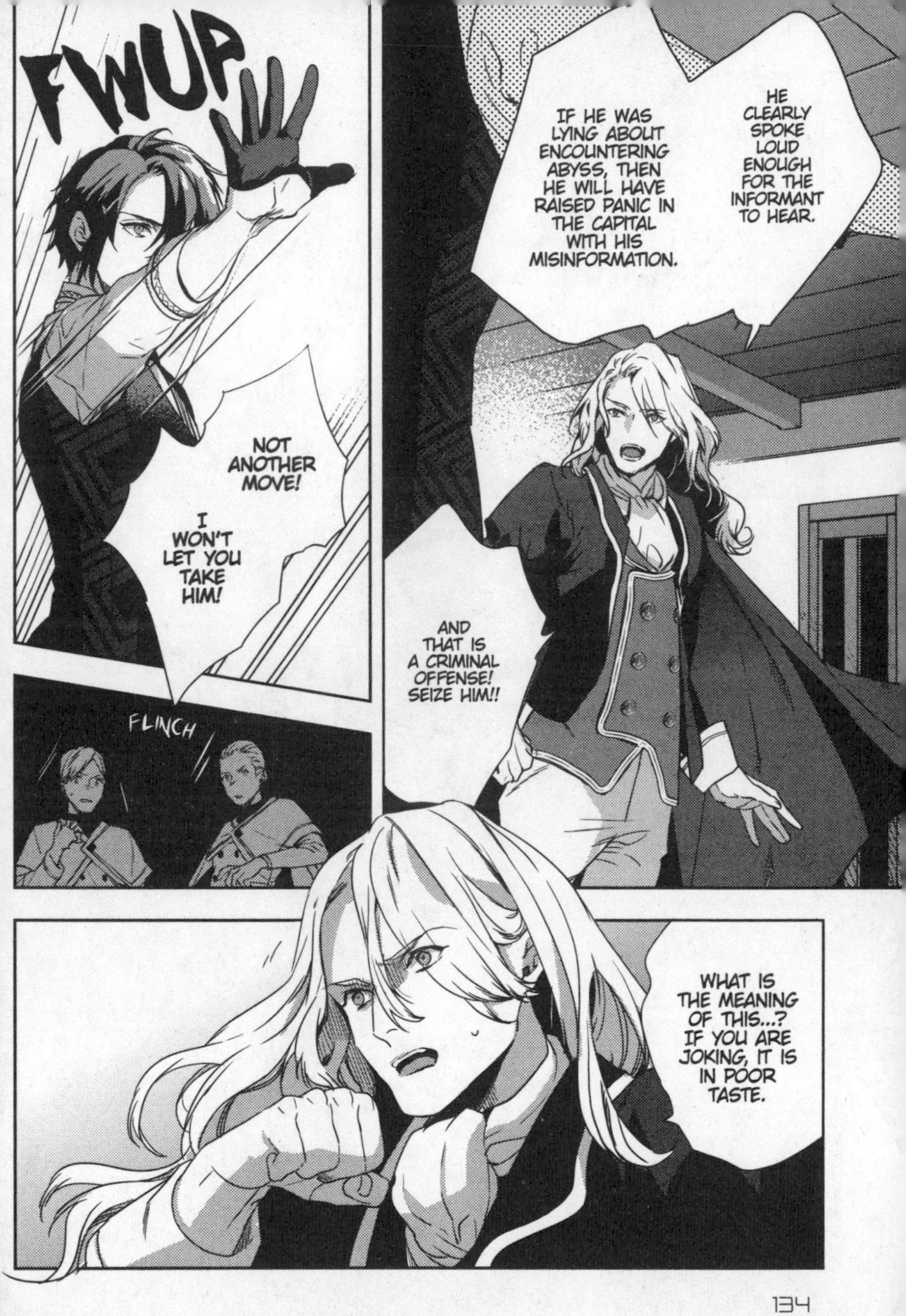
HE CLEARLY SPOKE LOUD ENOUGH FOR THE INFORMANT TO HEAR.
IF HE WAS LYING ABOUT ENCOUNTERING ABYSS, THEN HE WILL HAVE RAISED PANIC IN THE CAPITAL WITH HIS MISINFORMATION.
AND THAT IS A CRIMINAL OFFENSE! SEIZE HIM!!
FWUP
NOT ANOTHER MOVE!
I WON'T LET YOU TAKE HIM!
FLINCH
WHAT IS THE MEANING OF THIS...? IF YOU ARE JOKING, IT IS IN POOR TASTE.

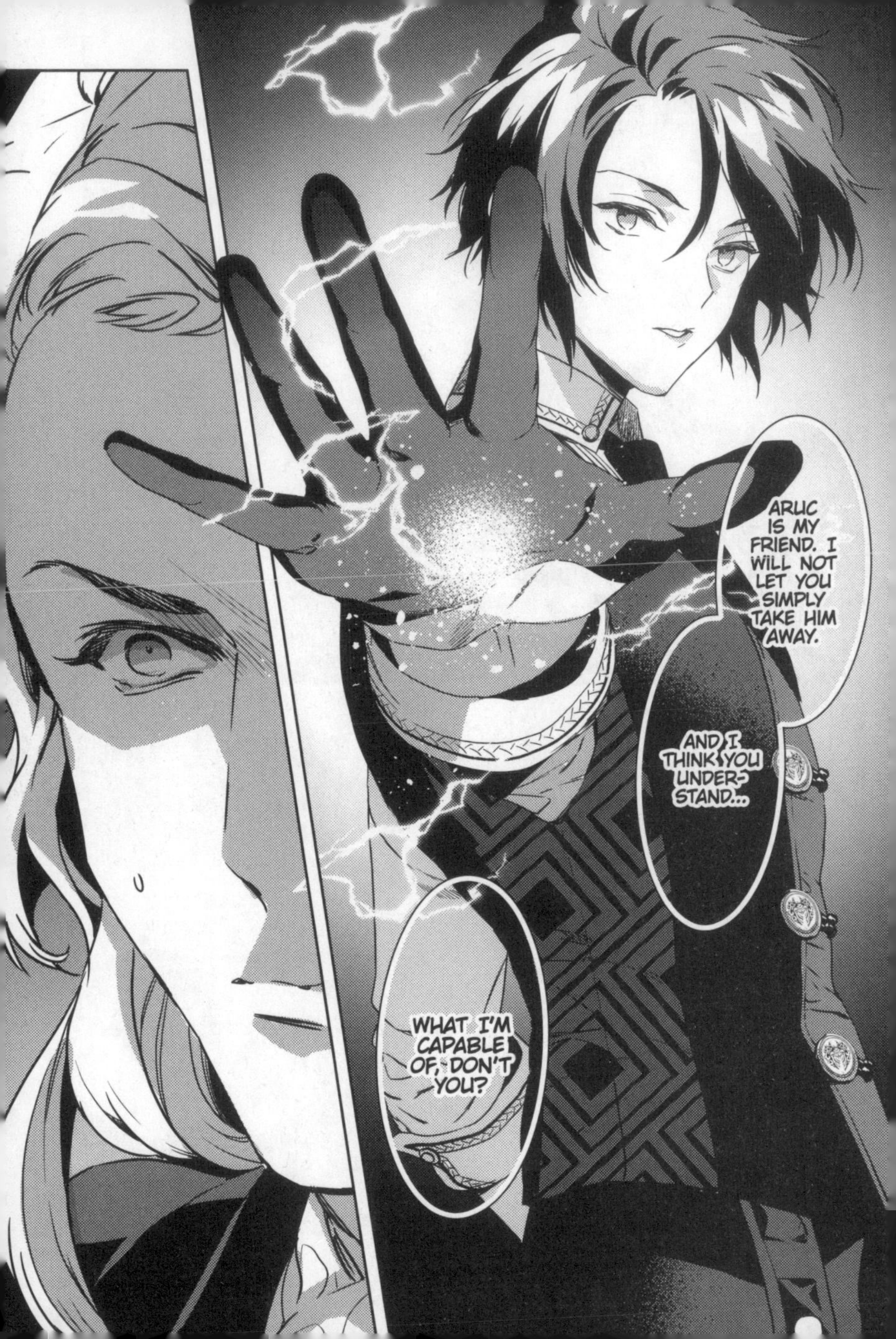
ARUC IS MY FRIEND. I WILL NOT LET YOU SIMPLY TAKE HIM AWAY.
AND I THINK YOU UNDER-STAND...
WHAT I'M CAPABLE OF, DON'T YOU?

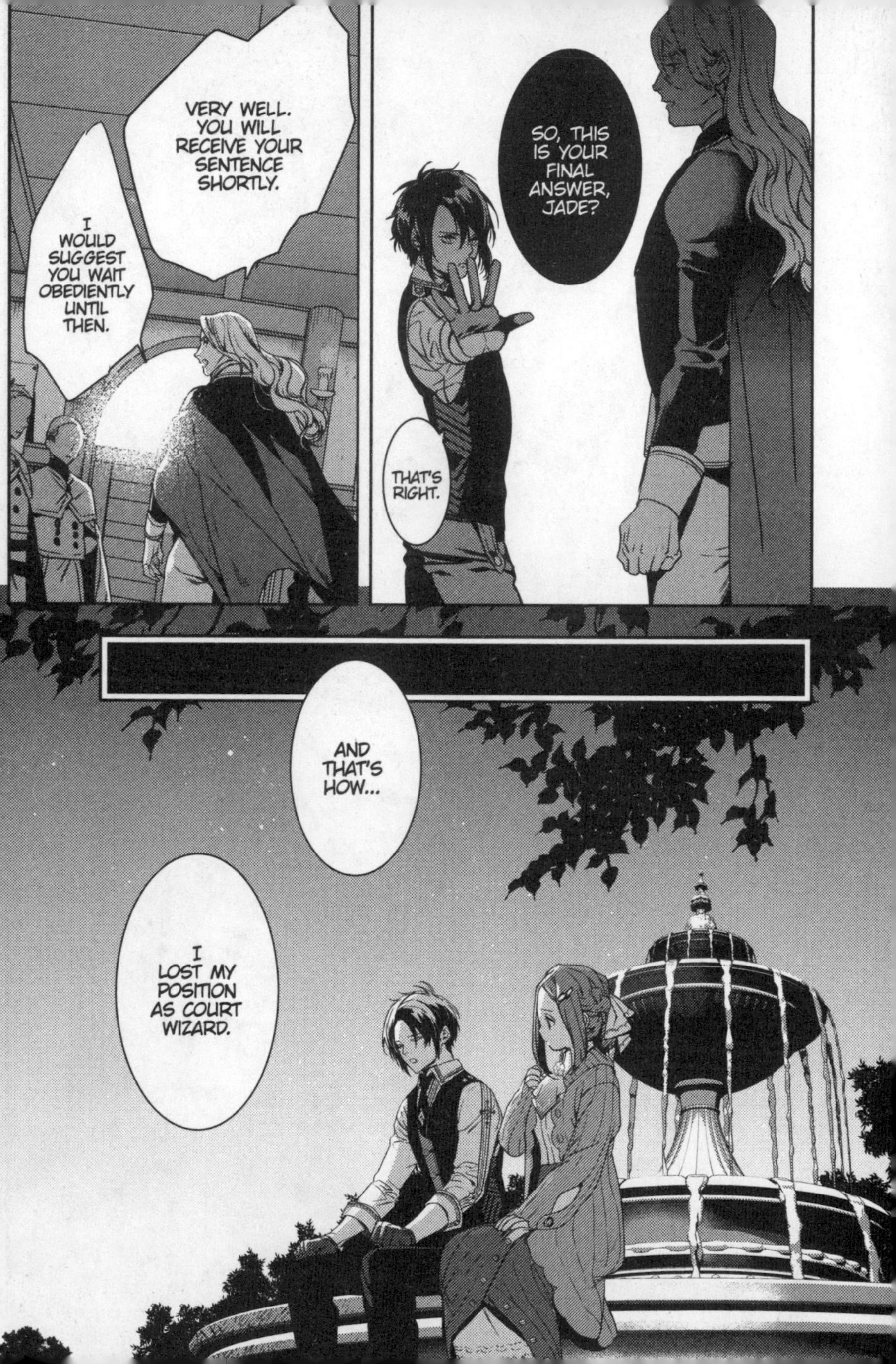
SO, THIS IS YOUR FINAL ANSWER, JADE?
THAT'S RIGHT.
VERY WELL. YOU WILL RECEIVE YOUR SENTENCE SHORTLY.
I WOULD SUGGEST YOU WAIT OBEDIENTLY UNTIL THEN.
AND THAT'S HOW...
I LOST MY POSITION AS COURT WIZARD.

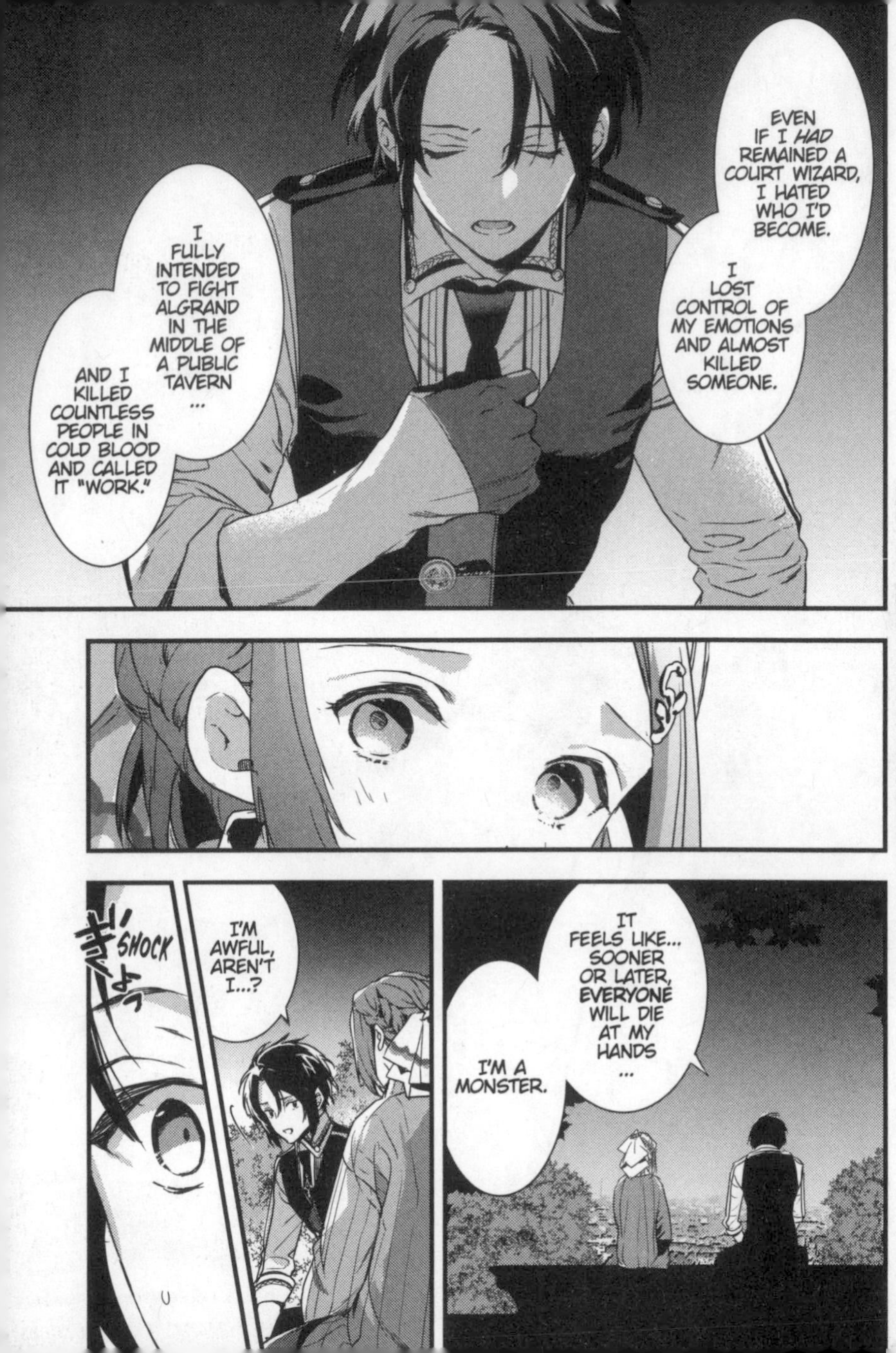
EVEN IF I *HAD* REMAINED A COURT WIZARD, I HATED WHO I'D BECOME.
I LOST CONTROL OF MY EMOTIONS AND ALMOST KILLED SOMEONE.
I FULLY INTENDED TO FIGHT ALGRAND IN THE MIDDLE OF A PUBLIC TAVERN...
AND I KILLED COUNTLESS PEOPLE IN COLD BLOOD AND CALLED IT "WORK."
IT FEELS LIKE... SOONER OR LATER, EVERYONE WILL DIE AT MY HANDS...
I'M A MONSTER.
I'M AWFUL, AREN'T I...?
ぎょっ
SHOCK

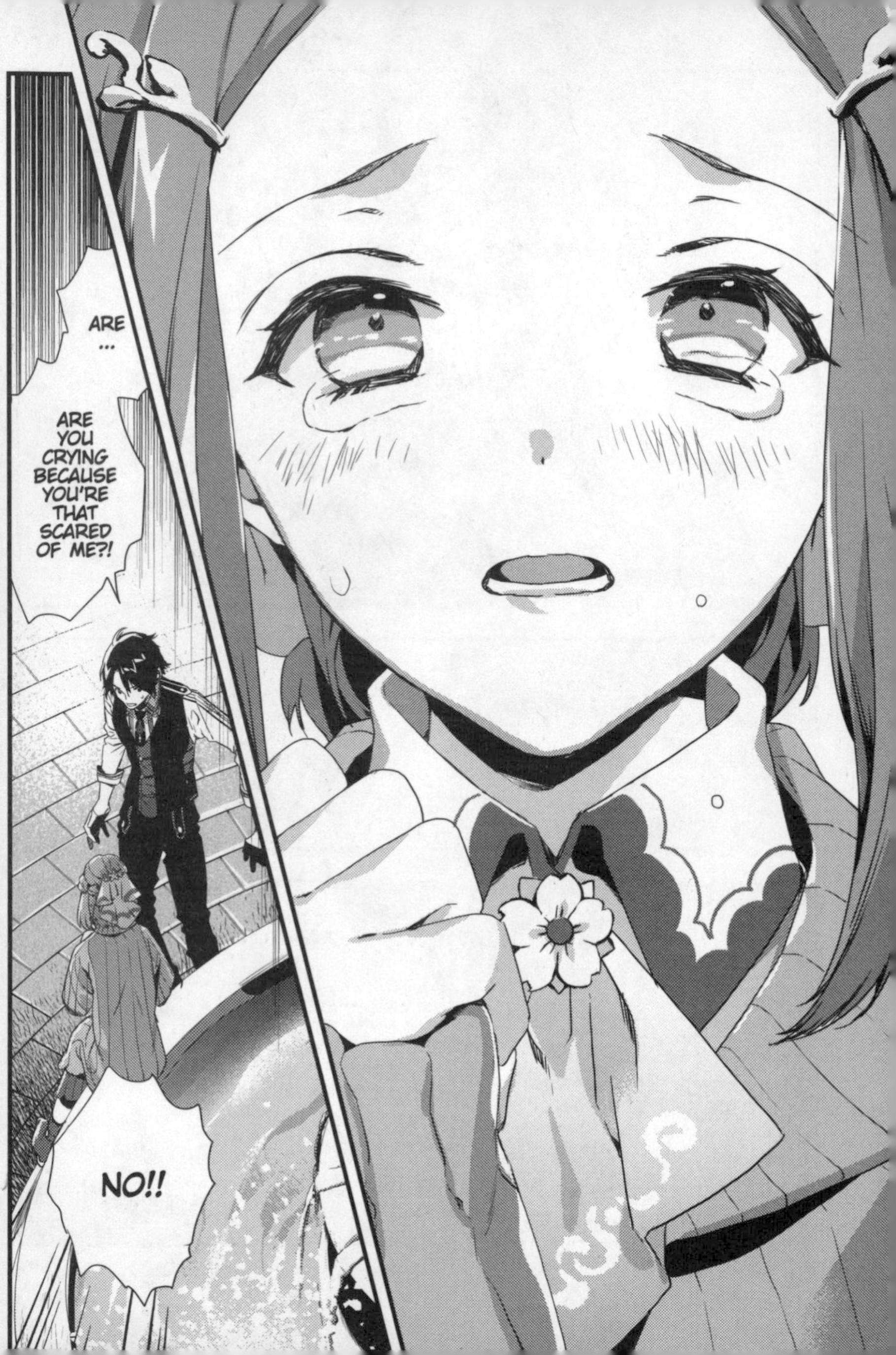
ARE ...
ARE YOU CRYING BECAUSE YOU'RE THAT SCARED OF ME?!
NO!!

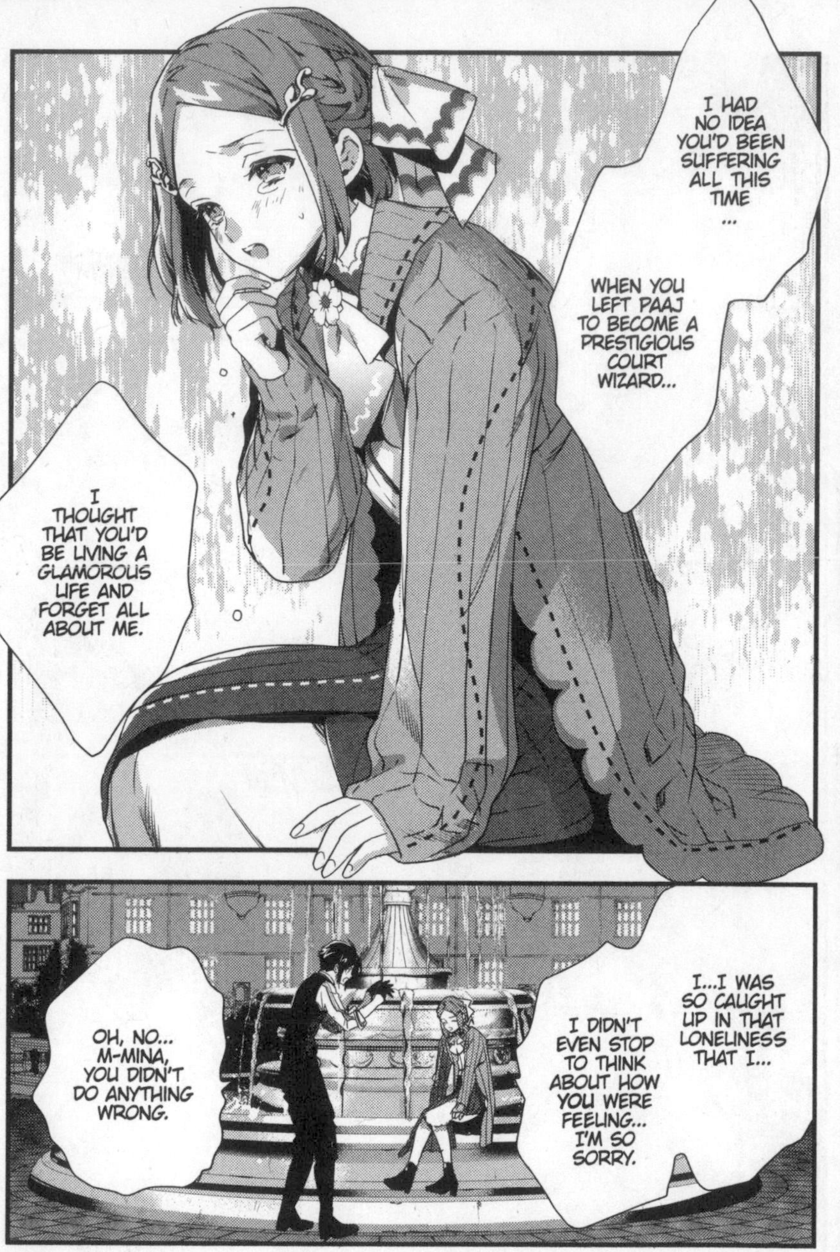
I HAD NO IDEA YOU'D BEEN SUFFERING ALL THIS TIME ...
WHEN YOU LEFT PAAJ TO BECOME A PRESTIGIOUS COURT WIZARD...
I THOUGHT THAT YOU'D BE LIVING A GLAMOROUS LIFE AND FORGET ALL ABOUT ME.
I...I WAS SO CAUGHT UP IN THAT LONELINESS THAT I...
I DIDN'T EVEN STOP TO THINK ABOUT HOW YOU WERE FEELING... I'M SO SORRY.
OH, NO... M-MINA, YOU DIDN'T DO ANYTHING WRONG.

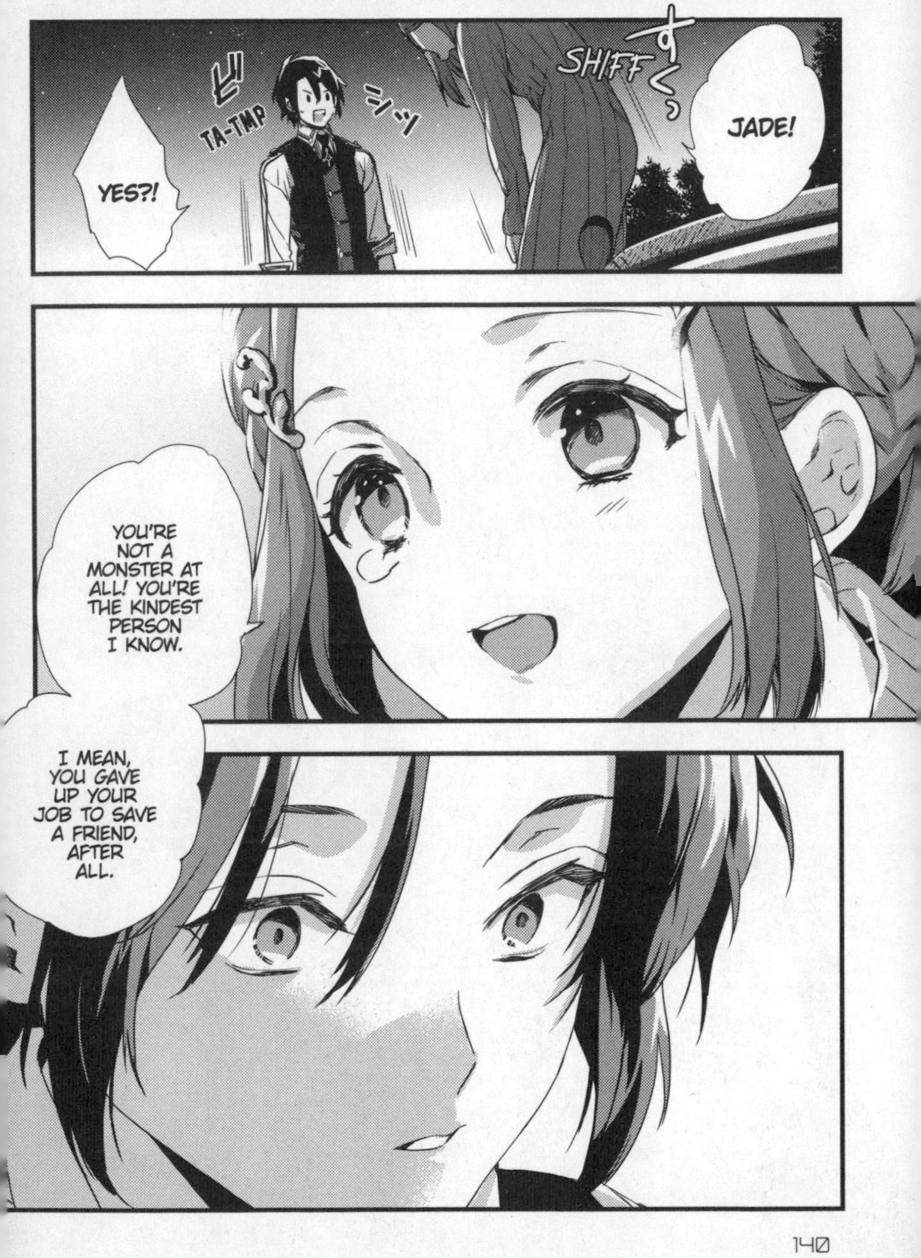
JADE!
SHIFF
すくっ
ビ
TA-TMP
シッ
YES?!
YOU'RE NOT A MONSTER AT ALL! YOU'RE THE KINDEST PERSON I KNOW.
I MEAN, YOU GAVE UP YOUR JOB TO SAVE A FRIEND, AFTER ALL.

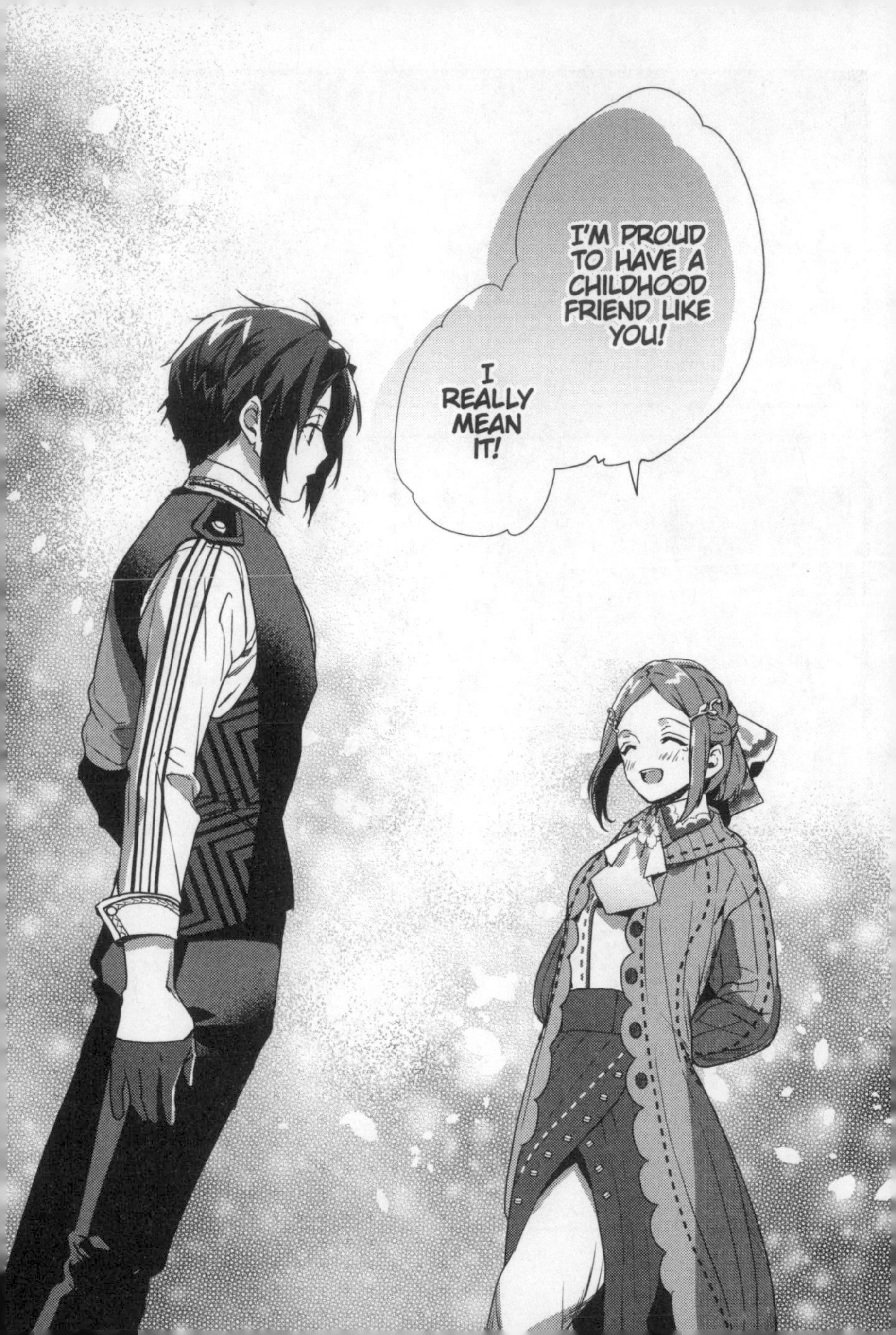
I'M PROUD TO HAVE A CHILDHOOD FRIEND LIKE YOU!
I REALLY MEAN IT!

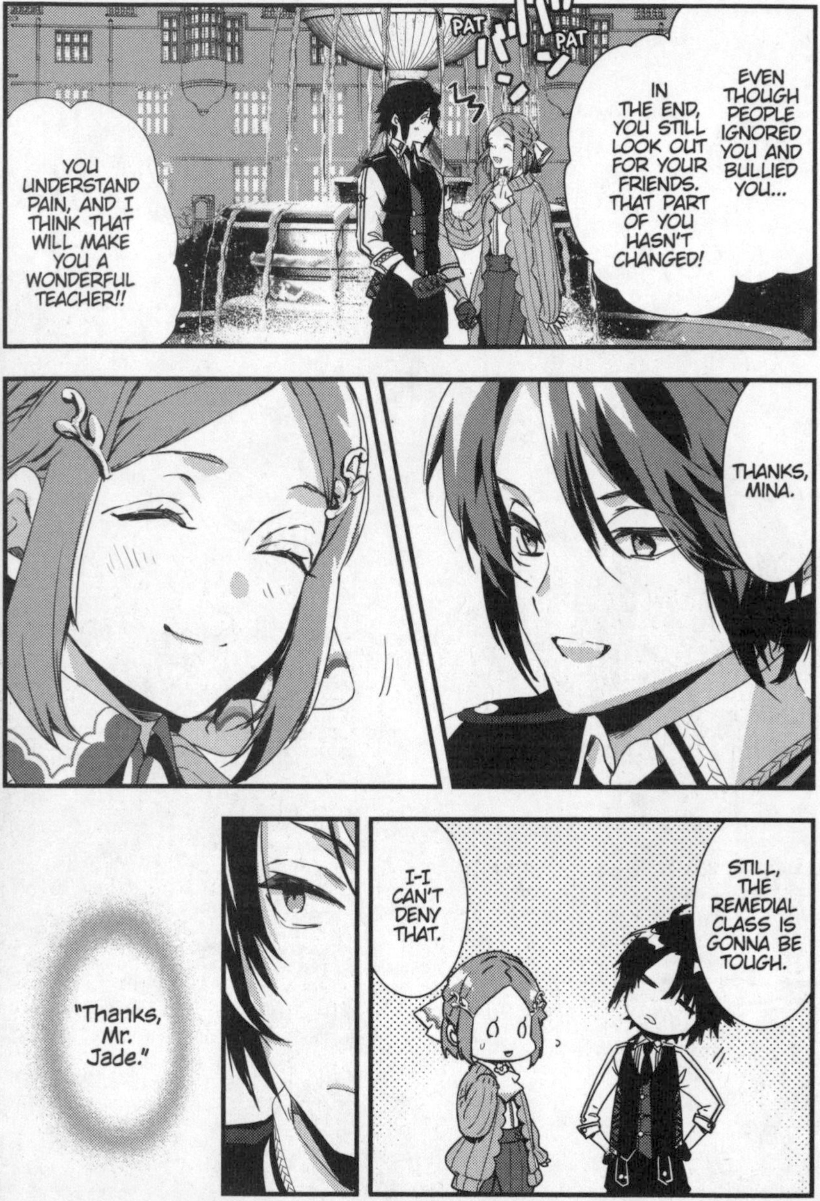
PAT PAT
EVEN THOUGH PEOPLE IGNORED YOU AND BULLIED YOU...
IN THE END, YOU STILL LOOK OUT FOR YOUR FRIENDS. THAT PART OF YOU HASN'T CHANGED!
YOU UNDERSTAND PAIN, AND I THINK THAT WILL MAKE YOU A WONDERFUL TEACHER!!
THANKS, MINA.
STILL, THE REMEDIAL CLASS IS GONNA BE TOUGH.
I-I CAN'T DENY THAT.
"Thanks, Mr. Jade."

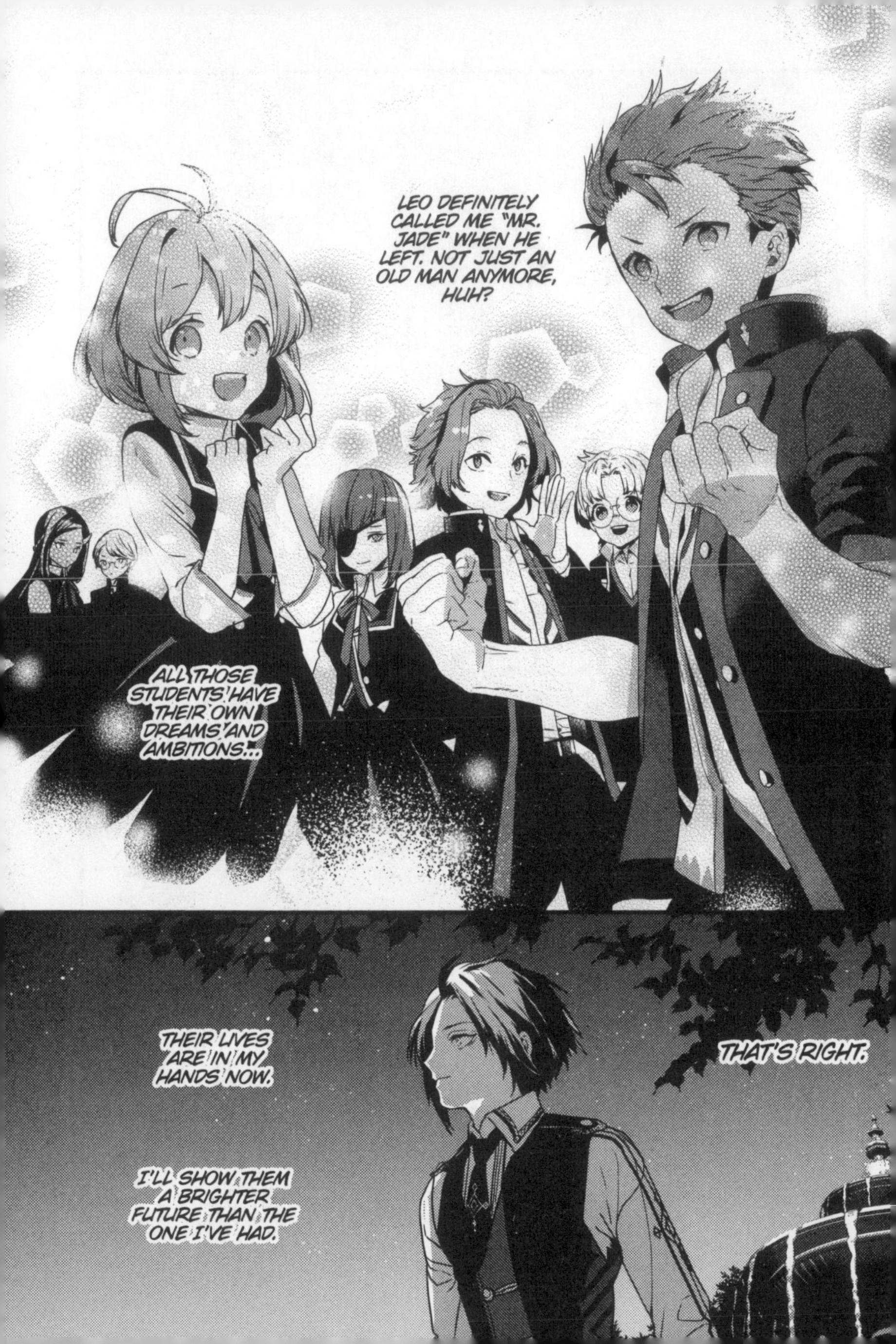
LEO DEFINITELY CALLED ME "MR. JADE" WHEN HE LEFT. NOT JUST AN OLD MAN ANYMORE, HUH?
ALL THOSE STUDENTS HAVE THEIR OWN DREAMS AND AMBITIONS...
THAT'S RIGHT.
THEIR LIVES ARE IN MY HANDS NOW.
I'LL SHOW THEM A BRIGHTER FUTURE THAN THE ONE I'VE HAD.

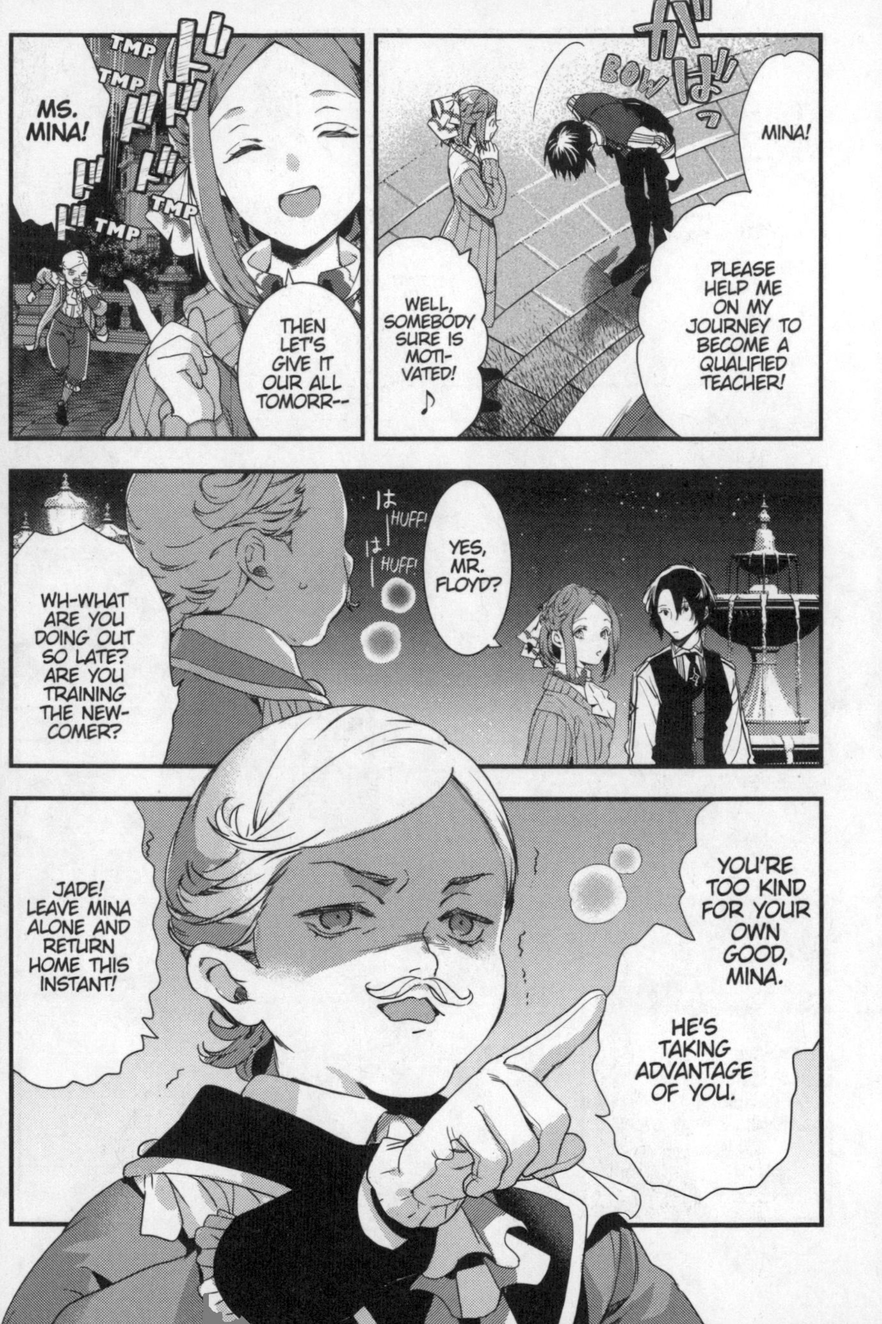
BOW
MINA!
PLEASE HELP ME ON MY JOURNEY TO BECOME A QUALIFIED TEACHER!
WELL, SOMEBODY SURE IS MOTIVATED! ♪
THEN LET'S GIVE IT OUR ALL TOMORR--
TMP TMP TMP TMP
MS. MINA!
HUFF! HUFF!
YES, MR. FLOYD?
WH-WHAT ARE YOU DOING OUT SO LATE? ARE YOU TRAINING THE NEW-COMER?
YOU'RE TOO KIND FOR YOUR OWN GOOD, MINA.
HE'S TAKING ADVANTAGE OF YOU.
JADE! LEAVE MINA ALONE AND RETURN HOME THIS INSTANT!

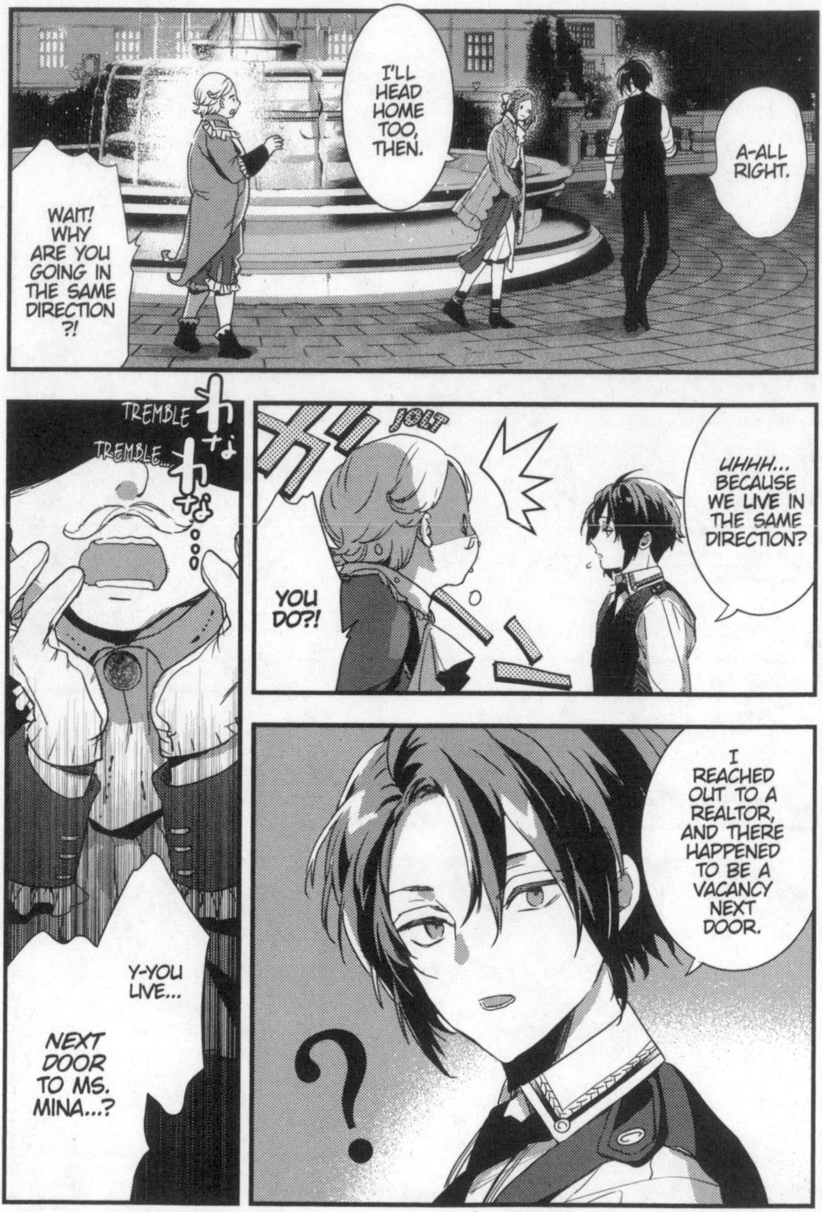
A-ALL RIGHT.
I'LL HEAD HOME TOO, THEN.
WAIT! WHY ARE YOU GOING IN THE SAME DIRECTION ?!
UHHH... BECAUSE WE LIVE IN THE SAME DIRECTION?
JOLT
YOU DO?!
I REACHED OUT TO A REALTOR, AND THERE HAPPENED TO BE A VACANCY NEXT DOOR.
TREMBLE
わな
TREMBLE...
わな
Y-YOU LIVE...
NEXT DOOR TO MS. MINA...?

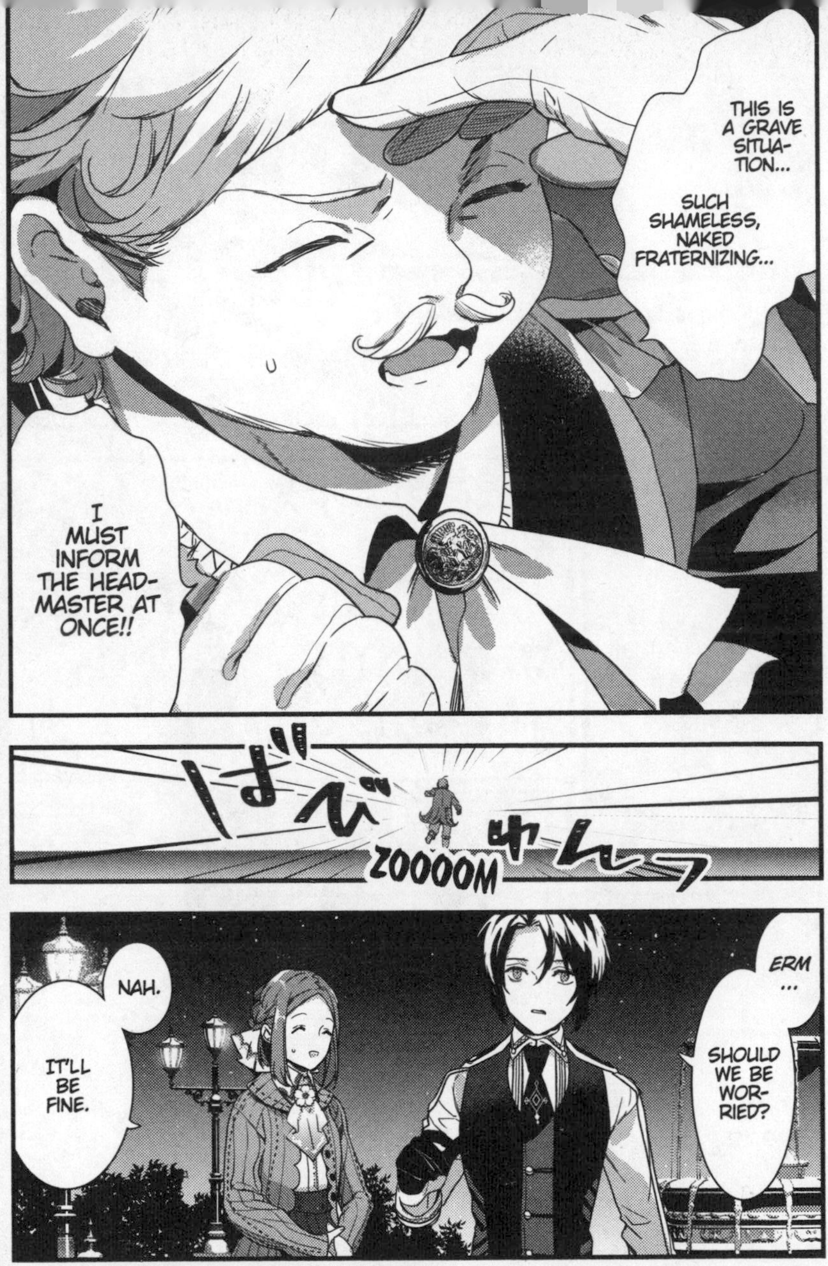
THIS IS A GRAVE SITUATION...
SUCH SHAMELESS, NAKED FRATERNIZING...
I MUST INFORM THE HEADMASTER AT ONCE!!
ZOOOOM
ERM...
SHOULD WE BE WORRIED?
NAH.
IT'LL BE FINE.

TO BE CONTINUED IN VOLUME 2.

Exclusive Short Story

The Magic
Academy
Faculty
Interview

Rui Sekai

BONUS SHORT STORY
The Magic Academy
Faculty Interview

After I was fired from the Royal Bureau of Magic, my old childhood friend graciously referred me to a teaching position at a magic academy. It was the day before the interview with the headmaster…

"How are you feeling, Jade? I know there's technically an interview, but the headmaster said you'd be hired as long as you're not a total weirdo, so try to relax," said Mina.

"So, in other words, if I don't get hired, that means I'm a total weirdo."

Even though I said that, I'd have felt bad turning her help down after all the trouble she went through. Meanwhile, if I failed the interview, I didn't know what else I would do. Probably just lose my mind. So

I decided to accept Mina's offer to help me practice.

"You worked in the capital for many years, right? You've got nothing to worry about. I already told you I'd help you prepare. Here, have some coffee."

"That's true… Thanks, this tastes great. So what was it like when you interviewed there?"

Sitting in my childhood friend's room, drinking the coffee she'd brewed for me, getting interview practice from someone five years my junior? I felt pretty pathetic.

But she'd gotten a lot better at brewing coffee. In the old days, neither of us drank it.

"Oh, thanks," said Mina. "Let's see, I remember I was asked why I chose this academy, what kind of teacher I wanted to become, what was my specialty in magic, what did I devote my time to as a student, and so on. Normal stuff, see?"

Normal indeed.

"What, is that *too* normal for you?"

"No, that's not it. I was just thinking about how I'm feeling a bit more anxious now. But first, I should think about how I would answer those questions."

Mina affected a much lower voice and slower cadence than usual. "So then why did you choose this school?"

"What, was that an imitation of Margrave Bendt?"

The juxtaposition between the voice and her face was awfully amusing.

"Oh, hush. It's important to get into character. Now answer the question: Why did you choose this academy?"

"I chose this academy because I lost everything I had, and then my friend recommended this position to me."

"Okay...Maybe we can be a little less honest on the day of. Now, what kind of teacher do you want to be?"

"One that's mildly tolerated by my students and colleagues, I guess..."

"Uh, are you okay, Jade? Your eyes are glazing over. I mean, ahem. Tell me what your specialty in magic is."

"I can use nature manipulation magics. I also enjoy spellcrafting and refining magic circles, so that's what I did research on. Among the arcane elements, I have a particular affinity for channeling darkness."

"You used to be so into fire and water, though! Okay, next, what did you devote your time to when you were a student?"

"Already giving up on your impression? Never mind, it doesn't matter. Umm... What I devoted my time to as a student... Do you mean outside of magic?"

"Yeah. I'd like to know what else you spent your time on."

By this point, it felt less like interview practice and more like she was just trying to get to know me.

"I practiced jōjutsu, a martial art that utilizes a short staff. My old mentor was extremely skilled at jōjutsu, so he inspired me to take it up as well. I got a lot of hits in, but I probably *got* hit at least ten times as much, hah."

"You better answer seriously during the actual interview, okay? Jōjutsu, huh…? You should show me sometime."

"Oh yeah? Want to spar?"

"Only if you take it easy on me."

"You're an old friend I owe a huge favor to. Do I seem like the kind of guy who'd seriously fight you?"

"Hmm…" Mina cocked her head in thought.

"Hey!"

"Just kidding. I know you wouldn't," Mina giggled. "All right, let's move on. I'm going to think of more questions that might be asked during the interview, so you better answer seriously."

"You were the one who went on a tangen—" I started to protest, but Mina smiled as if to say,

Leave it.

"Okay, next question..."

The day flew by as Mina helped me practice for the interview, and I ended up having dinner at her place. Tomorrow, the real trial would begin.

Knock, knock!

"It's Mina. I have Jade here with me," Mina announced. The large, imposing door in front of us could be none other than that of the headmaster's office.

"Come in," answered an equally imposing voice.

Mina opened the door, and there stood the legendary Margrave Bendt. I'd heard a great deal about him, but this was my first time meeting him.

"Thank you for coming. I am Bendt Elmtend, headmaster of this academy."

I knelt down, as was customary for greeting a member of aristocracy. "It's a pleasure to make your acquaintance. My name is Jade. Thank you for allowing me this opportunity to—"

"Jade. No need for such formalities. You may already know that I'm considered something of an oddity among margraves. Save the decorum for the capital. Go on, take a seat."

I did as he said. "Thank you, sir—"

Phhbbbt.

"..."

As soon as I sat down, the sound of a fart echoed loudly throughout the room. Perhaps the sturdy walls were built to better reflect sounds. Once the sound dissipated, there was silence.

Wait, what was that sound...? Did I fart? Pretty sure I would've felt something...

I started to break into a cold sweat. I didn't dare look Margrave Bendt in the eye. Instead, I stole a glance at Mina, who was standing beside me. Her face was ghastly pale, and she looked like she was about to faint.

"Ha ha ha! Looks like you fell for my little prank," the Margrave laughed. "You see, I got this at the general store. It's a new novelty product—I believe they call it a whoopie cushion. An apt name, to be sure. One of our students developed it." Margrave Bendt pointed at the cushion on my chair as he spoke.

"What...?" Flustered, I stood up and poked the cushion.

Phhbbt.

It made the same noise as before.

"Hmm," murmured Margrave Bendt, "I hoped it would calm your nerves, but Ms. Mina over here looks aghast. My apologies."

I gathered that Margrave Bendt wanted to wait longer before revealing the trick. But after seeing Mina's expression, he had to break the awkwardness.

"I'm, um, fine. Sorry to have worried you," Mina both looked and sounded terribly tired.

"Well then, let us proceed with the interview," Margrave Bendt continued. "Ms. Mina, would you take a seat as well? Feel free to sit next to Jade."

"Yes, sir." Mina glanced at the chair beside me. No doubt she was checking whether there was a whoopie cushion on it.

"Relax. I wouldn't use the same prank twice," said the headmaster.

Mina nodded, not fully believing his words, and gingerly sat down in the chair.

Grooooan...

It sounded like the death throes of the very earth itself.

"......"

Mina pulled something out from underneath the seat cushion. It was some kind of strange, bird-shaped toy. She stared at it for a moment and then gave its belly a quick squeeze.

Groooooooooan...

The dying earth roared once more.

"Bwa ha ha!" bellowed Margrave Bendt, "I

apologize, Ms. Mina. I do mean well. I simply can't help myself. Though, to my credit, I didn't lie! That's not a whoopie cushion, you see, it's—"

"No need to concern yourself with me, sir. Please, go ahead and conduct Jade's interview," Mina interrupted, smiling rigidly as she held the bird-shaped toy.

Margrave Bendt's expression stiffened. The awkwardness in the air was suffocating.

"V-very well. Let us start the interview. Mhm."

"Th-thank you."

I don't remember much about the rest of the interview. All I remember is the somber face of the bird toy being squeezed, Mina's smile, and the veins popping on the back of her right hand.

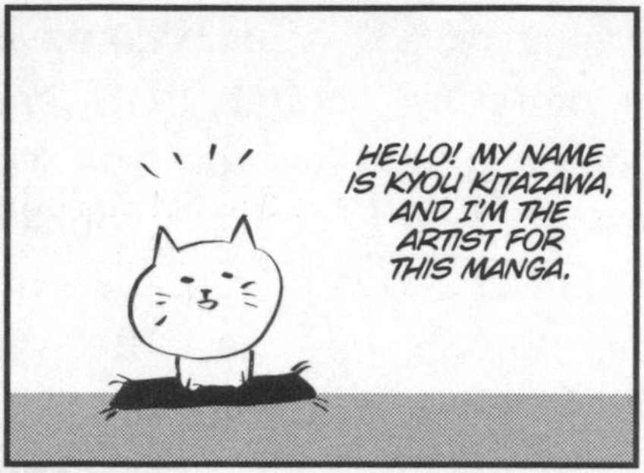
HELLO! MY NAME IS KYOU KITAZAWA, AND I'M THE ARTIST FOR THIS MANGA.

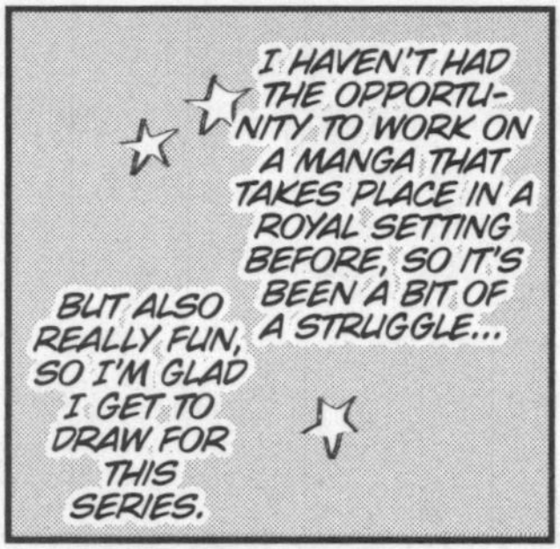
I HAVEN'T HAD THE OPPORTUNITY TO WORK ON A MANGA THAT TAKES PLACE IN A ROYAL SETTING BEFORE, SO IT'S BEEN A BIT OF A STRUGGLE...
BUT ALSO REALLY FUN, SO I'M GLAD I GET TO DRAW FOR THIS SERIES.

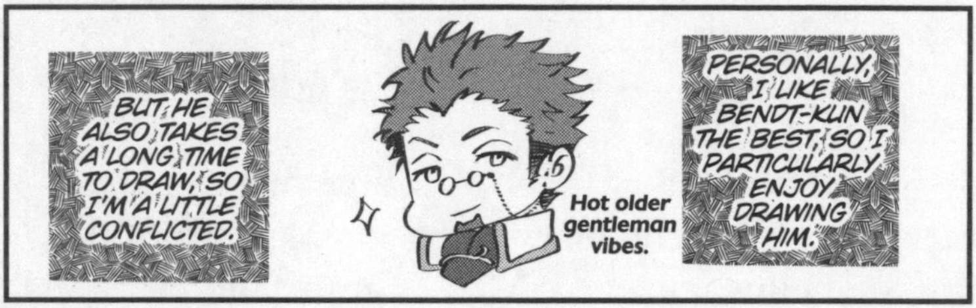
PERSONALLY, I LIKE BENDT-KUN THE BEST, SO I PARTICULARLY ENJOY DRAWING HIM.
Hot older gentleman vibes.
BUT HE ALSO TAKES A LONG TIME TO DRAW, SO I'M A LITTLE CONFLICTED.

I'D LIKE TO THANK EVERYONE WHO PUT UP WITH ME...

RUI SEKAI-SENSEI, WHO WROTE THE ORIGINAL STORY... KIYOMI TANABE-SENSEI, WHO DID THE STORYBOARDING... DABURYU-SENSEI, WHO CAME UP WITH THE BEAUTIFUL CHARACTER DESIGNS...

THE WONDERFUL EDITOR AND ASSISTANTS THAT HELPED ME WITH THE MANUSCRIPT, AND EVERYONE ELSE WHO CONTRIBUTED...

AND ABOVE ALL, THANK YOU, THE READERS!!

I HOPE TO SEE YOU ALL IN THE NEXT VOLUME!

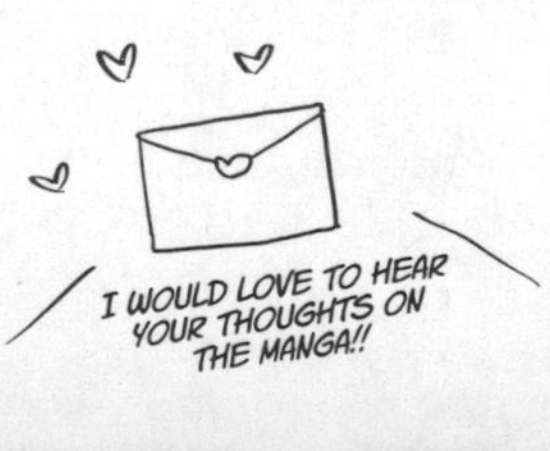
I WOULD LOVE TO HEAR YOUR THOUGHTS ON THE MANGA!!

Afterword

Hello, I am Rui Sekai, author of the original story. Nice to meet you all.

Thank you to everyone who purchased this volume. Many of you may not be aware of the original light novel, which currently has three volumes published in Japanese under the Saga Forest label of Hifumi Shobo. It is also available in e-book format, so for those of you who are interested, I would encourage you to take a look and enjoy the world of our old court wizard in a different way.

And for those of you who purchased this manga after reading the light novel, I think the beautiful and subtle art of this manga will convey a liveliness and intensity that is difficult to achieve with words alone. In closing, I hope you will continue to watch over these characters as they continue on their journey. Thank you.

April 2021
Original Author
Rui Sekai

世界るい